Hindu Nationalism

Hindu Nationalism

Origins, Ideologies and Modern Myths

Chetan Bhatt

BERG

Oxford • New York

First published in 2001 by
Berg
Editorial offices:
150 Cowley Road, Oxford, OX4 1JJ, UK
838 Broadway, Third Floor, New York, NY 10003-4812, USA

Berg is an imprint of Oxford International Publishers Ltd.

Library of Congress Cataloging-in-Publication Data
A catalogue record for this book is available from the Library of Congress.

British Library Cataloguing-in-Publication Data
A catalogue record for this book is available from the British Library.

ISBN 1 85973 343 3 (Cloth)
1 85973 348 4 (Paper)

Typeset by JS Typesetting, Wellingborough, Northants.
Printed in the United Kingdom by Biddles Ltd, Guildford and King's Lynn.

For Parul, Bina and Steve with love

Contents

Acknowledgements

I would like to thank the following friends and colleagues for their support, encouragement and discussions during the period of writing: John Solomos, Les Back, Mariam Fraser, Anton Pozniak, Parita Mukta, Jacqui Fairclough, Stephen Cowden, Vijay Prashad, Andrew Canessa, Arvind Rajagopal, Shabnam Hashmi, Fethi Acikel, Hiroki Ogasawara and Lilly Bhatt. I am especially grateful to Jane Hindley, Neil Washbourne, Kate Nash and Kirsten Campbell for their support and detailed critical comments. Bina Bhatt's extensive assistance was invaluable. I would particularly like to thank Pradip K. Datta and Thomas Blom Hansen for their important insights and suggestions, and Kathryn Earle for her consideration and patience. Finally, I would like to thank Robert Mitchell, Parul and Bina for their considerable support and help, and Stephen Cross for his suggestions for improvements, critical focus, intellectual acuity, and much more besides.

–1–

Introduction

On 16 May 1998, under the instructions of the Hindu nationalist Bharatiya Janata Party-led (BJP) government, Indian atomic scientists exploded three nuclear devices in the Rajasthan desert near Pokharan, and followed this with two further explosions three days later. The day of the first tests, Buddha Purnima, is traditionally celebrated as the day of birth, enlightenment and death of the Buddha. This was the second time that India had undertaken nuclear tests (the first was conducted on 18 May 1974 under the orders of Indira Gandhi's Congress government). The first three devices detonated were said to be a fission device (which India already had the capability of producing), a low-yield weapon that could be used for India's short-range Prithvi missiles, and a thermonuclear device with a destructive power of several kilotons. This third bomb, and its potential deployment in conjunction with the second stage of India's proposed development of its intermediate-range Agni missile (Agni II) would provide India with intercontinental ballistic missiles with a destructive intensity and spatial reach that had previously been the preserve of the nuclear superpowers. The tests were followed by a national-popular resurgence in India in celebration of the country's emergence, under a BJP-led government, as a nuclear superpower that had demonstrated India's strength and put its chief enemy, Pakistan, 'in its place'.

If the name of India's ballistic missile, Agni, the god of fire in the archaic Vedic texts was an older one, its symbolization in 1998 was novel, reflecting the eruption of mass social movements and a political party of government that represented a majoritarian, chauvinistic, anti-minority ideology of 'Hindu' supremacism. The Vishwa Hindu Parishad (VHP), the organization at the forefront of the upsurge of militant and violent Hinduism, and having close affinity with the ideological doctrine of Hindutva that also resulted in the formation of the BJP, called for a temple dedicated to Shakti (the goddess of power) to be built at Pokharan, some fifty kilometres from the site of the tests, the fifty-third addition to what it claimed are similar *Shaktipeeths* ('seats of strength') that symbolize Hindu power. The idea was mooted that sand from the explosion site be distributed across India in the 'tradition' of a religious offering, though the harmful consequences of 'radioactive *prasad*' resulted in the abandonment of this suggestion. The inevitable claim surfaced, one of many such enabling fictions, that nuclear weapons were traditional to Hinduism ('Om-made bombs'?), the Vedic god Agni adduced as proof that 'ancient Hindus' possessed nuclear bombs. The leader of the violent Bombay-based Hindu nationalist party, the Shiv Sena, declared that after the bomb tests, Hindus were 'no longer eunuchs' – reiterating a masculinist theme and an evocative anxiety that has animated Hindu nationalist ideology since its inception.

However, the triumphant Hindutva sacralization of weapons of mass destruction could have had only one consequence. By 28 May, Pakistan, under the government of prime minister Nawaz Sharif, had retaliated by exploding five fission bombs followed by one further bomb on 30 May in the Chagai Hills, Baluchistan. Pakistan announced its intention to nuclearize its intermediate-range Ghauri ballistic missile, while many of its population jubilantly celebrated the 'settling of its score' with 'Resurgent India'. The 'score' was certainly equalized as both countries now possessed a broadly equivalent destructive nuclear capability that had the capacity to kill millions in each other's major cities. While the development of nuclear weapons of mass destruction in south Asia had an autonomous trajectory, the BJP's decision to 'induct' India's nuclear weapons so soon after coming to power (March 1998) reflected a different history and ideological practice of 'Hindu nationalism', one that has been seen as peripheral to the Indian polity and social formation but has, since the early 1980s, moved to the centre-stage of Indian politics, state and civil society. The names of each country's missiles, Agni and Ghauri, symbolize, and have the capacity to make real exactly the imagined monumental conflict between a primordial Hinduism and a medieval Islam that the votaries of Hindu nationalism consider to be central to their political sociology.

The aims of this book are to provide a critical assessment of the ideological content to Hindu nationalism, and elaborate intellectual and historical influences that contributed to its development. The focus on ideologies and history is intended to supplement some of the existing and excellent literature published in recent years that has guided many of the directions of this book (Basu 1993, Jaffrelot 1996, Datta 1998, Hansen 1999, Ghosh 1999). The first three chapters are directed towards analysis of the main nineteenth and early twentieth century texts and personalities that were important in the development of Hindu nationalism. The methodological emphasis on idea, text and key personalities that symbolize the contours of Hindu nationalist thinking can inadvertently convey a holistic continuity to Hindu nationalism across a broad historical period. While rejecting the view of an uninterrupted historical development of Hindu nationalist ideology, and indeed highlighting critical epistemological and political discontinuities during the nineteenth century and throughout the twentieth century, one argument of the book is that one can trace a convergence in the substantive ideological *content*, if not the explicit political concerns, of Hindu nationalists across this period. This is a complicated argument, illustrated in the first two chapters, and its implications are that the generally dominant view of a distinct Hindu nationalism arising as a marginal movement during the 1920s, and of relatively little influence until the 1980s, requires modification.

Hindu nationalism, even in its recent 'cultural nationalist' forms, represents a dense cluster of ideologies of primordialism, many of which were developed during processes of vernacular and regional elite formation in colonial India during the second half of the nineteenth century. Chapter 2 presents a consideration of the impact of European varieties of 'primordialist' thinking from mid- to late-nineteenth century colonial India. The argument is that Hindu primordialist ideas developed in conjunction with evolutionary, 'physiological' and metaphysical conceptions of nation. This was not the result of an elementary and unmediated impact of European nationalist conceptions, but occurred through dialogic processes of negotiation and debate with such ideas, and through complex intellectual movement to and from colonial India and Europe. A key component of colonial Indian elite configurations of primordial nationalism was Aryanism, which in the Indian context represented the synthesis of a several intellectual strands arising from British and German Orientalism, and from processes of 'upper' caste, religious, regional and vernacular elite consolidation in colonial India. The theme of a variant 'Aryanism' continues throughout the book and is considered to be a definitive background to Hindu nationalism. Chapter 2 also examines the formation and impact during the later nineteenth century of Dayananda Saraswati's Arya Samaj movement, the 'Bengal Renaissance' and Bankimchandra Chattopadhyaya's affective religious nationalism, Bal Gangadhar Tilak's synthesis of archaic primordialism with politicized devotionalism, and other developments in regionalist nationalism, each of which imagined an overintegrated national future for India based on 'Hindu' precepts. The extraordinarily wide-ranging impact of neo-Arya Samajist ideologies in the twentieth century is also considered in Chapter 3.

Difficult questions haunt analysis of the relationship between the national movement for liberation from British rule and the projects of a distinctive Hindu nationalism. This is a complicated area to explore, since there were (it will be argued) several Hindu nationalist orientations that had a variety of strong associations with the national movement, both well before and after the emergence of M. K. Gandhi as a national leader. This is explored in Chapter 3 by examining the political trajectories of Lala Lajpat Rai and Lala Munshi Ram (Swami Shraddhanand) in the early decades of the twentieth century. These two political figures are used to symbolize the complexities and tensions between 'Indian' and 'Hindu' nationalism, and between 'anti-communal anti-colonialism' and Hindu majoritarianism during the troubled period of the 1920s. Both individuals were involved to differing degrees with the national movement and both can conceivably be called 'Hindu nationalists'. The divergence between strategies of non-cooperation with British rule, and strategies of 'responsive cooperation' with colonialism is also examined, the aim being to highlight the complex affinities between Hindu majoritarianism and 'responsivism'. In Chapter 3, it is argued that there was a strong degree of political continuity between 'Hinduized' versions of 'Indian' nationalism and the specific ideology of Hindutva that emerged in the 1920s. More contentiously, it is also argued that much of the substantial content of 1920s Hindutva was already ideologically established much earlier, including the idea that Indian nationality was primarily to be based on a 'common' Hindu civilization, culture, religion and 'race'. While aware of debates about the complex governmental, political, administrative, taxonomic, ideological and popular characteristics of 'communalism', the main focus of the book is on ideological Hindu nationalism – that Hindus did or should constitute 'a nation', and that Indian nationalism was solely or largely coextensive with, and to be based on, Hindu religious or ideological precepts. In this sense, what is usually referred to as 'Hindu communalism' is submerged under a narrative that essentially views the dominant forms of the latter as characteristically preoccupied with broader ideas of Hindu majoritarianism and 'Hindu nationality'.

The distinctive ideology of Hindutva that animates contemporary Hindu nationalism was expounded at length during the early 1920s by the Indian anticolonial revolutionary, Vinayak Damodar Savarkar. Chapter 4 critically, and in detail, explores the content of Savarkarism, the Hindu Mahasabha movement that he led after the mid-1930s, and the relationship of his ideology to strands of British evolutionist sociology. Savarkar is celebrated as a revolutionary hero in contemporary India because of his involvement, while in London during the first decade of the twentieth century, with revolutionary terrorist anticolonial societies. If the confluence of revolutionary nationalism with Hindu nationalism is apposite in his case, his activities during the 1930s also sharply demonstrated the difference between Hindu nationalism and the anti-colonial national movement.

In the mid-1920s, a new organization, the Rashtriya Swayamsevak Sangh (RSS), was formed in Maharashtra and was to become the foundational organization for the 'family' (*sangh parivar*) that comprises the main, though not all, Hindu nationalist organizations and tendencies in contemporary India. Chapter 5 explores the origin, ideology and organization of the RSS. Despite the claims of the RSS and its affiliated organizations that they are embedded in the 'traditional' ethos of Hinduism, they are products of nineteenth- and twentieth-century modernist nationalism and are characterized as India's own versions of authoritarian, xenophobic and majoritarian religious nationalism. It is argued that the RSS and its characteristic ideology of ordered and disciplined society, bodily control, hierarchy, conformity, and unanimist conceptions of collective Hinduism were formed in opposition to the national movement's strategies of disobedience, disruption, non-cooperation, equality and freedom. There has been significant debate about whether the RSS and its *parivar* can be considered 'fascist'. Both

Chapters 4 and 5 consider aspects of these debates by examining the RSS's and Savarkar's orientation toward Italy and Germany during the 1920s and 1930s.

Chapter 6 provides a descriptive narrative of the formation, growth and successes of the Bharatiya Jana Sangh from the early 1950s, and of the BJP from 1980. This chapter also focuses on the BJP's 'two' founding ideologies, 'integral humanism' and 'Gandhian socialism'. The functionalist ideology of 'integral humanism', formulated by Jana Sangh activist Deendayal Upadhyaya during the 1960s, is critically evaluated, as is the claim that it emerged from authentic Hindu *advaita* traditions. The chapter also considers how aspects of both socialism and Gandhian utopianism had a resonance for Hindu nationalist tendencies, especially in the critically important period of Indira Gandhi's Emergency in the 1970s. The more recent tensions between the BJP's policy of 'calibrated globalization' and the RSS's adherence to 'economic nationalism' are also explored.

Chapter 7 describes the origins of the Vishwa Hindu Parishad in the mid-1960s, and its attempts at the mass mobilisation of Hindu religious communities since the 1980s. The chapter examines the VHP's novel and experimental use of religious symbols, mythologies and practices in order to dramatically transform and politicize Hindu devotional traditions and direct them to concerns with landscape, territory and xenology. The VHP's use of semiotic methods relies on the condensation of a vast and disparate cluster of popular and folk religious meanings onto its chosen political symbols. While religious symbols have their own independent histories of change and development, the emphasis of the chapter is on the novel and synthetic use by the VHP of Hindu religious symbolism. Of significance in both Chapters 6 and 7 are the stated Hindutva intentions of the BJP and the VHP, exemplified their respective election manifestos and 'Hindu agendas' of 1998. It is argued that these have to be taken seriously as declarations of political intent in parliamentary and extra-parliamentary settings and pose a serious danger to India's constitutional secular, democratic and federal status once the parliamentary BJP comes to power without facing the burden of constraining coalitions.

–2–

The Primordial Nation of the Hindus

He:	Your task is accomplished. The Muslim power is destroyed. There is nothing else for you to do. No good can come of needless slaughter.
Satyananda:	The Muslim power has indeed been destroyed, but the dominion of the Hindus has not yet been established. The British still hold Calcutta.
He:	Hindu dominion will not be established now. If you remain at your work, men will be killed to no purpose. Therefore come.
Satyananda:	My Lord, if Hindu dominion is not going to be established, who will rule? Will the Muslim kings return?
He:	No. The English will rule.
Satyananda:	Alas, my mother! I have failed to set you free. Once again you fall into the hands of infidels. Forgive your son. Alas, my mother! Why did I not die on the battlefield!

Bankimchandra Chattopadhyaya, *Anandamath*, 1882

Introduction: Primordialist Conceptions of Indian Nationalism

If the nineteenth century is to be conceived as the period in which varieties of primordialist, ethnic, republican and civic nationalism flourished in Europe, there needs to be a suitable register within which to locate incipient and formative nationalisms under the conditions of colonial and imperial domination. The rise of, and tense relations between, nationalisms and patriotisms in colonial India was formidably complex and their trajectory is often underdetermined by post-Independence nationalist readings which seek to evoke a linear path in which the nationalism of the nineteenth century led inexorably to the liberated independent democratic and secular nation state of the twentieth. In colonized India, various 'indigenous' primarily elite and 'upper' caste ideas of nation, national belonging and national destiny were certainly set in motion in the nineteenth century. However, post-Independence readings of this earlier period tend to confer a telos onto the development of such nationalisms, whether these are conceived as the signal of modernity's progress towards secular nationhood, as the continuation of precolonial primordial destinies, or as 'derivative discourses' arising from the impact of the former in the recovery of the latter.

Nineteenth century colonized India was subject to complex processes of national, regional and, importantly, linguistic, caste, vernacular and religious elite formation. These processes were fuelled by changes in the spatially variegated organization and administration of the colonial economy, urban growth induced by both industrial and mercantile capitalism, a reconfiguration of feudal and caste relations and changes in the military, administrative, legal and educational apparatuses of colonial government (Bayly 1983). These economic and political processes are beyond detailed consideration here. However, the relations between the Indian merchant, industrial, landowner and feudal classes, the political, judicial, administrative, military and civil service elites and the emergent English-educated and especially vernacular intelligentsia neither form a reductive process of nationalist elite formation, nor were these relations pre-given as 'secular'. Of equal importance are apparently unrelated but concomitant processes of religious reorganization and reformation in the ostensibly 'traditional' structures of northern Indian caste Hinduism, Islam and Sikhism. These manifested most powerfully in what are often, and problematically, referred to as the 'reform' or 'revival' movements in northern Indian Hinduism and Islam, and typically located, from the middle of the century, in the towns and cities of the Punjab, Bengal, the United Provinces (now Uttar Pradesh) and what are now the states of Maharashtra and Gujarat.

Describing the intellectual import of these changes for subsequent formations of secular, religious or regional forms of nationalism is complicated by what may be conceived as 'external' intellectual influences, primarily those from Europe. The task is not simply to demonstrate how European nationalist ideas impinged upon and subsequently shaped varieties of secular or religious nationalism in the midst of deeper economic and social changes in nineteenth century colonial India. Rather, it is to uncover the extraordinary variety of intellectual currents that had moved back and forth between Europe and India since the eighteenth century, transmuting, magnifying, and gaining in importance up to and after the Victorian period. These ideas of nationalism were not uniformly received by the divergent elites in colonial India, nor could they easily or always be separated from patriotic loyalties to Empire among large sections of those elites, nor was there a sharp bifurcation of religious or nationalist sensibilities within them.

In so far as many of these currents had apparently European origins, or were influenced by Western intellectual discourses, nationalisms in colonial India can be conceived as 'derivative discourses' (P. Chatterjee 1986) or as 'catachreses' (Spivak 1993), as an example of 'hybridity' (Bhabha 1994), and indeed were 'invented traditions' (Hobsbawm and Ranger 1983). However, the use of such currently vogueish designations as if they are explanatory has the cost of a considerable and rather deterministic simplification of the complex relations and deep negotiations between apparently 'indigenous', regional and vernacular influences and apparently 'external' influences, both of which were to lead to religious nationalist movements in the nineteenth and twentieth centuries. Indeed, the designation of such processes as simply 'derivative' or 'hybrid' discourses only acquires power once the totality of nominally 'indigenous' influences is purged of religious or 'communal' significance under what is seen as the imposition of an overarching and often disagreeable 'foreign' secular, Western nationalism.

What is now conceived, in post-Nehruvian terms, as the story of the formation of an irreducibly secular nationalism in India, itself the conclusion to a universalizing movement for national liberation or independence, needs thoroughgoing problematization. This is not simply the (rather easily demonstrated) argument that Hindu (or Muslim) religious sensibilities were present or persistent in a national movement that was otherwise and primarily portrayed in the Nehruvian period as committed to secularism. Nor, conversely, is it argued that 'indigenous' varieties of Hinduism or a 'Hindu ethos' were necessary for or the dominant aspect of the national movement. It is however the argument of this chapter that an overarching process of the interpellation of discovered archaic and primordial Hinduism was a major, significant and before the 1920s often a dominating strand in the national movement such that secularism itself was neither sufficiently interrogated nor adequately developed beyond an elemental, if often strong and principled, commitment to anti-communalism. The combination or anti-communalism and anti-colonialism was, of course, neither equivalent to secularism nor could it form a sufficient ideological and cultural basis for a genuinely secular nation-state or, and more problematically, a 'secular civil society'. Given its importance, there was an absence of detailed, elaborate and sufficient national discussion of what secularism might mean across both state and civil societies until arguably *after* the Nehruvian period. Hence, the argument that a colonial Western-imposed secular nationalism, the latter viewed as coextensive with taxonomic configurations of religious blocs and communities, was itself responsible for or complicit in the rise of Hindu nationalism is therefore rejected (Nandy 1985, Nandy 1994, Nandy et al. 1995, Madan 1987, Madan 1993, Madan 1997). While advocating a genuine and strong distance from Hindu nationalism, such arguments can also unwittingly reproduce the epistemic resources of the latter. For example, Nandy's argument in 1983 that 'the alternative to Hindu nationalism is the peculiar mix of classical and folk Hinduism and the unselfconscious Hinduism by which most Indians, *Hindus as well as non-Hindus*, live' would find sympathy among those who make similar claims for 'Hindutva' (Nandy 1983: 104, emphasis added).

The Western Impact

A key development in the flourishing of nationalist ideologies in Europe in the nineteenth century was a turn towards specifically primordialist ideologies as a basis for modern constitutional nationality defined primarily through a perceived collective ethnic, or to use the language of the time, 'ethnological' belonging. The association between exclusivist forms of ethnic nationalism and ideologies of primordialism need not have been a necessary one, but frequently was, and had its roots in eighteenth century varieties of nationalist thinking that were to grow in force within Europe during the nineteenth century. However, the impact of these ideas in colonial India after the mid-nineteenth century is complicated by the way the emergence of these ideas in Europe in the late eighteenth and early nineteenth centuries was shaped by a converse engagement with the discovery of archaic Hinduism (McCully 1966, Marshall 1970, Edwardes 1971, Schwab 1984, Halbfass 1988, Trautmann 1997, Dalmia 1997).

The development of primordialist thinking in colonial India after the mid-nineteenth century and into the early twentieth century was inextricably related to processes of Indian elite caste formation. While regional nationalisms and local *patries* had existed in India before the colonial period (Bayly 1998), an overarching framework that served to provide ideological coherence for the idea of a primordial nationalism, primarily defined through an invention of archaic Vedic Hinduism, mainly gained force from the nineteenth century. 'Primordialism' here refers to the cultivation of primordialist thinking that gave shape and coherence to ideas of 'national unity' framed through discourses of archaic Hindu civilization, and which was instrumental in the concomitant development of the power of regional, vernacular and caste elites. Hence the term 'primordial' refers to an ideologically derived grid of intelligibility within which nationalism was understood, rather than to the linear development of an essential and extant ethnic unity among pre-given populations of India. While much ideological work was undertaken to give shape to nineteenth century Hindu nationalism, these projects were also divergent in locating the foundational content for their primordial nationalism. However, a key aspect to these projects was the idea of linear temporality, often linked to evolutionist ideas, in which viewing the past in linear terms was the first step towards imagining an overintegrated national future. If nomenclature and taxonomy, functionalism and positivism were epistemologically important for these projects, perhaps the definitive themes were new: vitalism, evolution and telos, palingenesis, survival and degeneration, 'social uplift' and 'social hygiene', spirituality, enumeration, a universalizing mission, and ideas of ethnology and race. As discussed in subsequent chapters, the way that apparently unproblematic narratives of 'upliftment' and 'hygiene' were inextricably linked to strong themes of religious 'upliftment' and purity betrayed a congruence between imperial and Hindu nationalist civilizing discourses.

Such ideas crossed both secular and religious forms of nationalism in nineteenth-century colonial India. Indeed, the period from the mid-nineteenth century until the turn of the century witnessed the flourishing of diverse intellectual projects preoccupied with the discovery of primordial Hindu belonging. To unproblematically categorize these as nationalistic or patriotic, within a milieu where patriotism often meant allegiance to Empire, is difficult. However they created the intellectual matrices for the kinds of Hindu nationalist thinking that were to follow towards the end of the nineteenth century. A definitive aspect of these ideas was their formation through a process of appropriation and interrogation of, as well as negotiation with 'Orientalist' and colonial scholarship related to the origins, languages and religions of the inhabitants of India. Here, 'Orientalism' is important not for its (allegedly) hermetic imagination of the non-West, but because of the complicated, indeterminate effects it had on those who were its willing or otherwise subjects. The dominant 'Orientalist' influence was inevitably British and in the English language, ranging from the eighteenth-century work of Charles Wilkins, William Jones and the Asiatick Society of Bengal, John Holwell, Nathaniel Halhed and Alexander Hamilton, through to the nineteenth-century work of Monier Monier-Williams and the British-German Indologist, Frederich Max Muller. However, it is important not to underestimate the influence of German 'Romantic' writers, from Herder, Frederich and August Wilhelm von Schlegel, to Goethe and Arthur Schopenhauer, nor to understate the exchanges between Indian writers and non-British Indologists and philologists (Halbfass 1988: 218). The idea that India was the cradle of all civilization (Voltaire, Herder, Kant, Frederich Schlegel among many others) or the original homeland of humanity (Schlegel, Schelling, even Hegel), that 'Hinduism' represented humanity's primal philosophy (Herder, Schlegel), or that Hinduism offered redemption for contemporary humanity (Schopenhauer), even that 'humanism' itself could be conceived as resulting from 'Hindu values' (Herder), as well as the associated ideas that privileged a transcendental cultural epistemology of a 'national soul' above any determination of the state (variously Herder, Fichte, Renan among others) were widely disseminated in Europe (Halbfass 1988, Bhatt 1999). What precise intellectual processes were at work in Arthur Schopenhauer's rejection of the veracity of Rammohan Roy's rendition of the Upanishads? Schopenhauer's own philosophy, written mostly in German and so, by and large, unavailable to the intellectual elites in India (who would have read and spoken vernacular Indian languages, English and possibly Persian) was conveyed by P. Deussen through lectures in Bombay and exchanges with Vivekananda during the 1890s (Halbfass 1988: 133, 239). What indeed are we to make of the claim that the *ethical* interpretation of the Upanishadic *ghosana*, *'tat tvam asi!'* acquired an importance in India, and a place seemingly at the core of *advaita vedantic* philosophy after it had been so interpreted by German philosophers (ibid: 240–2)? Conversely, what was the basis of the popularity among Indian elites of the curious proposition by Auguste Comte that his Positive Philosophy offered brahmins the means to 'free their theocratic country' from the foreign 'yoke' of Christianity and Islam (Flora 1993)?

R. C. Majumdar's view that Indians knew little of their history in the early nineteenth century, prior to the impact of Western scholarship, may seem brusque

(1971a: 290). However, the impact of English-language texts documenting, and English-language education diffusing, discoveries and speculations in philology and archaeology was nevertheless monumental. From the mid-nineteenth century, but especially after the early 1870s, this was evident in the conscious cultivation of the 'memory', indeed affective remembrance of India's archaic Hindu past by numerous societies and writers, in the burgeoning print media (newspapers, periodicals and journals), by nationalist and religious leaders and by British colonial officers and administrators (Marshall 1970) and Western religious societies, such as the Theosophists. This resulted in a glorification of India's archaic Hindu past. India's ancient civilization was demonstrated to be as old as that of the ancient Greeks and Romans and, it was speculated and then believed, may have been the progenitor of the latter. Its knowledge and philosophies demonstrated the super-iority of its religion and culture. Its religious texts illustrated not simply the religious and (frequently) 'racial' unity of its past, but pre-eminently its *national* unity, as *Aryavarta* (the land of the Aryans) or *Bharatvarsha* (the kingdom of Bharat). The Vedas, Upanishads, Puranas and the Epics illustrated that ancient Hindu civilization possessed not simply a cultural and moral greatness, but a highly developed ethical system, polity, civil society and social formation.

A key epistemological component of this intellectual discovery concerned a comparison between the vitalism, dynamism and resilience of the ancient Hindus and what was perceived as the degeneration and stagnancy of contemporary Hindu society. Conversely patriotism and nationalism were seen as the mechanisms by which Hindu society would be reinvigorated. Indeed, much can be written about how the Hindu trope of civilizational or societal degeneration, and a consequently necessary 'vitalism', travelled back and forth from Europe to India from the 1840s right through to the 1930s. It is also worth noting that, in this nineteenth-century linearist paradigm of Hindu glory, degradation and invigoration, there is by and large an absence of the view that Islam was responsible for the alleged degradation of Hinduism during the medieval period, or of the view that this linear history was driven forward by a logic of Hindu war against foreign, Muslim invaders. These two elements were written more forcefully into the imagined 'history' of Hindus towards the first decade of the twentieth century and were to become dominant in V. D. Savarkar's *Hindutva – or who is a Hindu?* ([1923] 1989).

Aryanism and Nationalism

One aspect of both 'Orientalist' scholarship and primordialist nationalist thinking concerned the invention of Vedic Aryanism as the ideological basis for either Indian or Hindu nationality (Thapar 1992, Bayly 1995, Bayly 1999). (It will be seen in later chapters how varieties of Aryanism continue to remain important for contemporary Hindu nationalism.) A key aspect of this was the discovery and consolidation of Vedic Aryanism in the eighteenth and nineteenth century by British and German disciplines of comparative philology, comparative mythology and, subsequently, comparative ethnology and their complex diffusion in colonial India.

The 'Aryan myth' in Europe was consequent upon eighteenth-century discoveries of the philological affinities between archaic Latin, Greek, Sanskrit and Avestan, and between these and other languages. Convergences were also discovered between the mythologies and deities of ancient Greeks and Indians; hence the hypothesis of a common linguistic origin. The common language group was variously named 'Indo-Germanic', 'Indo-European', 'Japhetic', 'Mediterranean', and, by Friedrich Schlegel, 'Aryan'. The word 'Aryan' was a corruption of the word which occurs in the Rig Veda as 'arya', and in the Zend Avesta as 'airiia'. The word also occurs frequently in later Buddhist and Hindu texts. The Rig Veda and the Avesta are identified as the oldest existing literature created by *arya*-speaking groups, and hence have had particular importance for tendencies with an investment in Aryanism.

The idea of a common linguistic origin was rapidly supplemented by epistemologically separate hypotheses of an original people and an original geographical homeland. This unwarranted equivalence between the burgeoning 'sciences' of comparative philology, ethnology and mythology was fuelled by a considerable scholarly and dilletantist literature during the eighteenth and nineteenth centuries, speculating on the Urheimat, Ursprache, Urvolk and 'Urmythus' of the Indo-European language family (Mosse 1966, Poliakov 1974, Schwab 1984, Trautmann 1997).

In the late nineteenth century, the British-German Indologist, Friedrich Max Muller, following Schlegel, popularized 'the technical term Aryan' to refer to the Indo-European language family, his view being that the term 'Aryan', because it was of foreign origin, could not be used for the purposes of ethnic or national chauvinism in Europe. By this time, the Rig Veda had been interpreted by European writers as demonstrating that a powerful warrior 'race', Aryans, had entered India and conquered 'the dark-skinned, stub-nosed' original inhabitants, the *dasyus*. The Rig Veda does have a distinct xenology of selves (such as some *arya*-speaking tribes) and others (the *dasyus*, the *mlecchas*, those who speak other languages, worship other Gods, have other customs, and indeed other *arya*-speaking tribes). The furious speculations about the 'original Aryan homeland' in Europe during the late nineteenth century exasperated Muller, who concluded that the homeland was 'somewhere in Asia'. However, the idea of an Aryan myth had travelled widely in Europe and various original 'homelands' were proposed, including India, Germany, the Caucasus, Eire, Persia, the Baltics, and 'Atlantis'. In the hands of first Arthur Schopenhauer and then Houston Stewart Chamberlain, Wagner and the Bayreuth Circle, 'Aryanism' became a vicious anti-semitism, reflecting an earlier Enlightenment and Romantic philosophical polarization between the

Hindu-Buddhist and the Judeo-Christian. The interpretation of the Rig Veda using the concepts of 'race' that were flourishing in nineteenth century France, Britain and Germany has been comprehensively rejected (Poliakov 1974, Trautmann 1997 for a excellent recent discussion).

For important intellectual strands in nineteenth century colonial India, an archaic civilizational Vedic Aryanism was also, if differently, important and became virtually a 'commonsense', an unquestioned backdrop, that provided a linear paradigm for what a future nationalism was to be. Aryanism also requires situating within a range of other reconstructive projects of regional, ethnic, caste or religious belonging that could considerably modify Aryanist thinking for more limited, vernacular or colloquial purposes. Aryanism in colonial India did not necessarily have the same kinds of association with 'race' that it primarily had in nineteenth-century Europe, nor does it now necessarily have the same connotations in India that it does in the post-Holocaust West.

Both race and Aryanism in colonial India signified a wide range of meanings and forms of methodological understanding that can be seen to constitute a distinctive nineteenth-century pedagogical field with its own thematic and lexical ramifications that were irreducible to, but were in negotiation and argument with those associated with the burgeoning racial Aryanism in France, Britain and Germany in the nineteenth century. Individuals as diverse as Vivekananda, Keshab Chandra Sen of the Brahmo Samaj, the Bengal novelist and writer Bankimchandra Chattopadhyaya, the Bombay judge, social reformer and nationalist Mahadev Govind Ranade, the social reformer Har Bilas Sarda, Bal Gangadhar Tilak, the 'Extremist' nationalist leader, the fiery revolutionary nationalist Aurobindo Ghose, Congress leader Annie Besant and the founder of the Arya Samaj, Dayananda Saraswati, employed conceptions of Aryanism within their various ideals of patriotism and loyalty to the monarch, religious reinvigoration, or reformist or revolutionary nationalism (Leopold 1970). The term 'Aryan' was widely used, including by national leaders such as M. K. Gandhi. Just as Frederich Max Muller had articulated the visit to England of Rammohan Roy as the 'return' of a lost Aryan cousin, for Sen, Aryanism demonstrated the patriotic unity of the British and Indians, cousins lost in antiquity who had, in the colonial period, rediscovered each other (Rothermund 1986, Trautmann 1997). For Besant self rule was to be the prelude to an international Aryan federation. Conversely, for Ranade, Ghose and Tilak, the European racial connotations of Aryan supremacy, and for the latter two the idea that Indians subjugated by the British could share a common descent, was anathema. For them, as for Dayananda and Sarda, Aryans were not necessarily racially constituted and were frequently characterized through a moral and dynamic propensity that was their genius. Nevertheless, for them, it was in India that Aryans had either originated or achieved the pinnacle of their culture and civilization which they had then bestowed on the world. There is an understated link between the universalizing conception of Hinduism as providing salvation, knowledge or redemption for all humanity, and the origin of this conception during the nineteenth-century fascination with Aryans as a world-dynamic force. Indeed, it could be argued that the nineteenth-century 'worldling' of Hinduism was inextricably related to such fascination. It is also worth noting that, even where the strictly racial or white supremacist connotations of 'Aryan' were rejected, a powerful xenological conception nevertheless remained.

The ethnologist, anthropometrist and Government of India Census Officer, Herbert Hope Risley had applied a racial Aryanist paradigm during the nineteenth century to 'explain' the existence of various castes, tribal groups and regional populations in India (Risley 1903, 1908); he portrayed dynamic Aryan man in India using a photograph of an aged, hirsute and fairly obese brahmin sadhu (plate XXV in Risley 1915). In the 1870s, he even attempted to describe India's political movements on the basis of differentiated caste-racial affiliations. This would, of course, have been disagreeable to Indian thinkers who were aiming to cultivate national unity. Moreover, Risley's work was also dominated by a racial supremacism that inevitably favoured the 'white' races. However, despite the rejection of this kind of racial Aryanism, an important characteristic of many Indian appropriations of a Vedic Aryanist paradigm was their thorough elision of populations that could not be seen to have shared in the fruits of ancient Hindu civilization: the tribals, the 'untouchables' and the shudra castes. Some writers, including Ranade, seemed to view southern Indians ('Dravidians') and tribal populations as inferior to or conquered by the chosen people or race of Hindu Aryans (Leopold 1970: 281). However, there is by and large either an instructive silence about these populations among other nineteenth-century Indian writers or a view that accommodates them as degenerate or errant wanderers from an original Aryan Vedism. The silence itself could betray a widespread and commonsense nineteenth-century view that considered brahmins as intellectually, morally, culturally or 'ethnologically' superior to the shudras, and the Aryan *dvija* ('twice-born' castes of brahmins, kshatriyas and vaishyas) as superior to the non-Aryans (Anaryans). As we see in the next chapter, it was exactly these populations of shudras, tribals and 'untouchables' that became the targets for a reinvigorated turn-of-century nationalist Hinduism that claimed primordial ownership of and authority over them.

This chapter examines three main developments in the nineteenth century within which varieties of primordialist thinking were to gain prominence: Dayananda Saraswati's Arya Samaj movement, the Bengal 'Renaissance' and its instinctive combination of Hinduism with nationalism, and Bal Gangadhar Tilak's conflation of regional Maharashtrian nationalism with a reconfigured and politicized martial-devotional Hinduism. These three northern Indian examples were divergent in their articulation of Hinduism with nationalism. However, their fabulation and configuration of archaic primordialism is illustrative of the themes highlighted above.

The Arya Samaj

The Arya Samaj, founded by Dayananda Saraswati (1824–83) in Bombay in 1875 and Lahore in 1877, is sometimes described as the first modern 'fundamentalist' movement to have emerged out of Hinduism (on the Arya Samaj and Dayananda, see Dayananda [1908] 1970, Lajpat Rai 1915, Ghose 1925, Upadhyaya 1939, Pareek 1973, Jones 1976). However, more usually, the Arya Samaj is viewed as one example of an overarching nineteenth century 'Hindu Renaissance' or 'revival', a neo-Hinduism, or a 'semitized Hinduism'. The analytical languages used to describe this period frequently use categorizations and dichotomies such as Hindu 'revivalists', 'reformists', 'traditionalists' and 'orthodoxy', these strictly religious taxonomies often differentiated from those used to describe nationalist movements and tendencies. Much of this analytical language requires problematization, at least in so far as an analysis of emergent nationalist strands is concerned. The nineteenth century certainly gave rise to a variety of what are often called 'Neo-Hindu' strands, but a focus on strictly religious reformation can elide a grander process in which the thinkability of nationalism for some was primarily figured from within a new Hindu religious and ethnicized framework such that, by the turn of the century, nationalism and Hinduism could be spoken of as synonymous, even by tendencies – Bipinchandra Pal is a good example here – that were seemingly *opposed to* sectarian communalism and Hindu majoritarianism. Indeed, what Vasudha Dalmia (1997) has been termed 'the nationalization of Hindu traditions' can considerably modify evaluation of the equivalence of 'secularism' with anti-communalism both within the Indian national movement and before and after Independence.

The name 'Arya Samaj' translates as 'The Society of Aryans' or, in contemporary usage, as 'The Society of Nobles'. The *oscillation* in the meaning of the term *arya* from indicating an 'ethnological' or 'racial' concept to indicating a quality of noble virtuousness is worth noting. Dayananda believed that the Aryans were the original human inhabitants of the world, living first in Tibet and then, after separating from the ignoble, unvirtuous, lowly and ignorant *dasyus*, moving to uninhabited India or *Aryavarta*, the best nation in the world. The Aryans then established an empire that ruled the world until the advent of the Mahabharata war. This idea of primordial humanity arising first in Tibet and migrating to India and then the rest of the world was prevalent in Europe in the *eighteenth* century and was accepted, by among others, Immanuel Kant (Poliakov 1971:186). The quality that defined the Aryans, according to Dayananda, was two fold. The *arya* was one who had knowledge, virtue and was noble, and the *arya* was one who worshipped only *one* God and had accepted the Vedic religion (Dayananda 1970). This ideal of virtue, knowledge and especially nobility is not strictly a racial conception, but nevertheless has strong territorial, environmental and xenological aspects; not everyone, especially those from outside the borders of India could, in Dayananda's conception, become 'Aryan'. There was also a strongly environmentalist component in his *Satyarth Prakash* in which the physical geography of India, as the best nation of the Aryans, led to their distinctive qualities and attributes of 'nobility' and 'virtuousness'. If those qualities appear to be empty signifiers, they were not innocent terms and were especially important, both within and outside Europe, in cultivating hierarchical conceptions of hereditarian privilege and nobility during both the eighteenth and nineteenth centuries.

Dayananda's social and political philosophy was predicated on the pristine and completed truth of some of the four Vedas, and sections of later Hindu texts that he asserted were in accordance with the Vedas. The Vedas were conceived by him to represent the literal word of God revealed to the ancient Aryans (an idea very similar to Friedrich Schlegel's earlier imagination of ancient India). This emulative idea of the Vedas as constituting 'the book' of the Hindus was supplemented by another conception of the Vedas as constituting the only true religion of humanity. This universalizing conception of Hinduism, the 'worldling of Hinduism', was influenced by some important strands of European romantic thinking and cannot be seen as unproblematically Indian in origin (Bhatt 1999). However, it has come to represent a potent invented tradition that combines a view of Hinduism's archaic and primeval nature with that of the first ever revelation to humanity (Dayananda 1970). This idea of Hinduism as constituting both a universal and a primordial revelation for all humanity has frequently been the mobilizing core of Hindu supremacism and performs considerable overarching ideological work.

Interestingly enough, Dayananda privileged the relatively ritualistic Samaveda (though the Rig Veda was by then known to be older and more authoritative) and rejected the authority and truth of the Puranas, Epics and Bhagavad Gita. Of importance here is that Dayananda rejected in its entirety the vast number of Hindu texts that were apprehended as 'sacred' within popular or devotional Hinduism. Indeed, he considered many of these texts as erroneous and responsible for the 'historical degradation' of Hinduism. This textual purging and simplification consequently meant that Dayananda rejected all conceptions of avatar and god mythology that dominated Hindu devotional traditions. This was a rejection of the beliefs and faiths of the dominant devotional movements centred on Rama, Krishna, Shiva and the goddess. Dayananda, while himself a brahmin, also rejected the privileged and unique role of brahmins in interpreting and expounding the Vedas. He vigorously opposed any form of idolatry, caste restrictions and untouchability, child marriage, and restrictions on the education of women. His ascerbic attacks on especially brahminic, popular or sectarian Hinduism, as well as on Christianity and Islam, were important both for distancing his Arya philosophy from these religions, and at the same time for emulating and modifying certain of their aspects. Dayananda believed that the Aryan fire ritual (*yagnas* or sacrificial fire rituals are widely practiced in many forms of traditional Hinduism) was one of few authentic Aryan Vedic practices remaining in Hinduism, whereas other Hindu rituals and sectarian practices were corruptions of the original revelation. Hence the fire ritual became central to Arya Samaj religious practice. Similarly, the idea of revelation and the literal word of God embodied in a text (accurately speaking, itself foreign to Hinduism), the infallibility of sacred books, a singular already written truth and one organizational structure ('the Vedic Church') were seemingly borrowed from the 'semitic' religions.

However, in vociferously rejecting *jati* (sub-caste), Dayananda nevertheless defended *varnashramadharma* ('the natural law of the four castes') and *varna vyavastha* ('the system of caste: brahmin, kshatriya, vaishya, shudra'), arguing that this functionally ideal method of social organization existed in the Vedic period and referred to the *non-hereditary* social classification of individuals based on their merits and actions, qualities or propensities. This was another important Arya Samaj invention that had an ambiguous basis in Hindu scriptures and which continues to strongly inform the contemporary Hindutva movement. Dayananda identified the corruption of the original caste system, and the degradation of Hinduism itself as occurring in the historical period documented in the *Mahabharata*, and in particular the war between the Kauravas and the Pandavas. The *Mahabharata* hence both documented this original degradation of Hinduism and, because of its sacred status within many contemporary Hindu and especially brahminic traditions, legitimized and enforced this degradation. Hence, Dayananda identified the causes of the degradation of Hindu civilization within Hinduism itself. (Interestingly, this particular theme was also prominent in both British and German Orientalism, and perhaps best stated by Friedrich Schlegel, who really set the paradigm for this in the early nineteenth century when he wrote of the 'slow and gradual declension' of India, which followed the original divine revelation. Much can indeed be said about how nineteenth-century Indian civilizational chronographies, and their epistemologies of time, were in debate with earlier European conceptions.)

Dayananda claimed for himself a revelatory mantle and believed that only he could authentically interpret the Vedas and those texts that accorded with Vedic teachings. His rejection of the exclusive role of the brahmins as interpreters of the Vedas did not mean that any other interpretations were valid or possible, and he placed considerable strictures on what an authoritative interpretation could be. Dayananda's ferocious attacks on brahminic, traditional and vernacular Hinduism, Sikhism, Jainism, Buddhism, Islam and Christianity were to earn him numerous enemies. However, of importance here was the specific and sustained attack by Dayananda and his followers on brahminism itself. Much of the early Arya Samaj literature, while inevitably written by brahmins, identifies other brahmins and the 'ecclesiastical' structures and practices of brahminic priesthood as responsible for the corruption of the original Vedic religion (Dayananda 1970, Lajpat Rai 1915). It is because of such views that some Christians and many British colonial administrators and governors often viewed the Arya Samaj as a positive movement for 'uplift' and reform (Lajpat Rai 1915: 36–50), albeit a movement that, for some, did not go far enough and accept the truth of Christianity (for example Lillingston 1901).

Dayananda, primarily because of his linguistic limitations, is typically characterized as a distinctly 'indigenous', if unorthodox Hindu reformer who Keshab Chandra Sen had attempted, unsuccessfully, to 'Westernize'. However, Joan Leopold has highlighted his direct and long-standing engagement with a range of Western writers and movements. These were not simply the fairly numerous Christian clerics and missionaries, as well as British officials, who met him, debated with him and reported his teachings within India and England, but included meeting with the British Sanskritist Monier Williams in 1876 and his then assistant, Shyamji Krishnavarma, meetings with the Indologists George Buhler and George Thibault, and extensive, if sometimes bitter, engagement with the Theosophists, including Olcott and Blavatsky herself. Dayananda was acquainted with the writings of a range of European Indologists, including Max Muller, Muir and Monier-Williams (Leopold 1970: 288–9). The Theosophical Society under Blavatsky and Olcott was already established in the US, Britain and India by the mid-1870s and was extremely influential in promoting a worldview based on Aryanist paradigms. Fascinatingly, from the mid-1870s until the late 1880s, there were extensive negotiations between Blavatsky and Olcott, representing the society, and Dayananda and the early Arya Samaj so as to merge the two bodies into a single organization. Olcott indeed viewed Dayananda as his own guru, and for a short period the Theosophists and the Arya Samaj were seen by the former and many members of the latter as a single society. Why these attempts at merging eventually failed is instructive. Whereas most Theosophists considered Americans, Europeans and Indians as 'Aryans', Dayananda rejected this for his view that only the inhabitants of *Aryavarta* ('India') could be so designated; and while most Theosophists were rejecting the monotheism, textual infallibility and clerical power of Christianity, Dayananda was seen as emphasizing precisely those aspects within his Vedic 'Church' and religion (Leopold 1970: 290–3). While Theosophy itself both diminished in influence and became occultist, and would have had much more to gain from merger of the two organizations than the Arya Samaj would, aspects of *its* version of Aryanism were to emerge in Congress and in some of the home rule leagues under the influence of the British feminist and Theosophist Annie Besant. A specifically Austrian and German version of the Theosophy movement ('Ariosophy') was later to provide much of the symbolic material for National Socialism (Mosse 1966, Goodrick-Clarke 1985).

The main activities of Dayananda and the early Arya Samaj centred on often large public disputes with brahmin priests. The Sanatan Dharm movement, formed earlier to defend Hindu orthodoxy and brahminism was quickly to become the Arya Samaj's main Hindu intellectual and indeed physical adversary (Jones 1989: 107–8) ; the importance of the Sanatanists, as well as the nineteenth-century Hindi language and cow-protection agitations, in supplying many of the political agendas and religious-political symbols for Hindu nationalism deserve fuller treatment than can be provided here (see Dalmia 1997). The Samaj's consistent and bitter attacks on brahminist orthodoxy and orthopraxy, while reconfiguring a simpler and 'purer' religious practice based on its interpretation of the Vedas, would require reconciliation in a later period. The tensions between the simplified formal rituals of invented religious nationalism and both the 'ecclesiastical' and vernacular practices of Hinduisms continue to exist today and in many senses provide the epistemic ground for varieties of religious, caste and regional nationalist thinking. However, in its formative period, the Arya Samaj's strong stress on nationalism and patriotism attracted many members of the emergent, English educated and typically 'upper' caste sections, some of whom had been disillusioned by both earlier reform movements (such as the Brahmo Samaj, which had split into three disputing factions by the last decades of the nineteenth century) and what was perceived as the backwardness of Hindu orthodoxy and superstition in the face of colonial or Christian 'social and ethical modernism' (Jones 1976).

After Dayananda's death (rumoured within the Arya Samaj to have been the result of poisoning by a Muslim concubine of his patron, a Maharajah) the first generation of Arya Samaj recruits expanded their *pracharak* ('preaching' or propagation) activities, especially in the Punjab, the north western Provinces and (what is now) Maharashtra. One major innovation of the Samaj, seen as another emulative strategy, was the *shuddhi* or conversion ritual. This 'purification' ritual was applied by the Arya Samaj's *shuddhi sabhas* (conversion councils) from the 1880s onwards. Initially *shuddhi* was used to convert to Hinduism elite *individuals* who had become Christians, as well as some 'lower' caste and 'untouchable' individuals, but it rapidly became applied to the collective conversion of *groups* whose 'ancestors had originally been Hindus.' This *shuddhi* innovation (and, arguably, the *pracharak* structure) did not have traditional precedents within Hinduism, and was to become extremely important for Hindutva organizations such as the Vishwa Hindu Parishad (VHP) a century later during their *paravartan* ('homecoming') campaigns among syncretic Muslims, Christians and tribal groups. It is a moot point, both in understanding the Arya Samaj in the 1890s and the VHP in the 1990s, how an unrepresentative, parochial, minority group, professing a strikingly anomalous ideology and developed entirely outside the institutions of traditional Hinduism, could believe that it had the legitimacy, authority and competence to speak for and act on behalf of Hinduism. The Arya Samaj was born under conditions defined by such a model: colonialism was predicated on the ideology that a minority of the population, the British, could claim, hold ownership over, regulate and administer the lives of the vast majority according to its normative rules of power, domination and exploitation.

The Demographics of Christianity and Hinduism

One of the key factors that influenced the institution of the *shuddhi* ritual by the Arya Samaj was the colonial census which (from 1871) regularly demonstrated an increasing proportion of the *Christian* population of India and a decreasing Hindu one. Significantly, prior to 1911, Arya Samajists, had demanded that they should not be categorized in the colonial census as 'Hindus', following the earlier Arya rejection of the label 'Hindu'. Subsequently, the Arya Samaj urged their members to report a Hindu religious belief. The Censuses of 1901 and 1911 were also extremely important in fuelling a militant Hindu nationalist idiom of Hinduism under *demographic* threat from Christianity and Islam in the early part of the twentieth century. This complicates linear understandings of Muslims as the pre-eminent 'other' for Hindu nationalism over the last century. The key *emulative* strategy of many nineteenth-century Hindu 'reform' and 'revivalist' movements was undertaken initially in relation and opposition to Christianity, rather than Islam. This is not at all to diminish the anti-Islamic activities of the Arya Samaj, but to situate more centrally the multifaceted importance that Christianity held for these movements. The anti-Islamic activities of Arya Samaj proselytizers were certainly important and consequential, and were to lead to extensive Hindu-Muslim violence in Punjab in the late 1890s. This was sparked by an Arya Samaj tract published in 1892 that portrayed Islam as a sexually perverse and corrupt religion based on war, violence, theft and deception. This monological view of Islam was based on colonial and Orientalist pedagogy and recurred in various forms until the present period. However, the conversion threat was not primarily or always located against what was seen as Islamic proselytizing but against Christian preaching and conversions. The Arya Samaj also focused on the activities of the Ahmaddiyas, a sect disowned as heretical by the dominant Deobandi and Barelwi Sunni traditions in northern colonial India. In this sense, much of the language, propaganda and thematics of the threat to Hinduism from Christian conversions that was mobilized by the Hindutva movement during the 1990s was already fully developed in the latter part of the nineteenth century. The substitution of Christianity by Islam followed most clearly from the first decade of the twentieth century, mainly after the formation of Hindu Sabhas (societies) and the Hindu Sangathan movement, though even the latter were to focus squarely on Christianity. While studies of this period have tended to concentrate on the constitution of Islam as a threat, hence identifying a monologic discourse that continues to the present period, it seems important to situate the complexities in early Hindu nationalist discourse within which Christianity was considered a pre-eminent threat. Similarly, and notwithstanding the importance of the nineteenth-century Urdu-Hindi language controversies and burgeoning cow-protection agitations in forming politicized anti-Muslim constituencies, of importance, especially in the period after 1905 and into the 1920s (when 'Islam' *was* seen as the dominant threat), is how British colonialism was conceived not as political domination and economic exploitation but because of its potential conversion of 'Hindus' to Christianity.

Fractures in the Arya Samaj

The Arya Samaj established several educational institutions and colleges for Hindu women. This reflected Dayananda's stress on educating Hindu women and preventing their conversion to Christianity. The Samaj also established a network of successful schools (*gurukuls*) and colleges. Of these, the Dayananda Anglo-Vedic College in Lahore, headed by Lala Hans Raj, and the subsequent Gurukula Kangri formed in Hardwar during 1900–2 by Lala Munshi Ram (Swami Shraddhanand) were the most important. The Arya Samaj educational system was very successful and provided an avenue for aspiring members of the emergent middle classes towards a modern education and a purified Arya world view that could combine simple religious practice and a self-avowedly depoliticized and loyal nationalism.

The Arya Samaj was continually riven by numerous extraordinarily bitter disputes and factions. It was precisely the success of the Dayananda Anglo-Vedic College that created one major fracture within the Samaj. This was between supporters of Hans Raj (the 'Cultured' or the 'College' party) and Munshi Ram (the 'Mahatmas' or the 'Gurukula' or 'Radical' faction). The dispute between the factions ostensibly concerned the curriculum of the Anglo-Vedic College, with the Munshi Ram faction demanding its radicalization – the teaching of 'Vedic' rather than 'Western' science, the prioritization of Sanskrit teaching, acceptance of strict vegetarianism, among other demands (on the disputes, see Lajpat Rai 1915, Shraddhanand 1961, Jones 1976).

However, the disputes reflected a deeper problem about the status and interpretation of Dayananda's teachings. There were two layers to this. Dayananda claimed the Vedas to be infallible, complete and universally relevant; similarly, all knowledge could in principle be derived from them. However, within the Arya Samaj, Dayananda's own teachings, especially his *The Light of Truth* (*Satyarth Prakash*, Dayananda 1908), were also considered infallible and complete by some factions and individuals. The College faction withdrew from the Arya Samaj in 1893 and established separate ritual gatherings. However, individuals from both factions were to become important in the further development of Arya ideology into one of Hindu supremacism. The political trajectories of two figures – Lajpat Rai and Munshi Ram (Swami Shraddhanand) – early representatives of both factions are explored in the next chapter in order to draw out the complex influences of Hindu nationalist thinking within and outside Congress and the national movement. The impact of neo-Arya ideology, and in particular its instinctive religious nationalism, was to be extraordinary and wide-ranging in the twentieth century, despite the fact that the original movement which gave rise to it was both uncharacteristic and parochial.

The 'Bengal Renaissance'

A different movement, revolutionary nationalism in colonial India, is located in the growth of a regional, vernacular intelligentsia in Bengal in the latter half of the nineteenth century, and the subsequent spread of nationalist ideologies and networks in the aftermath of the Partition of Bengal in 1905. However, after the mid-nineteenth century, especially among some key figures within the 'Bengal Renaissance', there was a confluence of Hindu cultural nationalist ideas with those of Indian nationalism. These developments occurred in the aftermath of the two consecutive splits in the original Brahmo Samaj founded in Calcutta in 1828 by Rammohan Roy. The first split in 1850, led by Debendranath Tagore (1815–1905), was ostensibly based on a rejection of Vedic authority and processes of 'internal' rational reform within Hinduism that had been initiated by Roy. Tagore promoted instead forms of customary Hinduism while arguing that intuitive knowledge as well as rationality should form the basis of the Samaj. The second breakaway in 1866 was orchestrated by the radical reformer Keshab Chandra Sen (1838–84) who had tried, to put it crudely here, to 'Christianize' Hinduism. This left Debendranath's group, the 'Adi' (original) Brahmo Samaj, arguing for the authority and supremacy of Hinduism against Sen's zeal for 'Christianity'. Of significance is that the various disputes in the Brahmo Samaj, and arguments about the specific contributions of Hinduism in relation to Christianity, led to exclusivist conceptions of 'Hindu nationalism' (Sen 1993: 29).

Two of Debendranath's close associates, Rajnarain Basu (Raj Narayan Bose) 1826–99) and Nabagopal Mitra (1840–94) were instrumental in promoting in Bengal some of the earliest ideas of nationalism based on Hindu superiority and exclusivity. The stamp of Hinduism, conceived as ancient, primordial and foundational, onto an incipient regional nationalism relied firmly on British Orientalist research into the antiquity of India (Majumdar 1960). These developments took place within an elite Bengali milieu in which the status of (aspects of) Christianity were contrasted with a Hinduism, which, among these same elites, was already unsettled because of the earlier fractious disputes within the Brahmo Samaj: which 'Hinduism', Vedic, Upanishadic or Puranic was to acquire prominence for nationalism? Of similar importance was a long-standing controversy, still of political relevance today, about whether Hinduism had the capacity or resources for universal ethics of the kind allegedly emergent in either Christianity or Western secular philosophical humanism. A resolution of sorts to both these debates was later provided during the famous controversy in 1882 between Bankimchandra Chattopadhyaya and the Scottish clergyman Dr William Hastie. The latter's attack on 'Hindu idolatry' was countered by Bankim's 'cultural' view of Hinduism in which the believer had undertaken to apprehend an idol as holy not because it was believed to be so, but because the believer, the latter already articulated by Bankim's in the language of ethical humanism, had 'made a contract with his own heart for the sake of culture and discipline' to treat the latter as an image of God (Flora 1993).

In 1866, the same year as Sen formed his breakaway 'Bharatvarsiya' Brahmo Samaj, Rajnarain wrote a 'Prospectus of a society for the promotion of national feeling among the educated natives of Bengal' (see Ghatak 1991: 35, see also Ispahani 1970, Majumdar 1971). By 1872, Rajnarain was promoting an exclusive Hindu nationalism based on what he perceived to be the superiority of Hindu religion and culture (*Hindu Dharmer Sresthata*), contrasting the latter with Christianity and 'European civilization'. The Hindus had, he said, forgotten their glorious past. Paraphrasing Milton, he foresaw

> the noble and puissant Hindu nation rousing herself after sleep, and rushing headlong towards progress with divine prowess. I see this rejuvenated nation again illumining the world by her knowledge, spirituality and culture, and the glory of the Hindu nation again spreading over the whole world. (Basu, quoted in Majumdar 1971: 295–6)

In a later text, *The Aged Hindu's Hope* (*Vriddha Hindur Asha*, 1886), Rajnarain made clear that his Hindu Mahasamiti and the 'Hindu nation' could not have a place for Muslims. While Muslims were free to form their own societies, nationality was to be based on Narain's conception of an Upanishadic Brahmo-oriented religion (the latter based on opposing an intermediary between the human and the Divine, defending a modified idolatry and defending a 'Vedic' conception of caste). The Mahasamiti's aim was to unite all Hindus under a concept of Hindu nation based on Hindu religion, customs and 'memory' of ancient glories. This nationalism precluded unity with Muslims since their religion and traditions were conceived as different. The flag of the Samiti should, he argued, bear the inscription: 'God and Motherland: Triumph of *Sanatan dharma*' (Ghatak 1991: 45). During the 1880s, Rajnarain also became preoccupied with Aryanism as the basis of Hindu nationality (Sen 1993: 57).

The dominant Brahmo emphasis on Hindu 'degeneration' and reforms in caste, widow remarriage, idolatry, overseas travel, untouchability, and child brides was rearticulated by Rajnarain through a gradualist and conservative reformism based on a 'return' to glorious, ancient Hindu or Aryan traditions that, it was claimed, upheld no distinction between religion, society, culture, civilization and nationality.

Rajnarain argued that the precepts for any societal reform had to be found not in 'evil' foreign influences but from precedents in ancient Hinduism. Similarly, it was because Hinduism comprehensively embraced all human knowledge, politics and economics that it could incorporate practices such as idolatry as 'inferior stages of religious belief in its own bosom in harmony with the nature of Man who cannot but pass through several stages of religious development before being able to grasp the Supreme Being' (Ghatak 1991: 43).

In 1867 an extremely influential annual 'Jatiya Mela' was started by Nabagopal Mitra. The Mela, which within two years had been renamed the 'Hindu Mela', was based on the 'Nationality Promotion Society' advocated by Rajnarain. The Mela aimed to promote national feeling, patriotism, unity and self help among Bengal's Hindus. Criticism of the Society for its exclusively Hindu orientation was countered thus: 'We do not understand why our [critics take] exception to the Hindus who certainly form a nation by themselves and as such a society established by them can very well be called "National Society"' (Majumdar 1971: 294).

Nabagopal, like Rajnarain, believed that 'the basis of national unity in India' was Hinduism. Moreover, 'Hindu nationality' embraced all Hindus in India regardless of region or linguistic difference: 'The Hindus are destined to be a religious nation' (Majumdar 1971: 295). The Mela went into abeyance by 1881 because of the formation of secular leagues and associations in Bengal. The ideological influence of both the Mela and of Rajnarain's lectures and writings has been described by Kamal Kumar Ghatak thus:

> The Mela's primary objective was the revival of the past glory of Hinduism. Its leaders talked of patriotism, freedom and Hinduism in the same breath. In fact, they found no contradiction in this. Neither Rajnarain Bose nor Nabagopal Mitra though of a common national sentiment which could enthuse the Hindus, Muslims and Christians of India in a feeling of brotherhood and unity. Nationalism and Hinduism were almost identical in their eyes. (Ghatak 1991: 38)

Of additional significance was the career of Chandranath Basu (1844–1910), and his popularization of the term *Hindutva* and its relationship to 'Indian history' that was to be consequential after the 1920s. Chandranath was very much part of the English-educated elite culture of Bengal in the nineteenth century. He worked as a librarian and a translator for the Bengal government and wrote regularly for Bankimchandra Chattopadhyaya's *Bangadarshan*. Amiya Sen has argued that he represented an intellectual bridge between 'reforming' varieties of Hinduism in the Bengal Renaissance and the conservative 'revival' of Hinduism. Chandranath's work represented a defence of brahminism, an argument for retaining 'traditional' caste, gender and marriage practices in Hindu society, an advocation of female chastity, restriction of Hindu women's education and civil rights, the upholding of male authority, an economic nationalism and an emphasis on Hindu rituals (Sen 1993: 210–13). His *Hindutva – an Authentic History of the Hindus*, published in Bengali in 1892 (Basu 1913) figured Hinduism in terms of its glorious archaic past and he aimed to demonstrate the superiority of Hinduism and its Gods in comparison with that of Christianity. In his *Hindutva*, 'history appeared . . . as the unfolding of man's innate spirituality' (Sen 1993: 215–16). It is significant that the birth of the concept of 'Hindutva' was so intimately related to the threat of Christianity during the colonial period. Chandranath's precise and novel link between 'Hinduness' and 'history' was to be decisive.

If these early stirrings of nineteenth century Hindu nationalism were overtaken by subsequent events, their impact in Bengal was important for crystallizing what was to later become both an anti-colonial patriotism and a 'Hindu communal consciousness' among the emergent Bengal intelligentsia (Datta 1999). Indeed, and conversely, the precise trajectories of Bengali elite formation in this period are intimately related to their role in furthering a distinctively Hindu oriented anti-colonialism that was based on the cultivation of a 'love' and freedom for a regionally or nationally conceived religious 'motherland'. This theme was emergent in various Indian nationalist and 'Hindu nationalist' Bengal intellectual circles in the later nineteenth century, and crossed from Debendranath Tagore to Bankimchandra Chattopadhyaya, Rabindranath Tagore, Aurobindo Ghose and the revolutionary nationalist sects of the early twentieth century.

Bankimchandra Chattopadhyaya and the Affect of 'Hindu Nation'

The novels as well as the journalistic, sociological and political writings and religious interpretations of Bankimchandra Chattopadhyaya (1838–94) present a complex legacy for both Hindu and secular nationalism (B. Chatterjee [Chattopadhyaya] 1986, P. Chatterjee 1986, Haldar 1989, B. Chatterjee, 1994, Kaviraj 1995, Kaviraj 1989, Sarkar 1996). Bankim is considered to be the 'father' of the modern Bengali novel and perhaps the most important figure in the Bengal Renaissance from the late 1860s. His huge body of work is subject to various interpretations. In particular, a regular distinction is made between his earlier writings, committed to humanistic forms of social, 'religious' and gender equality (the latter demonstrating the influence of John Stuart Mill), and his later ones that seem to celebrate Hindu nationalist supremacism, expound consistent anti-Muslim sentiments and erase his earlier and dramatic support for women's equality (this erasure was literal: later reissues of his seminal *Samya* did not contain the critical chapters on women's equality).

In the tradition of what is conceived to be secular nationalism, the themes of Hindu nationalism in Bankim's writings can be glossed. Conversely, for Hindu nationalists, his earlier writings for gender equality and a conception of sexual freedom, and his satirical, humorous and mocking prose directed against Hindu sadhus and Bengali babus is overwritten by his celebration of violent Hindu struggle against Muslims, and in particular his glorification of Hindu religious-territorial nationalism in his song, *Bande Mataram*, a virtual anthem for the contemporary Hindutva movement. As important for both secular and religious appropriations was Bankim's view that, while Western science (and indeed the West as the home of empirical science) was both valuable and important for Indian sensibilities to learn from, it was India and Hinduism that had provided advanced philosophical and religious learning that the west had barely reached, let alone moved beyond. The Kantian ideal of humanity as an end was in principle reachable not by Western utilitarian atheism, as some Western philosophers argued, but by a devotionalism to a humanized god – this was one of the distinctive potentials of Indian or Hindu philosophy.

Bankim can be rather effortlessly appropriated by or uncritically enfolded into apparently secular nationalist tendencies despite the thoroughgoing Hindu religious nationalist imaginary that not only permeated especially his later and most important writings but quite fundamentally structured them. Tanika Sarkar has argued for more subtle readings of his fictional writing that neither underplay the prominence of violent Hindu masculinities in his later novels nor understate his (earlier) humanist narratives that can embrace the poor, female or Muslim characters in his novels (Sarkar 1996). She has also argued for a more nuanced reading of the disruptions in his later 'Hindu nationalist' novels that can work against the exclusivist religious nationalism he was ostensibly promoting. The discussion below has a different aim: to highlight the Hindu nationalist themes in his work in the context of a telos of nationalist development that characterised his critical (and initially enthusiastic, but later diminishing) appropriation of Positivism (on Bankim and positivism, see his own essays in Chatterjee 1986, Gupta 1972, Forbes 1975, Flora 1993).

Bankim's later novels and writings were important for articulating an often rather didactic aesthetic of Hindu nationalism through their symbolisation first of the Bengal 'motherland' and then 'the Hindu nation' in visceral gendered and religious terms. While Bankim's novels were often occupied with apparently reforming concerns within Hinduism, especially in relation to poverty, equality and gender (*Samya*), in four of his novels (*Mrnalini*, 1869; *Rajsimha*, 1881; *Anandamath*, 1882; *Sitaram*, 1886) and in *Dharmatattva* (1888) and *Krishnacarita* these concerns were either displaced or intertwined with powerful themes of Hindu resilience and suffering, Hindu resistance to British colonialism, and what was conceived to be Muslim tyranny in Bengal or in medieval and colonial India. The merging of religion with nationalism in his novels is striking not simply because nationalism was often conceived as a battle against British colonists *and* Muslims, but because of his deployment of a powerful affective dimension as an integral component of what Hindu belonging to the Motherland must mean. Bankim recognized that political affect had to be made central to religious-nationalist affiliation. This sympathetic pity identified the sorrow at the historic plight of the symbolically conceived Motherland with the affect manifest in the inability of his masculine characters to exactly decide their future in the face of unanswerables, the aporias of and limits to their national condition. This was a consistent, *familial* and gendered theme in Hindu-leaning nationalist discourse: a cultivation and invocation of a strictly *grievous* emotional wounding as an abyss that both defined the Hindu man and turned him towards perpetually futile action against his 'enemies'. This theme of love for a suffering motherland was often crudely supplemented in Hindu nationalist discourse with past glories, the present need for militant action against perceived 'enemies', and future redemption. Of salience was a powerful metonymic relation established between domestic maternal suffering and affliction, the consequent affect of the son, and the imagined historical injury to the nation.

The affective configuration of Hindu nationalism in Bankim's novels may appear to sit uneasily with Bankim's critical sociological and philosophical commitments, notably to that distinctive combination of utilitarianism, strong positivism and social evolutionism that was flourishing, at least for a period, in nineteenth-century Bengal intellectual circles. Not only was Bankim familiar with the dominant trinity of Comtean positivism, John Stuart Mill's utilitarianism and Herbert Spencer's evolutionist sociology but had engaged with various other European writers. Aspects of what appears to be Kantian rationalism make an appearance in his writings, in particular the transmutation of Kant's conception of the faculties of mind in Bankim's distinctive idea of the harmonious cultivation of the human faculties (*Dharmatattva*, fifth and sixth *adhyaya* (chapters) in Chatterjee 1986). Bankim also appeared to be familiar with the abstracted conception of God and religious existence in German idealism (as demonstrated for example by Schelling, Fichte and Schleiermacher) which Bankim sought to displace with a humanized neo-Puranic God (Krishna) and a conception of *anushilan dharma* – a neo-Kantian harmonious cultivation of the human faculties in accordance with the necessity of action in a field that is defined by culture. In Bankim there was a displacement of an abstracted metaphysical-spiritual idea of religion for one in which the 'cultural cultivation' of religious affect was made central. He was also familiar with the work of some Indologists, such as William Jones and Max Muller, as well as the philosophies of Bentham, Hume, Rousseau, Locke and the Mills. However, Bankim's engagement with both Utilitarianism and Spencerianism was critical and he was to reject the atheistic and individual rights based thrust of utilitarian liberal political philosophy in favour of a view that inserted love, duties and obligations to the national or social collective under an overarching Hindu religious conception of humanism. Of all the objects of his 'faculty of love', the love for one's nation was of the highest kind (*Dharmatattva*, 24th *adhyaya* (chapter) in Chatterjee 1986).

The influence on Bankim of disciplines from Europe, such as British sociology, Orientalism and romanticism, can be seen in his strongly evolutionary perspective on Hindu national development and his conception of the development of 'Man', both of which were integrally related to the priority he gave to a neo-Puranic, neo-*bhakti* interpretation of Hinduism. There is certainly debate about Bankim's precise relationship to positivism. Bankim is both identified as the key proponent of positivism in nineteenth-century Bengal, primarily through articles that he himself wrote or published in his periodicals, as well as one of the stronger critics of the view that Comtean 'positive religion' could or should replace Hinduism (Flora 1993, Forbes 1975, B. Chatterjee ed. 1994). However, one cannot separate his commitment to a reconfigured humanized, intelligible Puranic conception of Krishna, ostensibly against his Brahmo or Christian adversaries, from his critical affiliation with a Comtean cosmology.

In his novel, *Anandamath*, redemptive Hindu nationalism was the necessary, but unfinished, conclusion to British colonialism. The latter was necessary for providing Hindus with knowledge of the physical world as the condition for Hindus to then comprehend *and feel* knowledge of the spiritual world and hence displace the 'vulgar, debased religion' that they possessed, manifested in his time in the aridity and rationalism of varieties of reformist Brahmoism. Hence 'English rule' was the prerequisite for revival of the eternal Hindu faith. However, the novel is also vigorously critical of the Hindu king and kingdom established after the overthrow of 'Muslim tyranny' in Bengal. The novel ends with the gaze of two ordinary, poor Hindu men for whom the tumultuous and violent Hinduism that structures the novel is abstracted from their daily lives, and is accessible to them only as rumour or fiction (Chatterjee 1992). This disappointment of Hindu nationalism at the end of *Anandamath* is also explicable in Comtean themes.

Comtean Positivism was an important resource for the project to promote Hinduism as a transforming, but nevertheless *perennial* religion that had travelled from an ineffable past and that could consolidate as a future nation. It may appear unusual that positivism could play such a role. However, it was of importance to the reconstructive conception of religious being in Bankim's work. Of additional significance is the distinctive positivist language of survival, degeneration and vitalism. Bankim's project can be seen as an attempt to simultaneously refute an abstract conception of God and an ineffable conception of nature or Spirit in both Upanishadic and Western post-Enlightenment traditions in favour of a conception of 'Man' or humanity in this world. Enlightened humanity had accession to God through both a semi-historicist understanding of the Puranic myths and a non-vulgar conception of devotion to an intelligible God, Krishna. Consequently, Bankim criticized the 'inscrutable power' that defined Herbert Spencer's conception of a transcendental nature, in favour of the positive conception of a 'religion of humanity'. The influence of Comte included Comte's 'law of three stages', his hierarchy of the sciences, his stress on natural science and the nomothetic rendering of humanity and society, his conception of the religious nature of 'Man', and his vision of religion as central not for individual salvation but for the collective redemption of an enlightened humanity (Forbes 1975: 134–5). These themes were explicitly propounded by Bankim in *Rajani, Dharmatattva and Anandamath*. Comte's 'positive philosophy', which made the natural and social world intelligible and could provide a basis for social progress and development though empirical investigation and the discovery of laws, is also clearly manifest in *Dharmatattva* and *Krishnacarita* (Chatterjee 1986). Of significance was Comte's 'law of three stages' of societal development, from the theological, to metaphysical abstract universalism to a positive philosophy of society in which the evidence of empirical investigation and reason provided the basis of societal organization. Importantly, Comte rejected a final or absolute conception of full knowledge in this final or third stage: absolute explanations were impossible and instead one proposed advancement through what could be known and intelligible in relation to the societal and historical norms that prevailed. In other words, the final limit point is not a conclusion to the threefold stagist development of societies but its aporia, though one in which humanity, through the development of its faculties, has acquired knowledge of itself and its society based on the prevailing historical and cultural circumstances.

In Bankim's work, each of these themes – the emphasis on empirical knowledge and a religion of humanity, this threefold developmentalism and this resolute aporia of the end-point – are manifest. There is therefore another possible reading of his critique of the Hindu kingdom at the end of *Anandamath*: the future is left open once the understanding of the potentials and corruptions of Hindu rashtra have been explicated as the only ground that has *as yet been possible and knowable* in a societal idiom that, nevertheless, cannot but reach towards an unfinished Hindu nation. In other words, what appears to be Bankim's muted return to social reform issues need not conflict with, but can enhance the performance of a Hindu nationalist imaginary.

One final point about Bankim's philosophy concerns his extremely careful trans-mutation of the figure of Krishna in *Krishnacarita* (and adjacently *Dharmatattva*). Bankim rejected what was conceived as the crude form of devotionalism within sectarian Hinduism, but he vigorously defended devotionalism and *bhakti*. He rejected the conception of abstracted, transcendental God or religion within traditional, Brahmo or Western metaphysical thinking, and yet defended the idea of God as accessible, intelligible, and humanised. He similarly vigorously rejected atheism and yet refused to concede to traditional conceptions of a Supreme Being, nor would he displace 'humanity' as foundational for his conceptions of religion or society. He rejected the abstract ritual textualism of Dayananda Saraswati and the appropriation of the soaring metaphysics of the Upanishads by the Brahmos, yet defended the absolute centrality of some kind of *transcendental religion* to human development. Bankim is often said to have created a new religion (*anushilan dharma*) based on a reconfiguration of Puranic, devotional religion such that Krishna symbolized a 'de-sexualized', ethical, militant ideal of what humanity could become. Here, the implied association between Puranic (rather than Vedic or Upanishadic) religion and politics is not the only consequence. This synthetic, rather than simply syncretic, association of 'Comtism' with Puranic Hinduism created a space that did not simply mimic neo-Vedantism using a different idiom, but made a closer relation between temporal politics, a necessary cultural field, and an apparently rationalized, humanist, scientific rendition of Hindu religion necessary.

Bal Gangadhar Tilak and Hindu Nationalist Activism

If the 'Bengal Renaissance' can be said to have created the grids of intelligibility through which nationalism could be naturalized in Hindu registers, a different and extraordinarily influential configuration of religious nationalism was being played out elsewhere. Bal Gangadhar Tilak (1856–1920), a Ratnagiri Chitpavan brahmin, became a central figure in the national movement until his death in 1920. He was the most important figure in the 'extremist' faction of the Indian National Congress and the most vociferous critic of the 'moderate' tendencies in Congress that sought degrees of accommodation with colonial rule and which wished to elicit a process of gradual social and constitutional reform. Tilak, alongside Ranade, Gokhale and Gandhi, is celebrated as one of the most important leaders of the national movement that led to independence. His secular credentials are demonstrated by uncompromising activism for the boycott and self-rule (*swaraj*) movements, rural reform, foundation of the Home Rule League in India (1914), and his role in the negotiations with Mohammed Ali Jinnah and the Muslim League in 1916 (the 'Lucknow Pact'), the latter serving as the basis for joint action between Congress and the League during Gandhi's non-cooperation movement (and allowing for separate Muslim electorates in provincial council elections and for greater than proportionate Muslim representation in all provinces except Bengal and the Punjab). Tilak founded two regional newspapers, the Marathi-language *Kesari* (The Lion) and the English-language *Mahratta*, that were the main mouthpieces for anti-British agitation in north-western India. Against the 'Moderates' who wanted to ensure cooperation with the British, Tilak also led the separate section of the 'Extremist' party during the December 1907 session of Congress at Surat ('the Surat split'). Tilak was imprisoned several times for his anti-British activities and gained the honorific *'lokamanya'* – 'revered by the people'. As a past leader of the national movement, his standing in contemporary India is perhaps second only to that of Gandhi.

....ile this is less apparent today, Tilak was important for cultivating a Hindu primordialism based on early Orientalist precepts about Indian civilization and combining this with a reconfigured and politicized form of public, urban Hindu devotionalism. The latter included the development of a new form of mass Hindu political activism in Maharashtra in the late nineteenth-century that depended on linking his bare Orientalist primordialism with two other ideological configurations, and in the process transforming the import of both: the novel politicization of the Hindu devotional idiom around the figure and competing and layered symbolism of the (then perhaps unlikely) God Ganapati (Ganesh); and the formation of politicized regional folk genealogies around the seventeenth-century medieval Hindu leader of the Mahratta confederacy, Shivaji. A partial rendering of the history of Shivaji and the Mahratta 'Empire' supplied potent symbols for the Hindu nationalist political imaginary of a 'Hindu state' and uncompromisingly militant aggression against Muslims. As with the Bengal intellectual 'upper' caste elite, the constitution and political sharpening of a regional, linguistic and elite-brahminical Maharashtrian *patrie* by Tilak was combined with a grander claim about Indian nationalism. The potential, in both the Bengal and Maharashtrian cases, that a distinctly regional nationalism could conflict with an Indian nationalism was one consequential dynamic. As important in both cases is how a regional nationalism became inextricably linked both to the political formation of upper (especially brahmin) castes and to the invigoration of Hindu traditions and symbols in the service of an 'Indian' nationalism and against colonial rule. Similarly, in both cases, one can see the transfiguration of symbols of Hindu religious devotionalism – the religious pantheon – into a nationalist pantheon.

Richard Cashman (1970, 1975) has argued that these processes were especially important in Poona and Bombay (now both part of Maharashtra). The Chitpavan brahmin community was threatened by a variety of colonial reforms in avenues for both educational attainment and government administration during the late nineteenth century, primarily because of colonial proposals that aimed to extend employment and education to non-brahmin castes. Cashman has argued that the Chitpavans, who together with other brahmin groups had traditionally held high-status posts in provincial administration and had benefited most from education, were viewed with revulsion by many British governors, officers and administrators. The latter saw the Chitpavan brahmin community of Poona as corrupt and deceitful, a locus of anti-British conspiracy, and wilfully obstructive of social reform initiatives that compromised what the Chitpavans viewed as their heritage in terms of serving the ruling power of the region. (The peshwa or chief minister elite had emerged from this community during the Mahratta confederacy; the Chitpavans also viewed themselves as both warriors and the priestly caste – *kshatriya brahmins* – inheritors of a glorious heritage under Mahratta rule.) Consequently, from the mid-1880s, there was considerable agitation from Chitpavan and other brahmin groups against the reservation of half the number of free college scholarships to the Deccan and Ferguson colleges for Muslims and 'backward' Hindu castes (Cashman 1975: 37–8). The status of the Poona brahmins was also threatened by the regional implementation of legislation for representation in the provincial legislative councils (1892). The previous year, the government had passed legislation that raised the female age of consent from 10 to 12 years. This resulted in considerable opposition to what was viewed as British interference in Hindu 'religious' and 'traditional' matters. A number of societies were formed, ostensibly protesting against the Age of Consent Bill but extending their activities to a general defence of brahminism, the latter seen as under threat. After 1893 in both Bombay and the Deccan, there was also considerable inter-religious violent conflict between Hindu and Muslim communities following the growth of militant cow protection societies, as well as Hindu protests against the restriction of music outside mosques.

Tilak's interventions during this troubled period are illustrative. Tilak had opposed the Age of Consent legislation for both pragmatic and political reasons. There was widespread opposition to the legislation among 'upper' caste Hindus; hence Tilak's support for the latter worked to further his political stature. Tilak also believed it was an illegitimate intervention by the colonial power in both Hindu religious matters and brahminic orthodoxy (Wolpert 1977). Similarly, prior to the Bombay and Deccan riots during 1893, Hindus in Poona had traditionally attended the annual Muslim festival of Muharram. However, in 1894, Tilak instigated a new public celebration by Hindus alone of Ganesh Chaturti. Prior to this, the annual traditional Ganesh celebration had primarily been a private or family affair among Hindus. Ganesh had also traditionally been a favoured deity primarily among the Chitpavan brahmin communities. Tilak instead publicly mobilized the symbol of Ganesh for the political forging of a mass movement among Hindus that both protested British rule and was marshalled against the Muslim Muharram festival, which hardly any Hindus thereafter attended (Cashman 1970). While the annual public Ganesh celebrations took on a momentum of their own among 'lower' caste communities, these were apolitical in comparison with the Chitpavan and Gujarati-speaking brahmin festivals, the latter explicitly exhorting Hindus to abandon associating with the Muslim festivals and to celebrate their martial Hindu, Aryan or Maratha heritage (Cashman 1975: 83–84). This was a practical example of the manner in which exclusivist Hinduism was mobilized so as to create fissures between religious communities and cleave apart the urban and public spaces of civil society into contending sections defined by nominal religious affiliation. The Ganesh festivals were to die down after a few years, partly because of the restrictive conditions upon them imposed by the British (though the festivals did re-emerge in the early part of the twentieth-century).

This distinctive and novel propagation of a devotional deity for a communal purpose that served as agitation against the British was supplemented with Tilak's next important intervention, that of instituting the figure of Shivaji as the pre-eminent symbol of Hindu militancy, anti-colonial agitation, Mahratta nationalism and finally as a symbol for Indian nationalism (see 'Is Shivaji not a national hero?' in Tilak 1919). While initiated as a memorial fund with associated festivals aimed at raising funds to refurbish the monument where Shivaji was buried, the Shivaji celebrations were to quickly turn violent under the conditions of both famine and plague that were affecting the Deccan and Bombay during the mid-1890s. Tilak used the Gita to justify violent means, symbolized in the manner in which Shivaji had killed Aurangzeb's general, Afzal Khan (see also 'Speech on the occasion of the Shivaji Coronation festival', in Tilak 1919: 62–4). Cashman has argued that Tilak primarily sought to mobilize Ranade's more moderate conception of Shivaji for the purpose of generating funds from the landed classes (Cashman 1975). Nevertheless, Tilak's was an ambiguous message, because the prominent abstraction of Shivaji's killing of Afzal Khan displaced the Muslim chief commanders of Shivaji's military force, his Muslim foreign secretary and various other close Muslim associates of Shivaji. Conversely, that Shivaji was captured and detained at Agra as a result of a military campaign by Mirza Raja Jai Singh, a Hindu and Aurangzeb's most important military general, and that Shivaji's escape from Agra was aided by his Muslim associates was similarly elided.

In his depiction of Shivaji, Tilak may have been justifying the use of violence against colonial rule but was simultaneously unleashing a communalized abstraction of India's medieval period. Violence was to be rehearsed as an ethical philosophy by Tilak in his *Srimad Bhagavatgita Rahasya* (*The Secret Meaning of the Bhagavad Gita*, Tilak 1936) written towards the end of his life. Here, Tilak defended the ethical obligation to the active principle or action, even violent action including killing, as long as this was undertaken according to the dictates of dharma, that is in a fashion that was selfless and without personal interest or motive. The idea that the *Bhagavad Gita* could be interpreted as providing *guidance* for temporal action had existed since the thirteenth century (Wolpert 1977: 260). However, Stanley Wolpert has argued that its use by Tilak to legitimate violence as a duty for which one could not necessarily find any moral or ethical principle beyond self-preservation and a disinterested disposition was novel (Wolpert 1977: 259, 262–3).

Such uses of Shivaji also demonstrated an appeal to those, like the Chapekar brothers, who viewed violent resistance to British rule as a *religious* duty and obligation on behalf of a greater Hinduism. Indeed, the articulation of revolutionary or violent nationalism as a religious obligation and a legitimate religious impulse was as important for the nationalist groupings that flourished in Bengal both during the nineteenth century and after the first Partition of Bengal in 1905. Several violent revolutionary Shivaji societies and clubs were also formed in the aftermath of his political elevation by Tilak. Similarly, the symbolic potency of Shivaji for Hindu chauvinist, anti-Muslim sentiments was not lost on the burgeoning 'upper' caste Hindu organizations that had come to be keen to celebrate 'Hindu victory' against Aurangzeb, and the glory of a 'Hindu empire' during the Mughal period. It was also to be a short step from a narrative of 'Hindu victory' against the Muslim Aurangzeb, to another narrative that Aurangzeb (who, like the Mughal emperors except the sixteenth century Babur, was born in India) was an illegitimate presence within, and an 'invader' of India. This late nineteenth century insertion of Shivaji into an emergent Hindu nationalist pantheon can be seen as one definitive stage in what, two decades later, was to become within the Hindu nationalist historical imaginary a monologic, unending, 800-year war by the Hindu nation against Muslim 'invaders'.

Tilak, Aryanism and Hindutva

If these strictly political interventions of Tilak in Maharashtra generalized the deity of Ganesh beyond its traditional 'upper' caste devotional constituency, and generated the figure of Shivaji as the pre-eminent symbol for Hindu and Mahratta power, Tilak's writings about ancient Indian history rehearsed the themes of primordialism that were discussed previously. Indeed, Tilak's political astuteness can be seen in combining an intellectual ground of archaic Hindu-Aryan primordialism with a populist reconfiguration of Hindu devotionalism and Hindu regional nationalism. This deeply political syncretism of the archaic-Vedic and the popular-devotional (*bhakti*) was to become an important method in later Hindu nationalism. In 1893 (the year before the Ganesh festival was instigated), Tilak published his *The Orion, or researches into the antiquities of the Vedas* (Tilak 1984). This was followed in 1903 by his larger *The Arctic Home in the Vedas: A new key to the interpretation of many Vedic texts and legends* (Tilak 1956). The former, critically inspired by Max Muller's writings, argued that the Aryan Vedic period be pushed back from the then-accepted date of 1500 BC to at least 4000 BC, when the vernal equinox was in the constellation of Orion and was allegedly observed and documented by 'Vedic seers'. Moreover Tilak, rather unfaithfully, drew upon the writings of Frederich Max Muller among others to present the argument that not only were the Aryans responsible for the first civilization in the world, but they had started the process whereby the world received civilization as such (Tilak 1984). This thesis was extended in *Arctic Home*, Aryan civilization both being pushed back even further to before 8000 BC, and being more advanced than the subsequent Bronze and Iron Age civilizations. Tilak reinterpreted both Vedic and Avestan deities as polar Gods representing a land that was the paradise of the Aryans, and that was destroyed by the advance of ice during the second glacial period. The original Aryan homeland was the Arctic (Tilak 1956). (It is of interest that a similar argument about human origins had been advanced by the French astronomer Jean-Sylvain Bailly in the eighteenth century, and had been later attacked by, among others, Hegel.)

If these tracts may now seem to be unimportant flourishes, Tilak was quite explicit even in 1906 about the importance of the Vedic Aryan heritage, not just for cultivating a common tie among Indians but for consolidating a future Hindu nation.

> Religion is an element in nationality . . . During Vedic times, India was a self-contained country. It was united as a great nation. That unity has disappeared bringing great degradation and it becomes the duty of the leaders to revive that union. A Hindu of this place [Benares] is as much a Hindu as one from Madras or Bombay. The study of the Gita, Ramayana and Mahabharata produce the same ideas throughout the country. Are not these – common allegiance to the Vedas, Gita and Ramayana – our common heritage? If we lay stress on it forgetting all the minor differences that exist between different sects, then by the grace of Providence we shall ere long be able to consolidate all the different sects into a mighty Hindu nation. This ought to be the ambition of every Hindu. ('Speech at Bharat Dharma Mahamandala', Benares, 3.01.1906, in Tilak 1919: 13–14)

More ominously perhaps was Tilak's view that the 'common factor' in Indian society was the *'feeling of Hindutva'*. Hindus, he argued, not only constituted the majority of India's population but that all Hindus were one because of their adherence to *Hindudharma* (Wolpert 1977: 135).

While it would be highly inaccurate to describe Tilak's ideological and pragmatic political projects as reducible to a bare Hindu nationalism, the severe elisions in his association of Hinduism with ideas of both primordial national belonging and Indian national destiny require noting. Hindu *dharma* and 'Hindutva' can by no means be said to have united, or indeed been a common sentiment among the populations of nineteenth-century colonial India; their attempted naturalization is itself an hegemonic claim that announced how these conceptions were constituted in politics. Tilak's claim about Hindu *dharma* and 'the feeling of Hinduness' situated these conceptions above and beyond the histories of societies and nations as transcendental ideas that paralleled the narratives of imperial progress and national destiny that they attempted to substitute. Similarly, the process whereby Hindu *dharma* could be articulated as the main basis for Indian nationality was a substitution of one narrative of the civilizing mission, the imperial, with another primordialist narrative of national formation and national progress that vigorously elided caste, both in the sense that the 'lower' castes and those outside the caste system were evaded, but also in the glorification of certain Hindu symbols, which was designed to appeal to brahminic, 'upper' caste and northern Indian constituencies during a process of political vernacular elite formation.

Other Influences

These themes were brought out explicitly by two of Tilak's associates in the 'extremist' wing of Congress, Lala Lajpat Rai (see next chapter) and Bipinchandra Pal (the three were called 'Lal-Bal-Pal' in the national movement). Bipinchandra Pal (1858-1932) argued that Indian nationality was a composite of its various religious communities and could not be a 'Hindu' or 'Muslim' India, and he could genuinely celebrate the contributions of Islam and Muslims to India (see Bipinchandra Pal, 'Contributions of Islam to Indian nationality' in Johari 1993, volume 3, book 2: 389–93). Pal was also to turn away from his earlier adherence to militant non-cooperation.

However, in an essay published in 1901, 'Reform on "national lines"', Pal explicitly advocated 'the thought structure of the Aryan race consciousness', the 'civic' Aryan social structure, and the genius of Aryan fellowship as key components that distinguished nationality in India (and ancient Greece) from other nationalisms. The civic, constitutional social polity of the Aryans was distinguished from the military, legalistic, despotic polity of the 'Semitic races', the latter defined by their uncritical obedience to the commands of God. It was precisely these differences in the structure of thought and society that constituted individual nationality, the latter conceived by him as the regulative idea in the historical evolution of nations and societies (Bipinchandra Pal, 'Definition of Nationality' in Appadorai 1973 vol 1: 476–8). Of significance here was a different opposition between the 'Aryan', conceived as Hindu, and the 'Semitic', conceived as Muslim (or Christian). This can also be seen as signifying a characteristically 'Indian' differentiation of the 'Aryan' from what was conceived as 'semitism'. The latter was not concerned with Jewishness as such, but could prefigure other groups within a 'semitic' register. We can discern here what might legitimately be called a current of Indian 'anti-semitism' that possessed its own distinctive characteristics based the perceived alterity of Islam and Christianity.

Bipinchandra Pal's Hegelianism, very similar to, though of lesser philosophical sophistication than that articulated by (Lala) Har Dayal, was extended by him in a book published at the turn of century that situated the nature of Indian nationality as the unfolding and development of 'Hindu Spirit' from an archaic past up to the boycott and *swaraj* movements of his time (Bipinchandra Pal 1910). In opposition to what he conceived as the dead secularism of the old Congress, the new national movement was defined exclusively by its 'intensely religious and spiritual character'. Religion and the new patriotism that demanded self-rule were inextricably intertwined such that the former, as *Vedanta*, was the evolutionary basis of the latter. To view the national movement through political, social or economic categories, he argued, was to misunderstand it altogether. The philosophy that stood behind the movement was religion, the philosophy of Brahman (the

Absolute). Indeed, the militant demand for 'self-rule' was itself an Hegelian return of the Hindu self to itself, after it had thrown off the 'hypnotism' of British rule. If a narrative of Hindu conflict with Muslims was absent from Pal's philosophical history, the overintegrated Hindu religious idiom within which this history was conceived by a central figure in the national movement is illustrative of the instinctive confluence of Hinduism with Indian nationalism.

Aurobindo's Dharmic Nationalism

The Bengal revolutionary Aurobindo Ghose (1872–1950), an important inspiration for the revolutionary and terroristic nationalist movements and secret societies that proliferated in Bengal after the turn of twentieth century, was as adamant about the relation between nationalism and Hinduism, though he was not averse to transforming this into an anti-Muslim narrative. Ghose spent much of his childhood and youth in England, where he received his schooling and his university education in classics and modern languages. He was to return to India as a young man and became embroiled in revolutionary activities until imprisoned in 1908, after which he fled to the French colony of Pondicherry and remained there for the rest of his life, becoming a spiritual teacher of an evolutionist metaphysics of human transcendence into 'the Supramental'. While accepting, like Bipinchandra Pal, *some* conception of a religiously composite Indian nationality, although one that was 'largely Hindu in spirit', (Ghose in Johari ed. 1993 volume 3: 32, 64), neither he nor Pal, who were both leading Congress activists and consecutive editors of the Bengal nationalist periodical, *Bande Mataram*, attempted to further Muslim inclusion in the national movement itself. Ghose, in several extensive commentaries on comparative philology and ethnology, accepted an indigenist version of Aryanism, but rejected the view of European Orientalists that Aryans had entered geographical India in pre-history or that there were fundamental racial or linguistic differences between the northern Indian Aryans and the southern Indian Dravidians (Ghose 1971, Ghose 1995). Like Dayananda, though with considerably more sophistication, Ghose viewed the Vedas as foundational to Hindu religion and Indian culture.

Ghose also conceptualized Indian nationalism in Hindu religious registers. However, for him nationalism was not simply related to Hindu religion: to be a nationalist *was* to be religious and vice versa. As he famously said in 1907:

> Nationalism is not a mere political programme: Nationalism is a religion that has come from God. Nationalism is a creed which you shall have to live . . . If you are going to be a Nationalist, if you are going to assent to this religion of Nationalism, you must do it in the religious spirit. You must remember that you are the instruments of God . . . [The national movement in Bengal after 1905] is a religion by which we are trying to realize God in the nation. (Ghose in Appadorai 1973, volume 2: 483)

Just over a year later, Aurobindo modified this: the advance and rise of India was the rise of *sanatan dharma*, a conception of Hinduism as a perennial religion. Nationalism was *sanatan dharma* (Ghose 1993: 48–50). Similarly, just as Bankimchandra had represented the nation as the Mother of the Hindu pantheon, for Aurobindo, nationalism was devotion to the Goddess. Ghose represented very clearly a curious but extremely powerful theme that travelled across the tendencies examined earlier in this chapter, namely the characteristically Hinduized sacralization of nation and nationalism, the view that the 'nation' was *literally* sacred. This idea was novel, and quite distinct from conceptions of 'national soul', and from the popular 'sanctification' of and 'reverence' for the Indian nation by the freedom movement. It was conceived by thinkers like Bankim, Tilak, Bipinchandra Pal and Aurobindo in solely Hindu idioms. The concept of 'sacred nation' was to be definitive of Hindu nationalist political philosophy in later decades.

Conclusion

The equivalence of Hinduism with nationalism in the latter half of the nineteenth century was more than a persistent or marginal tendency in the burgeoning movements of novel Hinduism, regional patriotism or revolutionary nationalism. This, however, is not to say that they were direct precursors to the varieties of Hindu supremacism that emerged in the 1910s, or the Hindutva movements that were formed from the 1920s and 1930s onwards and which, indeed, did claim them as their predecessors. While the ideological contributions of Tilak, Bipinchandra Pal or Aurobindo Ghose cannot be seen as unmediated influences on the militant Hindutva nationalism that emerged after the early 1920s, it would be as difficult to situate them as examples of secularism. The problem here is not one of taxonomic differentiation between an anti-communal nationalist who happened to be a devoted Hindu, or one for whom nationalism was to be largely defined by a Hindu 'ethos' and 'spirit', to a nationalist for whom India had to become a Hindu nation-state. The difficulties are present because 'religious' and 'non-religious' nationalist tendencies shared considerable epistemic space, and both of them can be opposed to a genuine secularism that was fleetingly glimpsed. In the next chapter, which primarily considers the trajectory of figures and movements unleashed by the Arya Samaj into the heart of the national movement in the early decades of the twentieth century, these difficulties become increasingly compounded.

–3–

Beyond the Arya Ideal

The Hindus are a nation in themselves, because they represent a civilization all their own. (Lala Lajpat Rai 1899)

The fact is that the best and the most glorious period of Aryan supremacy is yet a closed chapter to us. Almost the whole of the pre-Buddhistic period is shrouded in mystery. Even the literature that has reached us is so full of allusions, enigmas, signs, and names and is written in such an archaic language that the whole thing seems to be a mystery . . . Still we know and understand enough to be proud of, and to glory in the heritage which has descended to us from our 'barbarian' ancestors in the shape of national literature. And this must be the fulcrum of the lever with which we are to rise as a nation. It will not do to be unjust to our forefathers and to deny the idea of national love in them. (Lala Lajpat Rai [1902] 1966a: 37)

Introduction

The rise of a distinctive Hindu nationalist ideology and political movement with a coherent ideology of Hindu exclusivity, supremacy and nationhood is usually traced in historical scholarship to the troubled and violent – but puzzlingly short – period from 1919 (the end of the First World War) to the mid-1920s. It was indeed in 1923 that V. D. Savarkar's founding statement on Hindu identity, *Hindutva – who is a Hindu?* was published. Swami Shraddhanand's *Hindu Sangathan – Saviour of the Dying Race* was written the following year. The Rashtriya Swayamsevak Sangh was formed in 1924–6, and the Hindu Mahasabha was re-established and was to gain in political influence from the mid-1920s. These crystallizing events are seen as consequent to Hindu resentment at Gandhi's support for Khilafat, the role of the Muslim League in securing separate electoral representation, and the aftermath of the Khilafat agitation, all of which resulted in the consolidation of a distinct Hindu supremacist, anti-Muslim constituency whose demands were articulated by Hindu nationalist organizations that generally remained outside the fold of the national movement. This is indeed also the post-independence secular reading of the national movement itself.

However, in this register, Hindu nationalism can be seen as an external factor, subsidiary to the movement for independence and of relatively limited and minor importance until well after independence. As seen in the previous chapter, the tangible relationship between Hinduism and Indian nationalism, articulated primarily through a civilizational and cultural discourse of archaic Vedism supplemented by a politicization of devotionalism, had been politically and discursively established in the latter decades of the nineteenth century. In the formative activities of vernacular elites in colonial Maharashtra and Bengal, there was a substantive generation of a 'nationalist pantheon' built from symbols drawn from archaic Vedism, devotional Hinduism and medieval Indian history. This chapter continues this theme by considering several political figures and movements within and outside the national movement and Congress in the early decades of the twentieth century who extended Arya Samaj ideology to elaborate the relation between Hinduism and nationalism more sharply both against other religious communities and through a bio-power narrative of Hindus as under political, social, cultural, physical and demographic 'threat', even 'extinction' (Datta 1993, Datta 1999).

While substantial analytical distance must be retained between earlier varieties of Hindu nationalism and the specific ideology of Hindutva that emerged from the 1920s, much of what is conceived as a fully-formed ideology of Hindutva in the 1920s and 1930s was in its main ideological content elaborated before the 1920s and was to retain an ambiguous but important relationship to ideas of Indian nationalism. The explicit languages of 'Hindu nationalism' and 'Hindu nationality' were present at the start of the twentieth century, although the precise meanings of these terms for their proponents remain to be interrogated. A further argument, started in this chapter and continuing throughout the book is that, conceptually, *Hindu nation* as expressing a cultural, religious, ethnic and possibly 'racial' nationalism retained an ambiguous relation to the idea of a *Hindu nation state*, or a *Hindu government*, the latter representing territorially bounded sovereign political and administrative structures based on permanent 'Hindu majority rule'. Residing somewhere between 'Hindu nation' and 'Hindu state' is the indistinct conception of *Hindu sovereignty*. Notwithstanding the variety of archaic and medieval Indian language terms used to variously connote 'nation', 'state', and 'people' (including *rashtra, rajya, desh, qawm, gana, janapada, jati, watan*), an ambiguity regarding both '*Hindu rashtra*' ('nation') and '*Hindu rajya*' ('government' or 'rule') was foregrounded from the late nineteenth century. This reflected an elision of the distinctions between 'state', 'nation' and 'the people' that continues to characterize, and indeed give power to, Hindu nationalism. In pre-1920s formulations, however much embedded in Hindu idioms, there was also the absence of an unambiguously formulated conception of an ideological and cultural Hindu nationalism that was inextricably linked to the different idea of a constitutionally defined Hindu nation state or government and a 'Hinduized' civil society. Hence, there was an epistemological distance between the ideological, cultural, political and communal forms of Hindu nationalism proliferating in the late nineteenth and early twentieth century and a concept of Hindu nationalism in which territory, nationhood, citizenship, subjecthood, the constitutional nature of the state and a concept of 'the people' were cohesively articulated in Hindu registers. A claim for an exclusive 'Hindu state' or 'Hindu government' was not programmatically formulated prior to the 1920s, but instead retained in a vague manner. Taking the example of the former Arya Samajist, revolutionary Hindu nationalist and American-based founder of the Ghadar Party, Lala Har Dayal, his earlier proposals for an independent Indian nation state comprised detailed constitutional plans but were substantially different from his militant Hindu nationalist declarations of the mid-1920s, even though the latter articulated a 'Hindu Raj' (Brown 1975). If the concern of many Hindu nationalists was with elaborating a cultural conception of 'Hindu nation' in opposition to civic nationalism, this did not clearly articulate a 'Hindu state' explicitly defined through its constitution, governmentality, legislature, its relation to a 'Hindu civil society' and its structures of national and federal organization. However, if the imprecisions regarding Hindu 'nation', 'state', 'government' and 'people' were not resolved by Hindu nationalist ideologues, they were nevertheless held in reserve: one of the definitive characteristics of Hindu nationalism has been its discursive capacity to articulate Hindu 'people' with 'nation' while also invoking, indeterminately, 'state'. This had consequences for any potential theory of political power and governance that Hindu nationalism could be placed to offer in later decades.

This chapter also presents an overarching argument about a relatively strong degree of continuity in Hindu nationalist thinking from the latter decades of the nineteenth century and into the mid-1930s. It is an uncontroversial claim that the kind of Hindutva ideology formulated by Savarkar in the early 1920s was shaped by earlier influences but also represented an epistemological break from previous Hinduized forms of Indian nationalism (see, for example, Pandey 1993). The converse argument that stressing the novelty of Hindutva ideology in the 1920s elides the strong continuity of Hindutva with a range of what are usually encapsulated as modern 'Hinduized nationalist', 'Hindu-leaning' or 'proto-Hindu nationalist' strands that emerged from the latter decades of the nineteenth century has been countered by other writers. Peter Heehs, for example, has argued that the similarities between the post-1920s Hindutva and nineteenth-century 'Hindu revivalism' as represented by Vivekananda, Bipinchandra Pal or Aurobindo are basically superficial while the differences are deep (Heehs 1998: 117). More compellingly, 'Hindu-leaning Indian nationalism' did not demarcate Muslims as inherently exterior to an imagined nationhood, but very much within it and, so the argument goes, this is a definitive demarcation of Hindutva from earlier influences.

While acknowledging the force of such arguments, and without wishing to impute ideas of *logical* and unbroken progression, this chapter emphasizes the continuity between early forms of Hinduized Indian nationalism and later developments. The lack of an all-embracing and accurately descriptive label for these various 'Hindu-influenced' nationalist strands that can sharply and consistently demarcate them from the burgeoning Indian nationalism of the early decades of the twentieth century is itself instructive. However, the taxonomic problems reflect deeper issues about the conditions of possibility that allowed the coextensive imagination of redemptive Hinduism with Indian nationalism prior to the 1920s. Accepting the strong version of the continuity argument has a number of consequences, explored later, which can work against the grain of accepted secular histories and analyses of the Indian national movement, Hinduism in the modern period and Hindu nationalism itself. Expressed differently, it can be difficult to understand both the historical and contemporary appeal of Hindu nationalism if assessment of it is restricted to relatively marginal avowedly Hindu nationalist figures and organizations that only emerged after the mid-1920s. It is also the argument of this chapter that sharply bracketing Hindutva ideology in these historical and political ways can leave what is considered to be 'Hinduism' analytically untouched as if it existed transcendentally and separately from the dramatic political transformations occurring around and within it. Similarly, while the specific ideology of Hindutva has come to dominate contemporary Hindu nationalism, the latter is by no means completed by it.

This is as much a political problem as one of interpretation: the contemporary Hindutva movement does indeed legitimize its existence as the logical culmination of the nineteenth-century 'Hindu Renaissance', the movement for national liberation, and the ideologies of key figures ranging from Vivekananda to Tilak to Aurobindo. Even Gandhi's rather differently politicized Hindu devotionalism can be marshalled for this purpose. Hence stressing the continuity of Hindutva ideology with nineteenth-century movements and ideological currents can be viewed as providing contemporary Hindutva ideologues with the long intellectual 'Hindu heritage' that they crave. However, accepting the strong continuity argument does not result in the granting of any intellectual or political gifts to the Hindutva movement.

Various thinkers from the Arya Samaj, the Indian National Congress, the Hindu Sangathan movement, the early Hindu Sabhas and the pre-Savarkar Hindu Mahasabha, and the variety of revolutionary nationalist groups and Hindu 'proto-ecclesiastical' institutions can be accurately described as Hindu nationalists in the strong sense, rather than as Indian nationalists with Hindu leanings, exhibiting a proto-Hindu nationalism or being solely interested in Hinduizing extant Indian social, political or cultural traditions within the sphere of the private institutions of emergent Indian civil society. Though each of the latter characteristics certainly existed, they were often consequences of an existing Hindu nationalist thematic and lexical universe that existed prior to the 1920s.

The Troubled 1920s and 1930s

The period from the turn of the century, through the 1920s and into the 1930s was one of immense political change and upheaval in colonial India (Chirol [1926] 1972, Phillips et al. 1962, Majumdar 1971, Azad 1988, Kulke and Rothermund 1986, Nair 1991; these sources have been drawn on below and in parts of Chapter 4). In 1905, the colonial government under Curzon partitioned Bengal province so as to create a Muslim majority province made up of East Bengal and Assam with its capital at Dacca, leaving Calcutta, seen as the proud intellectual and cultural core of Bengal regional 'nationalism', grouped with what were seen as the backward, apolitical provinces of Bihar and Orissa. This 'vivisection of the Bengal motherland' was seen as (and almost certainly was) an attempt to isolate and marginalize the heartland of militant anti-colonial Indian nationalism, dominated by a politicized, Westernized Bengali-speaking Hindu intellectual elite. This action was welcomed by sections of Bengal's Muslim leadership, but virtually caused an open rebellion against the colonial government and an upsurge of politicized revolutionary nationalist action throughout India. Bankimchandra Chattopadhyaya's *Bande Mataram* ('Hail to Thee O Mother [land]'), from his novel *Anandamath*, was set to music by the Bengal poet Rabindranath Tagore and became the anthem for the Indian National Congress (for example, see Mukherjee and Mukherjee 1957). The Hinduized nationalist slogan, *Bharat Mata Ke Jai!* [Victory to the [Holy] Mother Land!] was also at that time a Congress slogan. Mass protest movements, boycotts of British and foreign products and British educational institutions in favour of Indian goods (*swadeshi*) and newly formed Indian schools and universities grew. Self-rule (*swaraj*) became an explicit Congress demand as a result of the partition of Bengal. As important was the massive wave of violent, terrorist forms of political agitation that grew as a result of Curzon's actions.

The bifurcation of both colonial political administration and nationalist political activity along Hindu-Muslim religious lines had a longer pedigree, but from this point it acquired a different resonance and a grotesque trajectory. In 1909, the colonial government introduced the Indian Councils Act ('the Morley-Minto reforms') whose purpose was to introduce a (severely limited) elective principle to membership of Indian Legislative Councils and increase Indian representation in the Supreme Council and provincial legislatures. It also guaranteed separate electorates and electoral seats for Muslims.

In 1906, Minto had received (and had actively encouraged) a deputation of Muslim leaders who wanted to safeguard the separate interests of Muslims within any proposed constitutional reforms. The successes of the Muslim delegation led by the Aga Khan coincided with the formal inauguration of the Muslim League in the same year through which demands were made to advance the separate political rights and interests of Indian Muslims. Resolutions passed at this founding meeting included support for Curzon's partition of Bengal, condemnation of the boycott movement against the British and loyalty to the British government, all of which aroused widespread resentment among many Hindus. The increasing violence in Bengal and elsewhere during 1909 and 1910, following the first Partition of Bengal, was met with extreme repression. However, under a new viceroy, East and West Bengal were reunified (1911), and a separate province comprising Bihar and Orissa was created. The capital of British India was moved from Calcutta, the heartland of the Bengal (Hindu-dominated) nationalist movement, to provincial Delhi, the former seat of Mughal power in India. The latter action was seen as a symbolic concession to Muslims for the loss of the short-lived, Muslim-dominated Bengal province, but was seen by many of Bengal's Hindus as another humiliation because of their involvement in the nationalist movement.

During and in the aftermath of the First World War, there was considerable pressure on the colonial government for increased representation of Indians – if not direct home rule – in return for the support by Indians of the war effort. The Montague-Chelmsford proposals from 1917, continuing a precedent established in the first decade of the century, admitted separate Muslim electorates. They increased the number of proposed Muslim seats in Bengal. Separate electorates, limited reforms and the proposals for 'dyarchy' were consolidated in the 1919 Government of India Act which was followed by elections in 1920.

In 1916, Tilak had signed a pact of nationalist alliance with the Muslim League ('the Lucknow Pact') which committed Congress to greater separate electoral and institutional representation of Muslims than had been legislated for in the 1909 Act. Britain was also at war against Mesopotamia (now Turkey), and Indian troops were mobilized in very large numbers during this military campaign. For sections of the Indian Muslim leadership, Indian troops were fighting for Britain against a Muslim power, the Ottoman Caliphate as represented by the Sultan. Consequently, some Muslims appealed to Muslim Afghanistan to create a military alliance against the British. This was the start of the massive south Asian Khilafat movement, which gained strength from 1919 and especially after the Treaty of Sevres of August 1920, which effected the break-up of the Ottoman Empire by the Allies, including Britain. The movement grew massively in India under the leadership of the brothers Shaukat and Mohammad Ali, who in 1920 led a *hijra* (emigration) from India into Afghanistan of some 20,000 Muslims in protest at Britain's role against the Ottoman Empire and their belief that colonial India was a land of 'apostasy'. This catastrophic action was considered necessary as British India was seen as at war with a Muslim power, and hence Indian Muslims had a religious obligation to leave India for a Muslim country. Many Hindus contrasted this action and the Khilafat agitations with what was seen as a lack of mass Muslim involvement in the struggle for national liberation.

Gandhi, who by 1920 had become the dominant influence in Congress following the deaths of both Gokhale and Tilak, launched his non-cooperation movement (the *satyagraha*, or 'truth-force' campaigns) and, in an attempt to build unity 'across the religious divide', committed Congress to make support of the Khilafat movement a key plank in its non-cooperation program. The Khilafat movement was linked by Gandhi to the massive 1920 *satyagraha* and boycott campaigns against the colonial Government that were launched in the aftermath of the 1919 Jallianwala Bagh (Amritsar) massacre and the repressive Rowlatt Acts of the same year. In 1921, partly as a result of the nationwide Khilafat agitations, a peasant rebellion in Malabar in Kerala was superseded by a violent uprising by sections of the Muslim Mapilla ('Moplah') community, some of whom installed their own 'caliphate' and forced the conversion of some Hindus to Islam. The atrocities committed during the 'Moplah Rebellion' led to India-wide revulsion and retaliatory violence against Muslim communities, commencing a pattern of communal violence that was to intensify after the mid-1930s. It was perhaps Gandhi's support for Khilafat and the subsequent events in Kerala that were to dramatically alienate some Hindus within and outside Congress and lead to the distinctive movement promoting the notion that India was to be an exclusively Hindu nation. It is significant that B. S. Moonje, a founder of the Rashtriya Swayamsevak Sangh, was part of the Congress deputation to Malabar in the wake of the Mapilla 'rebellion'.

The Muslim League had opposed Gandhi's support for the Khilafat movement and in late 1920 the League broke its alliance with Congress because of Jinnah's complaints about Hindu and Hindi language domination of Congress and the non-cooperation movement. This symbolized the collapse of the 'Lucknow Pact' of 1916. The Muslim League discourse of Hindu majority domination of Muslim minorities in the colonial legislatures and, ominously, in a future independent India was to become the key plank in the League's campaign from this point. However, the idea that India was 'two-nations' was already being articulated at the turn of the century by *Hindu* leaders of Congress and the national movement, such as Lajpat Rai, and was reiterated forcefully by Savarkar and the Hindu Mahasabha in the 1930s. The languages of majorities and minorities, religious nationalism and communal violence were firmly established by the early 1920s. Furthermore, Gandhi's decision in February 1922 to suspend *satyagraha* because of the killings of over twenty colonial police officers by anti-colonial demonstrators (the 'Chauri Chaura' incident), and his arrest and imprisonment soon after, were to lead to the collapse of the non-cooperation movement, and to serious rifts within the nationalist movement about the meaning, extent and reach of non-cooperation. The nature and meaning of non-cooperation had been the focus of considerable, complex debate and dissension for several years, both within and outside Congress, and the unfolding of several political tendencies either abandoning Gandhite methods or arguing for various degrees of cooperation with colonial rule during the 1920s was to be extremely significant for the shape of Hindu nationalist and Hindu communalist thinking. The question here becomes not one of whether Hindu nationalists were involved in the national movement but instead a different question about the nature of the dominant strategies advocated by Hindu nationalists regarding cooperation with British rule.

In 1935, the British government introduced two more Government of India Acts. The Acts were primarily aimed at extending the franchise and widening political representation, though with severe limits of British veto and a conception of 'dyarchy' in which the most important provincial powers and institutions were to remain British-controlled. However the Acts and the Communal Award of 1932, were as important for the further institutional codification of separate, mostly religiously defined minorities in the widening structures of electoral and political representation (electoral constituencies, electoral seats and reserved offices); these were extended from Muslims to Sikh, Christian, Anglo-Indian and European minorities, and reservations based on non-religious criteria were made in the case of, for example, women and labouring classes.

The British had also attempted to extend a separate electoral franchise to the 'untouchables' or 'scheduled castes' but withdrew following what was seen as a blackmailing 'fast unto death' by Gandhi in 1932, during which Gandhi made an agreement (the 'Poona Pact') with the reluctant dalit leader, Dr Bhimrao Ramji Ambedkar (1891–1956) to create, for a 10-year period, more reserved seats within the legislatures for the 'depressed classes' than the British had promised. Gandhi argued that the British proposals would cleave the scheduled castes from 'the Hindu fold' to which he believed they belonged. Gandhi articulated a domineering caste-Hindu ideology about 'untouchables' that was barely different to that of the Hindu supremacist groups he opposed. The salience of the inter-war period was that a disastrous communal framework based on bare religious affiliation and the language of majorities and minorities had become established, would be foundational to demands for the Partition of India, and would dominate both Indian and Pakistani politics, and the character and campaigns of Hindu nationalism and Islamism after independence.

From Arya Samaj to Congress to Hindu Mahasabha

Amidst these developments before and after the First World War, Lala Lajpat Rai's (1865–1928) symbolic trajectory from the Brahmo Samaj to the Arya Samaj, thence variously into and out of Congress, his alignment with the 'Extremist' section of Congress and some revolutionary nationalist activities, and then his emergence as a key figure in both the pre-Savarkarite Hindu Mahasabha and the Hindu Sangathan movement is both evocative and characteristic of the shape of Hindu nationalism in this period (Lajpat Rai 1965, 1966a, 1966b, Argov 1967, Nagar 1977.)

Lajpat Rai was important in the development of the Anglo Vedic College and was to head the 'College' faction of the Arya Samaj after its split. He had first come across Arya Samajists at the Government College at Lahore after 1881. He had previously been under the guidance of Pandit Shiv Narain Agnihotri, a Brahmo Samaj leader who was also initially associated with Dayananda and had subsequently fallen out with him, eventually starting his own Dev Samaj (on the latter, see Jones 1989: 103–6). Lajpat Rai joined the Arya Samaj in 1882 and rapidly became an influential figure. He became a legal representative in Jagraon and Rothak, and finally a lawyer, working first in Hissar, south Punjab and then in Lahore in the early 1890s. It was during this period, starting from 1893, that Lajpat Rai became practically involved in Congress activities. His interests in educational and industrial development (the latter becoming explicitly socialist in the following decades, particularly after his meetings with British socialists such as Hyndman) led to him becoming a member of the Indian National Congress Committee in 1901. While during his political career, Lajpat Rai was heavily involved in a wide range of social reform, industrial, anti-colonial and political activities, and in 1907 was deported to Mandalay Prison with Ajit Singh for revolutionary and seditionist activities, this chapter will primarily focus on those of his activities that related to specifically political Hindu concerns.

Prior to his serious involvement in Congress, Lajpat Rai had published a series of *Open Letters* to Sir Syed Ahmed Khan between October and December 1888 (Lajpat Rai [1888] 1996a: 1–25). In 1887, Syed Ahmad Khan had both criticized Congress proposals for representative councils as 'seditious', and had declared that the interests of Muslims and Hindus were not identical as far as political representation in the councils was concerned, claiming that proposals for representation would mean Hindu majority domination over Muslims. If this was an example of what was frequently viewed in Hindu nationalist discourse as the early stirrings of Muslim separatism and Muslim collaboration with the British colonial government, its trajectory was by no means set.

Lajpat Rai's critique of Syed Ahmad Khan used the latter's earlier patriotic declarations against himself, particular those that argued for a common nationhood based on geography and irrespective of religious, 'racial' or linguistic differences (Lajpat Rai [20.12.1888] 1966a: 17–25). However, while Lajpat Rai criticized Ahmad Khan for suggesting that the interests of Muslims and Hindus were different, he did not powerfully state in those letters that the interests of Hindus and Muslims were the same or defined by a common nationhood. It was this formative lacuna or asymmetry that constituted an important characteristic of early Hindu nationalism, and allowed the latter to slide between Congress nationalism and an instinctive Hindu supremacism until it faced a different ideological challenge after the 1920s. Elaborating on the Hindu contours existing in pre-1920s Indian nationalism is not a difficult task and is illustrated by a variety of currents in the national movement, both moderate and revolutionary. Some of these areas are at least partially illustrated by Lajpat Rai's own views about Hindu nationalism elaborated from the late 1890s onwards.

Lajpat Rai and Hindu Nationalism

In 1899, Lajpat Rai published an article for the Indian National Congress in the *Hindustan Review* in which he declared that 'Hindus are a nation in themselves, because they represent a civilization all their own' (Mathur 1996: 1). This was not a new idea even then (see Chapter 2). However, for Lajpat Rai, this idea was directly influenced by a conception of Hindu nationalism in the aftermath of the 'purification' of Hinduism by the Arya Samaj. In 1902, Lajpat Rai entered a debate occurring in the pages of *Hindustan Review and Kayastha Samachar* between an anonymous 'Hindu Nationalist' and Pandit Madhao Ram about the basis for creating a 'Hindu Nationalism' ('A Study of Hindu Nationalism' in Lajpat Rai 1966a: 37–44). Indeed, discussion about the idea of 'Hindu Nationalism' spread from the pages of *Hindustan Review and Kayastha Samachar* and into the *Times of India* between 1900-1902 (*Kayashta Samachar: A monthly record and review*, November 1902 Vol. VI. No. 5: 468–70).

Lajpat Rai agreed with the main prescriptions of 'Hindu Nationalist', arguing that these echoed his earlier writings (Lajpat Rai 1966a: 37). It was his areas of disagreement with the 'Hindu Nationalist' that are important here. The 'Hindu Nationalist' had asserted that the concept of nationalism was a modern, European idea that could be appropriated by Hindus in their project of coming to nationhood. Lajpat Rai disagreed both with the view that the origins of the national idea were to be found in Europe and with the view that Hindus had historically possessed no sense of nationality.

In several key passages of his response, Lajpat Rai expressed a series of gestatory ideas, many of which were to find their way virtually unchanged in Savarkar's definitive *Hindutva*. Lajpat Rai dismissed the argument that the term 'Hindu' was a Persian term of abuse invented by 'Mohammedan invaders'. He argued that it had a much more ancient history, and only became a pejorative term under Muslim rule because it signified the fall of the 'Hindu nation'. However (as Savarkar was also to reiterate) it was used in ancient times as a name that *others* – such as the Persians of the Vendidad – used to describe the inhabitants of India. This formative idea that the name 'Hindu' was a patronymic that had been conferred by a constitutive outside, rather than as emergent from within Vedic or other religious texts, is both highly significant and proved repeatedly troublesome for later Hindu nationalists who could find no such name in the archaic texts of 'Hinduism' itself.

However, while ancient Hindu literature did not use the word 'Hindu' as a self-description, but instead the term *arya*, for Lajpat Rai even these ancient texts contained the sentiment of nationality, expressed most strongly in Aryan battles against their enemies, the *dasyus*, *chandalas* and *mlechhas*. Against the view of 'Hindu Nationalist' that nationalism was a modern invention, Lajpat Rai explicitly situated the birth of 'Hindu nationality' in the Aryan Vedic period. This heritage, he argued, 'must be the fulcrum of the lever with which we are to rise as a nation'. He argued that the history of India had still to be written from 'a Hindu point of view', a task which would demonstrate Hinduism's ancient nationalism.

> We the English educated Hindus of the present day, who claimed to have imbibed the new spirit of nationality and patriotism from the West would really do well to study a few chapters of the Vedic literature with care and thought. (Lajpat Rai 1966a: 40)

In opposing the view that nationalism was invented in nineteenth-century Europe, Lajpat Rai used precisely the method and epistemology of the latter to discern what he believed to be an earlier idea of nationalism in the Vedas. The idea that the foundations of modern nationalism were to be found in archaic primordialism was a key component in the eighteenth- and nineteenth-century European invention of nationalism.

In accordance with Dayananda's critique of brahmins, Lajpat Rai situated the fall of the 'Hindu Nation' after the Buddhist period as resulting from 'the genius of a jealous and perverted, sometimes corrupt and selfish priesthood [who] built a vast and stupendous superstructure of conventionalities and formalities, with an almost interminable labyrinth of rituals and ceremonials' (Lajpat Rai 1966a: 40–1). These obscured the true role of religion as the mainstay of nation. (Interestingly enough, unlike Savarkar after him, Lajpat Rai was well-disposed to Buddhism and did not view the non-violence of the latter as responsible for the degradation of an original Hindu nationalism.) For Lajpat Rai, 'Hindu ritualism', and not the absence of the spirit of nationality, was the bane of the Hindus. This antagonistic separation of Hindu nationality from caste Hindu religious tradition was an archetypal Arya Samaj formulation that was to find its way into the 'post-religious' authoritarian nationalism of the Rashtriya Swayamsevak Sangh, but was also to become of source of tension within Hindu nationalism, both before and after independence. Lajpat Rai also situated the historical expression of Hindu nationality in the 'efforts of the Mahrattas and the Rajputs to throw off the foreign yoke and found a Hindu empire'. This transcendental conception of a temporal link between an ancient and a medieval 'Hindu nation' is significant and was stated most militantly by Savarkar.

After having stated that nationality did not imply a complete union in all the details of religious, social, economic and sectarian life, Lajpat Rai asserted a comprehensive definition of nationality:

> Run on a few basal principles in religion, on the community of a sacred language, and on the community of interests, the Hindus ought to foster the growth of a national sentiment which should be sufficiently strong to enable them to work for the common good in the different ways and according to the lights vouchsafed to each. Let us keep one ideal before us. *Let our ideal be sufficiently high to cover all, sufficiently broad and extensive to include all, who take pride in a common name, a common ancestry, a common history, a common religion, a common language and a common future.* We will not advance the cause of nationality by one inch if we decide to preserve an attitude of silent quietude and non-disturbing peace in all matters, religious and social. Such an attitude can only mean stagnation and gradual extinction. Struggle, hard struggle is the law of progress. Yes struggle we must, both inter se as well [as with] others. (Lajpat Rai 1966a: 43, emphasis added)

With one possible exception, the idea of a common 'race', perhaps indicated above by 'ancestry', this formulation of nation is virtually equivalent to that of Savarkar and vividly elides the distinction between a 'Hindu' and an 'Indian' nationalism.

As important was the thoroughgoing influence of Spencerian evolutionist political sociology, indicated above in the 'hard struggle' that was the 'law of progress'. This frequently defined the field of intellectual production for many colonial and anti-colonial currents. The consequences of this epistemology were brought out most clearly by Lajpat Rai in an article published in 1907:

> A question has often haunted us, asleep or awake, as to why is it that notwithstanding the presence among us of great, vigorous and elevating truths, and of the very highest conception of morality, we [Hindus] have been a subject race, held down for so many centuries by sets of people who were neither physically nor spiritually nor even intellectually so superior to us as *a fortiori* to demand our subjection. ('The one pressing need of India' [1907] in Lajpat Rai 1966a: 55)

This deceptively powerful formulation that encapsulated both 'Hindu weakness' and 'Hindu strength' has been foundational to successive waves of post-independence Hindu nationalism. The translation of the question, articulated in the colonial period, of why British colonialism had occurred into an *entirely different imaginary* of why Hindus had 'repeatedly failed to repel foreign invaders' over some ten to thirteen centuries is striking and considerable ideological and political content follows from posing the logic of a transcendental 'Hindu history' in this way. It was precisely this question that preoccupied both B. S. Moonje and K. B.

Hedgewar, from which they derived the Rashtriya Swayamsevak Sangh as the answer. In a densely fascinating way, a logic was started that severely minimized British colonialism within a much longer 'historical' frame of Hindu resistance to what were conceived as all 'foreign invaders'. This logic culminated in Savarkar's *Hindutva* ([1923] 1989), and Swami Shraddhanand's *Hindu Sangathan – Saviour of a dying race* (1926), both written in the midst of one of the most violent and troubled periods of anti-colonial agitation during the first manifestation of a genuinely mass anti-colonial movement, but which can be read with barely any indication within them that British colonialism was even present. (A similar theme preoccupied later Hindutva ideologues: the British colonial period was effectively dismissed or conceived as relatively benign, even civilizing and moral in character in comparison with the early or high medieval periods of Mughal rule, which were seen as periods of ruthless oppression and genocide of Hindus.)

The framing of colonial subjugation in such terms had distinctive intellectual conditions of possibility. As Lajpat Rai said:

> We do not require a Herbert Spencer to tell us that the social efficiency of a social organism as such, depends upon the sense of social responsibility amongst the members of such an organism. The greater and the intenser [sic] the sense of responsibility amongst the individual members, regarding the safety and welfare of the whole, the greater and the stronger the efficiency of the organism. ('The one pressing need of India' [1907] in Lajpat Rai 1966a: 55)

Lajpat Rai's political speeches frequently employed Spencerian themes of organicism, social flexibility, adaptability and adaptation, efficiency and inefficiency, survival and extinction. In particular, Spencer's critical combination of ideas of the *collective survival of the fittest* with *individual liberty from domination* was to have significant resonance in colonial India. Spencerianism allowed for the development of a specifically naturalistic, 'physiological' and 'biological' theory of imperialism and anti-colonialism (see Chapter 4).

Lajpat Rai claimed that Hinduism did contain an organic sense of responsibility and survival, since it had continued to 'reign supreme' even after 'twelve centuries of Islamic propaganda backed by all the forces of political ascendancy and moral superiority which is the anchor sheet of a virgin religion and a conquering creed', and after a further '100 years of active evangelical work done in the name of Christ'. The fact that Hinduism existed at all was testimony to its strength and power. This was a key teleological and functionalist component of evolutionary sociology: the elementary fact of the contemporary existence of a social phenomenon was evinced as proof both of its inherent functional fitness and an indication of its telos. In essence, this was a naturalistic theory of imperialism, a transmutation of Spencer by those fighting colonialism. The use of Spencerian themes would inevitably lead to a focus on Hindu biological and physiological 'fitness', reproductive 'efficiency' and the necessity of strengthening the fertility of Hindu women.

One consequence of conceiving both nationalism and colonialism in naturalistic and 'physiological' terms was the requirement to explain a strong and powerful Hinduism able to resist other 'conquering' religions *and* the 'historical weakness' of Hindus unable to repel 'foreign invasions'. Both themes, central to Lajpat Rai's political epistemology, were to travel through Savarkar's formulation of Hindu identity and then into the 'man-moulding' activities of the RSS. Lajpat Rai articulated the strength and resilience of Hindus through their simple existence in the face of repeated 'foreign invasions'. (Interestingly enough, in the eighteenth-century Herder had used an idea of brahmin-Hindu religious and cultural resilience, which he argued the British could barely scratch the surface of, to make the case for the cultural depth and incommensurability of his nationalism concept.)

What then was the cause of the 'weakness' of Hindus and Hinduism, demonstrated most clearly for Lajpat Rai by the elementary fact of British colonial domination? He argued that this was primarily because of *individual* selfishness, greed and calculation that prevented organismic consciousness of the greater society and nation. The political remedy for Lajpat Rai was to inculcate a 'sense of social responsibility which requires each and every member of the organism to place the interests of the community or the nation over and above those of his own' (Lajpat Rai 1966a: 57). While individualism could be identified by Lajpat Rai with the 'selfishness' of, for example, the brahmin castes, there is another sense here in which the individualism of political rights and that of economic and social possessive individualism were problematized. A political sociology of the collectivity, drawing on influences such as Spencer, were mobilized to provide an organic view of the overintegrative capacities of Hinduism, the latter indeed dovetailing neatly into extant colonial discourses about Hinduism's amalgamating properties.

In his conceptions of nationalism, Lajpat Rai discussed Hindu nationality in a 'commonsense' and naturalized way as an integrative function that elided its difference from Indian nationality. This is an historical and theoretical issue of considerable importance during a period when distinct and sophisticated political languages of secularism were not available. After the 1920s, the distinction between Hindu nationalism and anti-communal (but not necessarily 'secular') Indian nationalism was to be politically forged, but a naturalized British discourse of group communalism and group rights substituted for a deeper elaboration of the meaning of secularism as constituting a substantive field distinct from a principled 'anti-colonial anti-communalism'.

Hence, Lajpat Rai both appeared to accept and frequently stated that Hindus and Muslims had something like a common national destiny, and severely castigated Syed Ahmad Khan for suggesting otherwise, and yet articulated Indian nationality as a Hindu nationalism. The faithful and imaginative holding of both these positions continued to be reproduced in Hindutva literature after the 1920s and is still central for what are viewed as the 'moderate' tendencies in the contemporary Hindutva movement. Lajpat Rai cultivated associations with both Gandhi and Jinnah, with 'moderates' and 'radicals' in Congress, *and* with organizations that explicitly called for 'Hindu Raj' and Hindu self-organization against Muslims. This was a convergence between an Indian nationalist who happened to have been raised within and affiliated to a Hindu religious tradition, and a Hindu supremacist for whom Hinduism was nationalism.

Lajpat Rai's view of a Hindu nation represented a general intellectual current manifested around the turn of the century in colonial India. The distinctive aspect of this was the view that Hindus were historically a nation, and that they were a nation solely because of the associated view that Hinduism was an ancient civilization. There were various examples, often associated with Arya Samajist currents, which articulated a similar equivalence between the alleged historical existence of a Hindu nationality in India that was claimed to be primordial precisely because of another, different claim that there existed a primordial civilization that was in all its important aspects 'Hindu'. The term 'civilization' was neither neutral nor unrelated to a longer intellectual project that disputed, while emulating, British claims about the civilizing mission while vehemently criticizing, and offering historical explanations for what were perceived as the uncivilized, barbaric or degenerate aspects of Hinduism. This intellectual equivalence between imagined nationalism and imagined civilization was extremely important and the civilizational method was indeed definitive (on the importance of civilizational aggrandisement for Hindu nationalism, see Bhatt 1997: 195–7, Bhatt 1999). The early Hindu nationalist organizations indeed had a civilizing mission that promised another ostensibly 'indigenous' path into modernity for those wayward populations that were deemed to require 'upliftment' into Hinduism, a mission that continues to this day.

The Superiority of the 'Hindu Race'

One illustrative tract, written in the early 1900s by Har Bilas Sarda (1867–1955), an Arya Samajist social reformer and legislator now perhaps best known for his sponsorship of the Child Marriage Restraint Act (1925), and who could not easily be considered 'extremist' in his political views and activities, was entitled *Hindu Superiority: an Attempt to Determine the Position of the Hindu Race in the Scale of Nations* (Sarda [1906] 1975). This large uneven tome is striking for a variety of reasons. It engaged with and appropriated, if rather selectively, Orientalist and Western assessments of Indian antiquity while deploying a racial conception of the Hindu. Its fundamental thesis of an original, primordial Hindu nation that fell because of Hindu disunity was complemented with an eighteenth- and nineteenth-century European view of India as the cradle of world civilization. All ancient civilizations from America and Africa, through Europe to China were conceived by Sarda as originally Hindu and consequential upon a global ancient Hindu system of colonization and world conquest. According to Sarda, the ancient Hindus were virile, brave, strong, chivalrous patriots. Hindu women had complete equality with men; their oppression was a subsequent introduction by non-Hindus. Ancient Hindus had also comprehended all the arts, philosophies, jurisprudence, political and economic science, religion and the natural sciences which had been subsequently discovered or vindicated by the west. In line with Arya thinking, he defended the 'scientific' nature of the *varnashramadharma* while rejecting sub-caste. Typically, for its time, it located the downfall of the Hindus as of their own making.

The importance of *Hindu Superiority* did not reside in its claims, many of which pre-existed it, but rather its fragmentary, autodidact and dilletantist methodological approach in which *Western* texts of uneven veracity were deployed to demonstrate, *under modern colonial conditions*, the *ancient* achievements of *Hindu colonists*. The 'indigenous' idea emergent in the British imperial period that Hindus had also been colonists and empire-builders is suggestive. The book was published in 1906, the year after the Partition of Bengal and the rise of violent and terroristic movements against British rule. Yet, apart from asides against James Mill's chauvinism, its main concern with British colonialism was to demonstrate that ancient Hindus already possessed the art of good government and law, and indeed had given it to the world, and that the origins of both Christianity and of ancient English paganism (such as the druids and Stonehenge) were Hindu. But perhaps the most important aspect of *Hindu Superiority* was the development of a phantasmatic space of archaic Hindu greatness, evinced through religious texts mediated through Western understandings, which was understood to be equivalent to an unbroken essence of Hindu nationhood. It is instructive that the positive content of this nationhood resided in exactly those qualities of character, strength, valour, chivalry and patriotism that were associated with *British* ideological promulgations of self, and seen as lacking in their colonial subjects.

The Early Hindu Mahasabha and the rise of Hindu Sangathan

Many of these pre-1920s currents were to take organizational forms that were to become especially important during the early 1920s. In 1906, the year that the All-India Muslim League was founded in Dacca and was received by the Viceroy, Minto, a Hindu Sabha (society) was formed in Punjab (a region that had also seen the first stirrings of the Muslim League) to promote Hindu interests within a framework, similar to that of the League, of complete loyalty to the British government. In a meticulous assessment by Richard Gordon, it has been argued that the early Hindu Sabhas were heavily restricted in their influence beyond a very few urban centres, were loosely formed conservative associations of middle-class men (such as lawyers, *zamindars* and *taluqdars*) from the kayastha, bania and brahmin castes, and tended to be affiliated with the Sanatan Dharm orthodoxy, rather than Arya Samaj modernizers (Gordon 1975). The influence of Arya Samaj activists upon their ideology and activities was hence nominal. However, not only do we see the presence of Arya Samaj activists in the early Sabhas but also that their interventions were decisive in formulating a wider ideological Hindu communalism.

Lal Chand and 'Hindu Nation'

One of the influences behind both the formation and politicization of Punjab's Hindu Sabhas was a series of letters written by Rai Bahadur Lal Chand (1852–1912), an Arya Samajist and first President of the Dayananda Anglo-Vedic College, to *The Punjabee*. These were published as a pamphlet in 1909 entitled *Self-Abnegation in Politics* (Lal Chand [1909] 1938) and presented a prominent series of themes about Hindu self-deprecation in the face of Muslim communal interests in the aftermath of the Partition of Bengal and the Morley-Minto proposals. Lal Chand's themes about the 'lack' of Hindu self-pride, the 'shame' in calling oneself 'Hindu' and Hindu 'self-abnegation' in the face of minority religious demands are resonant in the contemporary Hindutva movement. Muslims, he argued, had extra-territorial support based in Constantinople and were seeking a 'Muslim Raj' in India, whereas Hindus, who had no support outside the walls of Hindusthan, were weak, gullible and disunited.

Lal Chand's key targets were Congress, and the Indian press which supported it. Within Congress, he claimed, the term 'Hindu' was 'forbidden' and 'tabooed', and Hindu nationality, Hindu sentiments and Hindu interests were 'obliterated' or submerged under 'Indian' grievances. We were, he said, 'afraid to utter the word Hindu' (Lal Chand 1938: 21). Conversely, Congress was keen to pass resolutions supporting 'purely Mohammedan interests'. A common and united nation may be a high and sentimental ideal, but was an impossibility when differences of race and nation existed (Lal Chand 1938: 4). The 'physiology of nations' demanded strength in the face of challenge.

> [It] looks to me the very height of folly and absurdity to go on crying for a united nation when one important community, by its words and actions, make it persistently and absolutely clear that they do not desire nor seek union. The remedy when such evil exists is not to say we are one, but to declare emphatically that we are two. (Lal Chand 1938: 5)

Lal Chand's letters were uncompromising in their open sectarianism, explicit advocation of Hindu communal interest, and of their expressed fear that those professing Hinduism in India would diminish in numbers as the British facilitated the rise of a Muslim leadership and consequent 'Muslim domination' of India. Conversely, he held that in their quest for an Indian nation, Hindus had adopted a 'suicidal self-abnegation' in politics. To illustrate this, he presented examples of proportionate communal numerical representation in provincial councils and municipal administration in Punjab, Bengal, the Sind and elsewhere, within the judiciary, the police and army, educational institutions and in land distribution, within which he argued Muslims had been overwhelmingly favoured. Similarly, he vehemently criticized the privilege attached to Persian ('the badge of past slavery') and Urdu, rather than the Sanskrit or vernacular 'Hindu' languages. The letters aimed to demonstrate the oppression of and discrimination against Hindus and Hindu culture: 'This is the pass to which the Hindus, sons of the soil and its most ancient inhabitants, have been reduced' (Lal Chand 1938: 33). 'This is the depth of the degradation into which we have fallen. When shall we open our eyes and begin to see, speak and think as Hindus?' (Lal Chand 1938: 42).

Lal Chand made the plea for Hindus to form a separate nation (Lal Chand 1938: 20). The love for one's country, he argued, was based on the predominant *communal ideal* based on common descent and love of one's community. Conversely, the love for the geographical 'tract' in which communities settle was secondary:

> Communal love, in fact, is the root of the majority of the sentiments which we love and cherish, not excluding even religion . . . The idea is to love everything owned by the community. It may be religion, it may be a tract of country, or it may be a phase of civilization. But these are mere outward clothes of the inner feeling. This then is the fire I wish to rekindle. (Lal Chand 1938: 103)

Blaming Congress for Hindu 'imbecility', Lal Chand proposed that Congress be dispensed with in its entirety. In its place, he advocated forms of Hindu communal self-organization for furthering and strengthening the Hindu interest, 'untrammelled by any consideration whatever for the interests of the other community' (Lal Chand 1938: 101). This would involve bringing all Hindu sections onto a common political platform where they would realize they are 'merely branches of the same stock and community' (Lal Chand 1938: 118).

> I also intended and I have evidently succeeded partly to instil into the Hindu mind what some people choose to call sectarianism; but which I regard as the very breath of life, viz, that a Hindu should not only believe but make it part and parcel of his organization, of his life and of his conduct, that he is a Hindu first and an Indian after. (Lal Chand 1938: 70)

Lal Chand argued that given the 'weak' position of the 'Hindu community', such organizations would fight for their interests within the legislative and administrative machinery of colonial government, to reconcile with rather than seek to antagonize the ruling powers (Lal Chand 1938: 100). He even opposed colonial self-government or a form of Dominion status as 'chimerical', partly because the British would not voluntarily grant it, but mostly because Hindus have 'abjured and neglected' work for themselves in 'pursuit of a mirage' of a united nation (Lal Chand 1938: 117–8). Instead, Lal Chand advocated the substitution of Congress Committees by Hindu sabhas, the Congress press by a Hindu press and the organization of a Hindu Defence Fund for the protection of Hindu interests against those of the Muslim League – 'there ought to be political agitation [but] conducted in the interests of a purely Hindu cause'.

One of the most prominent aspects of such views at the end of the first decade of the twentieth century, only a few years after the Partition of Bengal and the rise of revolutionary terrorist anti-colonialism, increasing demands for Home Rule in India and abroad, and Congress negotiations for some form of self-rule or increased representation of Indians in government is not simply the Hindu communal consciousness they inspired. It is also the concomitant setting into play a substitutionist logic, which was to become extremely important in the further development of Hindu nationalism over the decades that followed, in which Indian reformist or revolutionary struggles against British colonialism were counterposed to a demand for Hindu communal interests within the framework of British colonialism. This can be seen as a change in Hindu nationalist ideology from a preoccupation with demonstrating the political capacity of Hinduism as an 'Indian nationalism' equivalent or superior to British ideas of nation, to an accommodation with British colonialism within which a separate politicized public sphere of Hindu communal interests defined the 'national interest'. It is significant that Lal Chand explicitly argued (indeed, warned) against making proposals, such as self-rule or independent status, which he believed would be detrimental for future generations of Hindus. This can be seen as major change in Hindu nationalist ideology and demonstrated how from this point Hindu nationalism developed in accordance with the manoeuvres of the British.

Until about 1915, the activities of the early Hindu Sabhas remained confined to cities in the Punjab, an Arya Samajist stronghold (Gordon 1975: 150). However, its 1909 Provincial Hindu Conference, held at Lahore, was attended by Lajpat Rai who made a speech on the 'Desirability of Feeling of Hindu Nationality and Hindu Unity', during which he reiterated his earlier statement of 1899 about Hindus constituting a distinct and separate 'nation' (Mathur 1996). In 1913, the Hindu Sabha undertook to form an India-wide (Sarvadeshik) Hindu Sabha to 'safeguard the interests of the Hindu Community throughout India' and the following year, the first Akhil Bharatiya (All India) Hindu Mahasabha Conference was organized at Hardwar during the Kumbh Mela. Further meetings were held during 1915 that defined the objectives of the All India Hindu Sabha:

a. To promote greater union and solidarity amongst all sections of the Hindu Community and to unite them more closely as parts of one organic whole.
b. To promote education among members of the Hindu Community.
c. To ameliorate and improve the condition of all classes of the Hindu community.
d. To protect and promote Hindu interests whenever and wherever it may be necessary.
e. To promote good feelings between the Hindus and other Communities in India and to act in a friendly way with them, and in loyal Co-operation with the Government.
f. Generally to take steps for promoting religious, moral, educational, social and political interests of the community.

Note – The Sabha shall not side or identify itself or interfere with or oppose any particular sect or sects of the Hindu Community. (Shraddhanand 1926: 109–10)

Notably, the Sabha framed its objective of loyal cooperation with the colonial government. Indeed, the All India Hindu Sabha did not organize annual national meetings during the mass *satyagraha* and boycott periods of 1919 or 1920, partly because it was by then a moribund organization but also because it tended to remain aloof from the explicit non-cooperation strategy of Congress. However, in its session of April 1921, during which the Sabha was renamed the 'All-India Hindu Mahasabha', the objective of loyal cooperation was appended with the aim of evolving 'a united and self-governing Indian nation'. While cow protection societies and leagues had existed for over a decade, the Mahasabha launched further campaigns against 'the slaughter of cows for the military and the export of beef, cows and bullocks to other countries' and resolved non-cooperation with the British administration until cow slaughter had ended.

The Hindu Sabha viewed Hindus as part of an 'organic whole', and it viewed itself as above the many doctrinal or sectarian differences within Hinduism. This was a reflection of the persistent antagonism between Arya Samaj and Sanatan Dharm representatives whenever the issue of religious or caste reforms arose and from which the Mahasabha attempted to distance itself. It is curious that an overarching, all-embracing, non-sectarian ideal of militant 'Hinduism', the model for both Savarkar's *Hindutva* and much contemporary Hindu nationalism, arose not directly from antagonism to Islam or Christianity but as a result of a deep, sectarian conflict between two novel nineteenth-century *Hindu* movements, the 'fundamentalist' Arya Samaj and the brahminic Sanatan Dharm. Prior to the 1920s, the Mahasabha had opposed communal representation – with the significant proviso that if communal representation was to take place, Hindus should be represented commensurate with their numerical weight in the population. But by the early 1920s, it considered its role as representing, defending and strengthening the separate public sphere of Hindu communal interests.

The influences upon and leadership of the Hindu Mahasabha from 1924 included N. C. Kelkar, Lajpat Rai, Madan Mohan Malaviya and B. S. Moonje, important figures in the next phase of the development of Hindu nationalist ideology and practice. (However, it should be noted that both Motilal Nehru and M. K. Gandhi presided over major Hindu Mahasabha events and indeed some Congress leaders were to ask the Mahasabha to merge with it after Independence.) After 1922, under the leadership of Malaviya (whose precise relationship with Hindu nationalism requires much further elaboration), the Mahasabha's annual meetings coincided with the annual meetings of the Indian National Congress, within which it was to play an increasingly influential, if complex political role, remaining ideologically distant from the non-cooperation strategy of the Swaraj Party, while aligning itself with 'responsive cooperation' factions within Congress and with remnants of the Hindu Sabha movement of the previous decade (Gordon 1975).

From 1925, the Mahasabha, which was committed to a strategy of co-operation, allowed its provincial sabhas to contest provincial elections and its elected officers to take up government posts. The Mahasabha strategy of exclusively promoting its candidates was directly related to its opposing Muslims, representatives of non-brahmin parties, and those it considered prejudicial to 'Hindu interests' who were elected to the legislatures; conversely, its own candidates were seen to safeguard what it viewed as 'Hindu interests'. Under Malaviya, the Mahasabha had made significant inroads into the political machinery of Congress, opposing both the Gandhian and Swarajist factions and their (divergent) strategies of non-cooperation. By 1926, the Mahasabha had not only claimed the right, within Congress, of its local Sabhas to nominate their own candidates for local elections but had attempted to get Congress to abstain from provincial elections where the Mahasabha proffered an alternative candidate representing 'Hindu interests'. Communal organizations had been blacklisted by Congress in 1925 and 1926. The Swaraj Party, then controlling Congress, was to curtail the influence of the Mahasabha, viewing the later as a communal organization (Gordon 1975). Congress later resolved in 1934 to forbid any of its members to simultaneously belong to the Hindu Mahasabha, the Rashtriya Swayamsevak Sangh or the Muslim League.

From the early 1920s, the attention of the All-India Hindu Mahasabha turned towards the issue of religious conversions and *shuddhi*, and the formation of the All-India Shuddhi Sabha in 1923 under the aegis of the Arya Samaj. This had two aspects: campaigns to 'reclaim' 'neo-Christians' and 'neo-Muslims', and eventually any Muslims, into Hinduism; and campaigns to 'purify', 'uplift' and 'return to the Hindu fold' those belonging to 'untouchable' or *adivasi* (tribal) groups. During the Arya Samaj *shuddhi* campaigns of the previous century, these strategies had been extremely problematic for Hindu orthodoxy and for various regional caste and *jati* leaderships who had refused to accept 'converted' individuals and groups or to dispense with the strictures around untouchability or caste commensal rules.

Similar issues confronted those in the Hindu Mahasabha who argued for caste reforms. This area is worth dwelling on by considering the Hindu Sangathan movement, because it was through the issue of 'conversions' that the next key stage of Hindu communal-nationalist ideology was forged and continues to resonate strongly today.

Shraddhanand, Biopolitics and Hindu Sangathan

In 1909, Lt Colonel U. N. Mukerji of the Indian military service had published an influential pamphlet, *Hindus – A dying race*, based on his articles to *The Bengalee*. Using the results of the 1901 Colonial Census, he had argued rather simplistically that in just over 400 years, Hindus ('the Indo-Aryan race') would cease to exist both because of the relative increase in the Christian population (due to missionary activity) and the increase in the Muslim population (resulting from conversions to Islam and allegedly higher Muslim birth rates). This terrifying invocation of *biological* Hindu extinction (Datta 1999) had a remedy: a focus on those groups of the Indian population that were otherwise considered marginal – the 'tribals' and 'untouchables' who were seen as willing if misguided fodder for Christianity. The pamphlet hugely influenced an Arya Samajist, Munshi Ram (1857–1926), who had become a *sannyasi*, Swami Shraddhanand, and was a key founder of the Hindu Sangathan movement that emerged from the revitalized Hindu Mahasabha of the early 1920s.

Swami Shraddhanand was previously leader of the 'Mahatma' faction during its dispute with the Dayananda Anglo-Vedic 'College' faction within the Arya Samaj that led to its first major split. He subsequently headed the Punjab Arya Samaj (becoming president of the Punjab Arya Pratinidhi Sabha) and founded his own Gurukul Kangri (school) in 1900, which was itself subject to bitter internecine disputes about curriculum and doctrinal purpose. Similarly, vicious disputes about the status and fallibility of Dayananda's teachings continued to affect both Arya Samaj factions. Shraddhanand, like the previous head of the opposing 'College' faction, Lajpat Rai, was also to be involved in Congress activities in the 1920s; to differing degrees, both were associated with Hindu Mahasabha activities from the same period.

In the period from 1905 until 1919, Shraddhanand had severely criticized anti-British political agitation, whether revolutionary or reformist. When the Arya Samaj had come under suspicion for seditious activities, particularly after the arrest and deportation of Lajpat Rai and Ajit Singh in 1907, Shraddhanand, while opposed to the arrests, portrayed the Arya Samaj as a loyal, non-political, purely religious organization having no subversive or seditious aims (Shraddhanand 1926, Shraddhanand 1961, Jordens 1981). He viewed politics as in essence an impure diversion from religious learning. However, he had strongly agitated for a range of reforms within Hinduism, mostly within the framework of Arya Samaj ideology but with significant modifications that were to be consequential for his militant Hindu nationalism.

Shraddhanand had remained aloof from the national movement until he met Gandhi. According to one of his biographers, it was Gandhi's religious simplicity and commitment that transformed Shraddhanand towards active support for the *satyagraha* and non-cooperation campaigns (Jordens 1981). Shraddhanand is frequently viewed as a central figure in the 1920s anti-Rowlatt *satyagraha*, and often portrayed as a major and unique symbol of Hindu-Muslim unity, especially because of his preaching of national unity from the pulpit of the Jama Masjid in Delhi and his singular bravery in the face of armed colonial police. However, his active involvement in the non-cooperation movement and Congress spans just a few years from 1919 until 1922, when Congress opposed participation in his *shuddhi* campaigns. Thereafter, from 1923, he devoted himself to Hindu nationalist and Hindu communal interests on an India-wide scale. Again, his trajectory into and out of Congress, like that of Lajpat Rai, muddies an easy understanding of the 'secular' foundations, and indeed anti-communalism, of Congress.

In 1912, Shraddhanand met U. N. Mukerji in Calcutta who explained to him his fear of Hindu extinction (Shraddhanand 1926: 14–15). Shraddhanand claimed to have then spent the next thirteen years as a student of statistics, analysing the census reports for 1901, 1911 and 1921. These resulted in his book, *Hindu Sangathan: Saviour of the dying race*, written in 1924 as the 'solution' to Mukherji's *Hindus – The dying race*.

> The great Aryan Nation is said, at the present moment, to be a dying race not because its numbers are dwindling but because it is completely disorganised. Individually, man to man, second to none on earth in intellect and physique, possessing a code of morality unapproachable by any other race of humanity, the Hindu Nation is still helpless on account of its manifold divisions and selfishness. (Shraddhanand 1926: 127)

Shraddhanand's influential tract was important for its reiteration of the fear of Hindu extinction, and because it proposed a solution, *sangathan* or the strategic organization of Hindu society, to the perceived problem of Hindu numerical decline and degeneration into the system of sub-castes. *Hindu Sangathan* knitted together Shraddhanand's quite dogmatic Arya Samajist philosophy into a political programme for Hindu organization while presenting a renewed framework for interpreting Indian history and the place of Hindus within it. *Hindu Sangathan* was written within the same few years as Savarkar's *Hindutva* (while it does not refer to the latter, Shraddhanand does commend Savarkar in other texts). It can be seen as a product of the consolidation of Hindu nationalist ideology in the 1920s following Gandhi's withdrawal of the non-cooperation movement, and in the political aftermath of the Khilafat agitations.

Hindu Sangathan is a prominent example of the products of late nineteenth-century and turn-of-century 'neo-Vedic' ideology, bearing the unmistakable stamp of the Arya Samaj. For Shraddhanand, who based his historical methodology on primarily colonial and Orientalist writers, ancient India had been ruled by the Aryan race for 'millions' of years and had colonized and given birth to the entire civilized world. (The term 'Aryan' would have been based on the ethnological and anthropometric studies of Herbert Hope Risley and his collaborators, studies adjacent to the colonial censuses that Shraddhanand claimed to have read and that were readily available in India.) Aryan colonists, he claimed, had been sent from India to both poles, to bring civilization and knowledge to both hemispheres. The Aryans, who gave the ancient name of *Aryavarta* 'to our motherland' possessed 'a real civilization which has not been equalled even up till now' (Shraddhanand 1926: 1). Similarly, the Aryan social polity was an ideal organized according to the *varna vyavastha* or system of four castes, which, according to Shraddhanand meant the organic and functional organization of society according to one's 'attributes and works, quality and action, character and conduct' rather than because of heredity. This displacement of individual heredity for a hierarchically defined social organism retained biological tropes while apparently claiming to dismiss hereditarianism. As with Lajpat Rai, Shraddhanand usurped and strategically reversed colonial discourse, while demonstrating a modernist preoccupation with biopolitics and population demographics.

The 'downfall of the nation', according to Shraddhanand, occurred because of the rise of pride and jealousy, as shown in the Mahabharata war between the Pandavas and Kauravas, and the rise of a brahmin aristocracy that reduced the other castes to servility. The system of *brahmacharya*, in which the brahmin-Hindu renounced the world and sought spiritual education, was replaced by heredity, blind faith, superstition and fetish worship. Sub-castes mushroomed, untouchability (the 'panchamas' or fifth 'caste') arose and with it grew the shudras and 'untouchables', a third of the population, living under 'a social and economic tyranny unparalleled in the history of the world'. If this is one reason for 'the dying of the Hindu race', Shraddhanand was also at pains to highlight at length what he viewed as the conversions by violence, force, fraud and inducements of those groups by Muslim conquerors and Christian missionaries. (These long sections of Hindu Sangathan could be virtually reproduced unchanged today and would be barely distinguishable from the propaganda of the Vishwa Hindu Parishad.)

While Shraddhanand was clear that it was the tyranny of brahminist orthodoxy that often drove some groups to Islam or Christianity, he also needed to demonstrate the resilience of 'Hinduism' in the face of the corrupt and dishonest methods of conversion allegedly used by Islamic and Christian proselytisers. In this sense, deeply resonant today, the strength of Hinduism is simply that it existed despite the fraudulent attempts to disparage it. There were precise intellectual conditions of possibility by which the Arya Samaj, an explicitly unorthodox, and initially an avowedly non-Hindu movement, could undertake conversion campaigns legitimately while considering those undertaken by Christianity or Islam as inherently illegitimate.

Shraddhanand proposed several remedies to restore to Hindus their 'ancient status in the world'. He recommended the revivification of the practice of *ashram dharma*. Opposing the Hindu Sabha's lower minimum ages for the marriage of boys and girls, he urged Dayananda's prescriptions of 25 years for males and 16 years for females. Shraddhanand's reasons were twofold – his belief that the progeny of younger adults was biologically weaker, and hence a source of weakness for the 'Hindu race'; and that the recommended ages allowed for the education of youth, and the institution of *brahmacharya*, whose knowledge would filter down and strengthen the Hindu community. He also proposed that all child widows be allowed to remarry, and provided various remedies for unconsummated marriage or widowhood (Shraddhanand 1926).

Shraddhanand also urged the revival of the *varnashramadharma* while urging the destruction of the system of sub-castes. The 'resurrection' of the system of only four main castes and the abolition of all sub-castes may appear a paradoxical, if not entirely anomalous solution to the problem of untouchability, particularly for a person like Shraddhanand who opposed untouchability. However, this was a dominant strand in Hindu nationalist thinking that attempted to articulate the Vedic and *Manudharmashastra* caste system, which was considered sacred, while opposing sub-caste, since the latter was considered to be the basis of Hindu weakness and division.

Of considerable importance was the use of the warning in the *Manudharmashastra* of the degradation and doom, symptomatic of the advance of the Kali Yuga, that can befall a society once shudras become the majority of the population. Both Shraddhanand and Lajpat Rai used this section of *Manu* to argue against untouchability and for the necessity of 'purifying' the 'scheduled castes' and 'reconverting' them to Hinduism. (This particular section of *Manu* is also frequently quoted in later Hindutva literature.) *Manu* is the most important text of archaic religious jurisprudence for the legitimation of brahmin and kshatriya caste superiority and shudra, 'untouchable' and women's inferiority and suppression by the caste Hindu traditions. The use of *Manu* to argue against untouchability or for 'purification' is disingenuous and can only make logical sense once its founding precepts about caste hierarchy and shudra subjugation have already been accepted as necessary and legitimate. Indeed, the section of *Manu* that warns against shudra 'over-population' explicitly begins by stipulating the solely *hereditary* rights enjoyed by brahmins to provide guidance on justice (*dharma*), rights which a shudra can *never* possess. As *Manu* in its characteristically direct manner states, if a shudra did dispense advice on righteousness (*dharma*), the kingdom would go under like 'a cow in the mud'. The deeply political and biological nuances in the way was *Manu* was used need to be noted. Of importance here is the manner in which caste was articulated in a 'Malthusian' language of social checks on biological population demographics, a coupling of *Manu* and Malthus that highlighted a radically different socio-political agenda.

Shraddhanand urged that brahmins abolish intra-caste differences, and that the Rajputs, Khatris, Jats, Gujjars and others

> be one recognised society of protectors of nation. All the castes and sub-castes engaged in trade and agriculture should be included in the vaishya caste. And the rest should constitute the Shudra caste and serve society. There should be free marriage relations, to begin with, within the castes, and Anuloma marriages should not be interfered with. Then gradually Pratiloma marriages should be introduced. And lastly, character and conduct should become the determining factors in fixing the Varna of a Hindu. But interdining among all the castes should be commenced at once – not promiscuous eating out of the same cup and dish like Muhammadans, but partaking of food in separate cups and dishes served by decent Shudras. (Shraddhanand 1926: 136)

Why shudras could only be placed to serve the other castes, which does not in fact alter their social position, is not explained. Similarly, to argue that this was a tract of its time, and simply reiterated a modernized version of Hinduism's allegedly transcendental capacity 'to include and hierarchize' (Dumont 1980) would be misleading since Shraddhanand was writing during a period when strong anti-caste discourses were well established.

Shraddhanand's partial opposition to *jati*, aspects of gender inequality and untouchability has to be considered within his narrative against what he perceived as the threatening demography of Islam and Christianity. His prescriptions on child marriage were directly related to his belief that early marriage and conception led to physically weak children and thus physiologically weak Hindus. His belief that young widows be allowed to remarry was precisely related to his fear that young widows could not procreate if they remained unmarried. He compared traditional Hindu prescriptions about child marriage and widowhood directly with Muslim and Christian age variations in marriage and widowhood, as well as the allegedly more prolific Muslim birth rate. Christians and Muslims, he argued, also married later and thus had biologically stronger and numerically greater progeny. Similarly, his attacks on the Hindu Mahasabha for earlier passing a resolution against untouchability that (in the face of Sanatan Dharma opposition) nevertheless did not go so far as to allow 'untouchables' to draw water from a common well, attend any Hindu temple or wear the sacred thread, was compared directly to Muslims and Christians who could use the same water wells as caste Hindus. 'Muslim prostitutes', he argued, were allowed to dance in front of temples that 'untouchables' could not enter (Shraddhanand 1926: 136–7). In each of the caste and gender reforms he proposed, the treatment of 'untouchables' by brahmin and other caste Hindus was explicitly contrasted with the favourable treatment enjoyed by Christians and Muslims.

One of the most consistent arguments of Shraddhanand concerned 'the untouchables', who he argued should be immediately brought into the shudra caste after a purification ceremony. They numbered some 75 million individuals who were prey to conversions 'by beef eating religious denominations' because of the stubbornness of a mere four million orthodox brahmins. 'Untouchables', including 'tribals', he argued, once belonged to one of the three higher castes of Hinduism. They had become 'socially degraded' probably because of their 'moral degradation' but once 'uplifted' and having reformed their way of life and morality, 'nothing should stand in the way of their regaining their former positions.' It is clear throughout the text of *Hindu Sangathan* that the mass of those outside the Hindu caste system were important precisely because of their numerical and demographic strength for Hinduism and of the fear, consistently projected by Shraddhanand, that they would be lost to Islam or Christianity, and thence contribute to the extinction of the Hindu race. His was not an argument that scheduled castes should as of right, and with reference only to their condition, enjoy greater freedoms and liberties; it was rather that Christians and Muslims already had such liberties whereas those who were only important because they could potentially become incorporated as low castes within a hierarchical Hinduism and increase its numerical strength, did not. This orientation whereby the strategy towards populations outside the caste system should be to bring them into a hierarchical system of caste was definitive of *sangathan*, and is a key characteristic of today's Hindutva movement.

Syncretism and Repugnance

The main practical remedy Shraddhanand proposed to prevent the decline of the Hindus was to oppose the 'evil' of conversions to Islam and Christianity. He recounted an incident in 1923 during which, while Congress was meeting with Khilafat leaders, the All India Kshatriya Mahasabha had resolved to 'take back' 450,000 Malkana Rajputs into the kshatriya caste. The Malkana Rajputs practised a form of religion that was syncretic and comprised Hindu and Islamic beliefs and practices, but they were often seen as Muslims. The first large-scale 'reconversion' campaigns Shraddhanand highlighted as indicative of the growth of the Hindu Sangathan movement concerned *not a Muslim population but a syncretic one* that could not be categorized unambiguously by 'Hindu' or 'Muslim' labels. Of similar importance was Shraddhanand's concern that 'Muslim proselytizers' had targeted this same community. Shraddhanand proposed in 1923 the formation of the Bharatiya (All-India) Hindu Shuddhi Sabha to undertake India-wide conversions, initially of those termed 'neo-Muslims', but often comprising communities with syncretic religious traditions. This syncretism was interpreted by Shraddhanand as the 'casting of yearning glances towards their Hindu brethren for the past two centuries or more' by communities whose entry into Hinduism was forbidden by orthodoxy. He hence urged the 'reclamation' of these 'strayed brethren', the neo-Muslims and neo-Christians.

Two conspicuous processes, the logic of modernist demographic enumeration and the imperative of unambiguous classification, are glaringly obvious throughout Shraddhanand's text. These process of numerical and categorical reasoning are distinctive to modernist configurations of the populace, groups and nations. As Datta has argued, groups that could not be enumerated or categorized under dominant religious classifications were problematized by Hindu communalism (Datta 1999). Of additional importance here is the logic of purity and danger highlighted by Mary Douglas (1991) in which the target groups for Hindu supremacism were not Muslims and Christians but those who offended and created revulsion for the Hindu chauvinist sensibility because they could not be nominated as Christians, Muslims or Hindus. Instructively, a circular by E. A. Gait, census commissioner for the 1911 census, proposed syncretic 'Hindu-Muslim' categories and the classification of 'untouchables' as 'not Hindus'. This was received by Arya Samajists and Hindu leaders in the Punjab and United Provinces as the potential 'loss' of sixty million 'Hindus', and resulted in the political galvanization of Hindu 'orthodoxy' against the census categories, combined with an intensification of Arya Samaj *shuddhi* activities (Lajpat Rai 1915: 227–33).

The central thrust of these activities was about the disciplining and 'purification' of Indian groups and communities that were economically, politically and culturally marginal, and yet numerically large – 'untouchables' and hybrid communities were important because they could be nominated as 'Hindu'. As important was the different civilizing mission, based on 'purification', 'social hygiene' and 'upliftment', whose intellectual conditions of thinkability were those of British colonialism itself: how could a minority claim political hegemony over a majority, if not by modernist processes of nominal reasoning, as subjects of the British King-Emperor, or as subjects of a Hindu nation? Finally, Shraddhanand urged the adoption of Hindi and the Devanagari script throughout India, and, as the first step towards Hindu national solidarity and unity (*sangathan*), building of a Hindu Rashtra (Hindu Nation) *mandir* (temple) in every town and major city, which would hold at least as many people as the major mosques in northern India. The Hindu Rashtra *mandir* would be based on the worship of the cow as mother, the goddess of knowledge, and the motherland.

The Vagaries of Non-cooperation

Shraddhanand was shot and killed by a Muslim in 1926, the year that *Hindu Sangathan* was published. However, the Hindu Sangathan movement and the Hindu Mahasabha grew in strength from the mid-1920s under the guidance and leadership of Madan Mohan Malaviya, Lajpat Rai and B. S. Moonje. From 1921, coinciding with the end of Gandhi's mass *satyagraha* campaigns, to the middle of the decade, there were significant and instructive developments in the national political field. The mass arrests of nationalist activists and the outlawing of Congress by the British in 1921 resulted in the imprisonment of Gandhi, Jawaharlal Nehru, Lajpat Rai and other Congress leaders and activists within the national movement. This created considerable factional dissension within Congress regarding the strategy of non-cooperation with the British.

While Gandhi was imprisoned, Motilal Nehru (1861–1931) and Chitta Ranjan Das (1870–1925) formed a faction within Congress, the Swajarist group (1922) which became the Swaraj (Self-Rule) Party (from 1923–7). The Party had the initial aim of contesting the elections to the Central Legislative Assembly in 1923 while adopting a policy of indiscriminate walk outs and 'uniform, continuous and consistent' obstruction of all processes of legal policy making in the colonial legislature. However, even during their formative stage in 1922, the Swarajists had internally split between those wishing to continue the formal Congress policy of non-cooperation by obstruction and those who advocated entry into the legislatures with the aim of 'responsive cooperation' with the British. A key factor in the split of the Swaraj Party 'from top to bottom' was the impact of the Malaviya group organized through the Hindu Mahasabha, which was important in explicitly aligning 'responsivism' with Hindu communal demands (Gordon 1975, Hasan 1991). The Swaraj policy was later changed to 'resistance to the bureaucracy [in so far as it] impeded the nation's progress towards Swarajya'. It is here worth analytically distinguishing the complex political tendencies in and around the Swaraj Party and noting the salience of the last one: absolute non-cooperation, unreconstructed Gandhianism, forms of limited cooperation still having the aim of self-rule, 'responsive cooperation', and 'responsive cooperation' solely in order to secure 'Hindu interests'.

Lajpat Rai joined the Swaraj Party in 1923 and worked for the elections in the Punjab that year. While throughout the initial period of dissension he remained with the Congress group, he typically articulated intermediate positions between absolute non-cooperation and 'responsive cooperation' while supporting the latter (see, for example, Lajpat Rai 1966b: 316–22). In 1925, the Swaraj Party was riven with serious conflicts because of the rise in strength of the 'responsivist' group, led by M.R. Jayakar, N.C. Kelkar and B. S. Moonje, the latter a foundational figure in the newly formed Hindu nationalist Rashtriya Swayamsevak Sangh, which evolved in the period 1924–6.

Similarly, and in a complex but parallel development, Madan Mohan Malaviya and Lajpat Rai, both leading figures in the Hindu Mahasabha, were to form variously an 'Independent Congress Party' and a 'Nationalist Party' (in 1926) again with the aim of 'responsive cooperation' with the British government. Conversely, by the end of 1929, Congress had passed its historic Purna Swaraj (Absolute Self-Rule) resolution declaring complete freedom from the British. While it would seem to be an elementary matter to present a narrative in which the non-sectarian national movement was determined to oppose and obstruct British rule, while those with Hindu nationalist leanings chose at virtually every turn to cooperate with British rule, this would be a simplification, because there had historically been non-sectarian 'moderates' within Congress who supported varying degrees of cooperation (such as Gokhale), while 'Hindu nationalists' such as Tilak had consistently taken 'radical' positions of absolute and immediate self-rule. However, in the crucial if extremely complex period of the mid-1920s, it *is* striking that the major figures involved in the national movement who opposed absolute non-cooperation – Lajpat Rai, Madan Mohan Malaviya and B. S. Moonje – were also important in the by then burgeoning and militant Hindu nationalist organizations that existed within and outside the Indian National Congress.

Lajpat Rai, 'Cooperation' and Hindu Communal Interests

Lajpat Rai's political trajectory and concerns after 1924 until his death in 1928 form an illustrative ideological map of the kinds of complex positions that were ostensibly central to the national movement but clearly favoured Hindu communal interests and generally opposed Muslim ones. Lajpat Rai lobbied for purely Hindu interests and consistently argued against the 'policy of appeasement' of Muslims. He provided strong leadership for the Hindu Mahasabha (of which he was President in 1925), Hindu Sangathan and the *shuddhi* movements, urging the growth of the latter against the corresponding *tabligh* and *tanzim* activities among Muslim communities. He opposed the politicization of the Hindu Mahasabha, and talk of 'Hindu Raj' or 'Muslim Raj' while bemoaning the historic weakness of Hindus, claiming that Hindu Sangathan and Indian nationalism were entirely compatible and necessary for each other. Lajpat Rai was an extremely influential member of Congress who accepted the need for Hindu-Muslim unity, that Hindus and Muslims shared a common interest, even a composite nationality (Lajpat Rai 1966b: 157–9, 162–3). But he had already declared in 1917 that he was 'a Hindu nationalist'. While a willing supporter of non-cooperation ('Speech at 35th session of Indian National Congress, Nagpur, December 1920' in Lajpat Rai 1966b: 67) who was extremely critical of Gandhi's suspension of civil disobedience (Lajpat Rai 1966b:

88, 91), he consistently adopted a more pragmatic position towards absolute non-cooperation and absolute independence, typically arguing that these were legitimate aims, but the reality of political possibilities demanded a more compromised position, if not their absolute rejection.

His conception of the politically possible delineated his movement towards an explicitly Hindu communalist position within a few years. In discussing the 'Hindu-Muslim problem' during 1924, following his resignation from Congress, Lajpat Rai (using Spencer) bemoaned the growth of the idea of absolute freedom and absolute rights in religious matters, at the expense of duties towards the nation: 'All organic relations depend upon the mutual obligations of the members comprising the organism. No part of the organism has any absolute right' (Lajpat Rai 1966b: 176). While consistently viewing communalism as an invention of British statecraft, he traced its growth to the principle of separate communal organization, cooperation with the British and opposition to self-rule of Sir Syed Ahmed Khan and the Muslim leadership that followed in his wake – 'the Aligarh School of Muhammadans became characteristically anti-Hindu and pro-Government'. He portrayed Islam as an intolerant, dogmatic religion in comparison with Hinduism, which despite its caste system, was 'the most tolerant of all great religions in the world'(Lajpat Rai 1966b: 184, 186–7). Gandhi was criticized for asking Hindus to concede to Muslim religious demands while never making a similar request to Muslims; similarly Gandhi's assertion that Muslims had accepted non-cooperation 'was absolutely unwarranted'. Remarkably, he said that untouchability must have arisen as a result of Hindu 'non-cooperation with foreign rulers who happened to be beef-eaters' (Lajpat Rai 1966b: 189–90). However, the 'enemies' of previous centuries were now neither foreigners nor rulers and were an integral part of the Indian nation. Despite this, he argued, Muslims leaders over the past fifty years had implanted the idea in the Muslim masses that Hindus were 'Kafirs'.

While Lajpat Rai also consistently blamed the Arya Samaj, as well as Vivekananda and Sister Nivedita for fostering an intolerant Hindu communal consciousness, he viewed this as a response to what he perceived as earlier Muslim communalism and cooperation with British rulers, first through the formation of the denominational Aligarh College and then the subsequent fostering of a logic of separate representation and separate electorates. Lajpat Rai conceded that some of these activities may have been necessary for Muslim advancement into education and government, in a manner that Hindus already enjoyed. But the fact that Muslims were underrepresented in government posts was their own fault for not taking sufficient advantage of education under British rule, and not the fault of Hindus who did.

Lajpat Rai's narrative which depicted Muslim communalism as exclusive, self-seeking, anti-national, anti-Indian and in complete alliance with the British, whereas

Hindu communalism was both a response to Muslim separatism and represented a 'cult of political freedom' from British imperialism, was central to his justification for the flourishing of Hindu communalist organizations from the mid-1920s. This discourse was pivotal in legitimizing Hindu nationalist strategies of cooperation with the ruling British power and of opposing both the Congress and the national movement, especially strands in the latter that were to remain committed to absolute non-cooperation, obstruction of British rule and immediate and complete independence.

Lajpat Rai argued that many Muslims *had* genuinely committed themselves to the non-cooperation movement, but 'in very many cases, their nationalism seemed to be secondary to their Pan-Islamism' (Lajpat Rai 1966b: 196). Muslims, he argued, were opposed to the British mainly because the British had been at war against other Muslim countries, and not because of their unconditional love for India and its freedom. 'Divided allegiance and divided love cannot produce either good nationalists or good patriots' (Lajpat Rai 1966b: 197). Moreover, it was only in India that exclusivist and Pan-Islamic Muslims could be found, whereas in every other Muslim country, the task of nation-building had predominated. Conversely:

> Hindus cannot be anything but Indians. They have no other country and no other nation to look to. They cannot, therefore, be accused of any kind of Pan-Hinduism, in the sense in which the term is used in relation to Islam. Hinduism and Indianism are, in their case, synonymous terms. (Lajpat Rai 1966b: 203).

Lajpat Rai's discussions of the *shuddhi* and *sangathan* movements were couched in similar terms. While critical of Swami Shraddhanand and the earlier Arya Samaj *shuddhi* activities, he defended *shuddhi* as 'non-political', and its adoption by the Hindu Mahasabha as 'partly political, partly communal and partly humanitarian'. The *shuddhi* movement, he argued, had come to stay and had to be accepted; it could not be stopped as long as non-Hindu agencies were undertaking proselytizing work. Similarly the *sangathan* (Hindu Sabha) movement need not be inherently anti-Muslim (though Lajpat Rai also said that the fact that it was anti-Muslim was 'the only thing that keeps it alive'), but, in comparison, *tanzim* activities were 'obviously anti-Hindu' (Lajpat Rai 1966b: 209).

The thrust of his analysis of communalism was criticism of Muslims and of Muslim communal representation since, he argued, this was the surest way of not achieving *swaraj*. After iterating a fear among some Hindu leaders that Muslim communal representation of electorates was designed, with the assistance of foreign Muslim states, to establish Muslim rule of Hindustan, Lajpat Rai argued on the one hand for proportional communal representation in the provincial legislatures and local bodies where Muslims were in a majority; but on the other hand opposed separate electorates, the principle of 'effective' minority representation in the provinces where Muslims were in a minority, and communal representation in government service or educational institutions.

In 1923, Lajpat Rai argued that Muslims should have four states (the Pathan province, western Punjab, the Sind and eastern Bengal), but he added, 'it should be distinctly understood that this is not a united India. It means a clear partition of India into a Muslim India and a non-Muslim India' (Lajpat Rai [1923] 1966b: 213). He used the term non-Muslim India because 'all that the Muslims are anxious for is a guarantee of their own rights. All other communities they lump into one as non-Muslims' (Lajpat Rai 1966b: 211). Lajpat Rai is indeed credited with being the first major leader of the national movement to propose the theory of two exclusive nations in India and is said to have proposed this from the late nineteenth century.

His message in 1924 to both Muslims and Hindus is worth quoting at length, since it encapsulated the ideological map of a primordial, majoritarian Hinduism that grew rapidly from 1923–25.

> For God's sake don't threaten us with Jehad. We have seen many Jehads! For the last twelve hundred years, we have heard that cry every day of our national existence. Yet, Jehads have not succeeded in killing us, and God willing, no threat of Jehad will influence us by one hair's breadth in our determination to continue to live. We are prepared to subordinate our communal life to national life. For united national existence we would do anything, but we shall not submit to threats or to coercion. It is true that Muslim distrust of Hindus can successfully block the avenues of Swarajya, but brother Muslims! don't forget that active Hindu hostility may also be productive of some harm to the Islamic world. Away, then with these threats and distrust. Let us live and struggle for freedom as brothers whose interests are one and indivisible . . . India is neither Hindu nor Muslim. It is not even both. It is one. It is India. To the Hindus, I will say, 'If there are any among you who still dream of a Hindu Raj in this country; who think they can crush the Mussalmans and be the supreme power in this land, tell them that they are fools, or to be more accurate, that they are insane, and that their insanity will ruin their Hinduism along with their country . . . You have no one outside India to help you. You are like a lonely waif in the world and your position is extremely delicate.' (Lajpat Rai 1966b: 221)

Leaving the Swaraj Party

Lajpat Rai's withdrawal from the Swaraj Party is equally instructive. Lajpat Rai opposed 'unreserved' non-cooperation because in his view the national movement was too weak and disunited to paralyse the administration or bring it to a standstill. Characteristically arguing that the principles of non-cooperation were correct, he nevertheless opposed the practice of uniform obstruction, because the movement had not 'correctly estimated the facts and conditions of national life'. After resigning from the Swaraj Party in September 1926 and forming the Nationalist Party, with Madan Mohan Malaviya, Lajpat Rai argued that non-cooperation had been frustrated because of the separatism of the Muslim community (Lajpat Rai 1966b: 316). Hence, the policy of non-cooperation or obstruction by only Hindus would also fail. Conversely, the Muslims would continue to cooperate with the British to secure their own rights, the acceptance of which would reduce the Hindu community to a position of inferiority and subordination. 'What would be the position of the Hindus after 10 or 20 years hereafter if the present alliance of the Government and the Muslims continues and the Hindus continue to allow themselves to be influenced by the mentality of [non] co-operation and boycott?' (Lajpat Rai 1966b: 319). Contrasting his nationalism with that of the Swaraj Party, he said his nationalism would be consistent with 'justice' to the Hindu community, and it would not abide the formation of national unity at the cost of 'Hindu rights'. While rejecting the conversion of all Muslims in India to Hinduism and establishing a Hindu Raj, and while claiming that his policy was not that of unfettered cooperation with the British, he urged instead what he called a 'balanced' and 'reasoned' approach to the issue of cooperation: 'I do not want to change masters' (Lajpat Rai 1966b: 320). Hence, the answer to Muslim communalism was Hindu communalism, cooperative with the British and in accordance with the separate sphere of exclusively Hindu interests.

Such sentiments were to gain greater force in Lajpat Rai's activities as president of the Hindu Mahasabha and in his Sangathanist activities. In his speech to the Bombay Hindu Provincial Conference in 1925 (as President of the Hindu Mahasabha) the theme of 'Hindus in danger' was very strong: 'it was incumbent on Hindus to take active steps to repel the attacks and to resist the attempts that are being made to destroy their unity and communal existence' by Muslims, the latter wishing to become 'the dominant communal entity' in India. Failure to do this would mean Muslim domination. He asserted that if organizing Hindus 'is anti-Muslim or anti-national, than I frankly confess that the Hindu Sabha movement is both' (Lajpat Rai 1966b: 247). Hindus should cultivate internal unity and unity with the Christians and Parsees (Lajpat Rai 1966b: 249). Similarly, in a reference to the upsurge of the Non-Brahman movement in Maharashtra in the early to mid 1920s, he argued that the brahmins must 'destroy' the movement for the separate political existence of the non-brahmins and bring into the shudra fold all 'untouchables'. He argued, using the *Manudharmashastra*, that a nation in which shudras were a majority and the *dvija* (or 'twice-born') castes were a minority is 'doomed'. Hinduism was a living organism and life implied adaptability and growth; hence, Hindus had to 'move every nerve' to become communally efficient and united (Lajpat Rai 1966b: 252–3). The ancient *varnashrama* system had to be restored and modified according to contemporary exigencies. The Hindu Sangathan movement, he said, had to face the odium of orthodoxy (Sanatan Dharmis), and an unpopularity within the anti-sectarian national movement that wanted to keep the Hindu community 'eternally inefficient'. One may ask why 'untouchables' should become shudras and not brahmins; it is indeed curious how gently brahmins were dealt with by Lajpat Rai and Shraddhanand given their views about the abject and deplorable state brahmin selfishness and 'inefficiency' had brought Hinduism to. Of additional significance was the fact that the national movement's attempts, under uniquely difficult political circumstances, at cultivating a non-communal, non-sectarian political strategy was viewed by Lajpat Rai as a matter of *inefficiency*.

If these Spencerian, organicist themes are prominent (and were propounded in a similarly forceful way by Swami Shraddhanand, who was indeed explicit about the metaphoric usefulness of bodily tropes), it should not be surprising that Lajpat Rai, like Shraddhanand, focused on the biological and physiological weakness of the Hindu race, which could only be remedied by the reproductive strengthening of Hindu women:

> The Hindus of today are inefficient, lacking in courage, lacking in enterprise, lacking in the zest for life, lacking in enthusiasm, lacking in solidarity, scattered units of a once great race *because* the condition of their women is not what may be called healthy. (Lajpat Rai 1966b: 255, emphasis added)

The answer to this 'physical disability' was to attend to 'our girls', living in ignorance and superstition, physically poor because of the social restrictions of Hindu orthodoxy and early child marriage, while girls in other countries 'are at school, developing their muscles and nerves, hands and feet by suitable exercise' (Lajpat Rai 1966b: 255) He contrasted this with 'ancient times', during which Hindu women were independent, assertive, self-reliant, physically competent and as free as men, and produced brave, kind, self-confident, able-bodied and strong Hindu children.

Conclusion

One of the most striking aspects of the period from the turn of the century into the mid-1920s examined in this chapter is just how significant the preoccupations of the Arya Samaj of the previous century were in configuring the non-Gandhite ideological universe for both Hindu internal reform and Hindu political assertion within and around the Congress, the non-cooperation and national movement. While Lajpat Rai and Swami Shraddhanand represented ostensibly adversarial positions, their remedies for Hindu reform and political organization were very similar and reflected the preoccupations of earlier Arya Samajist 'rationalist' reform of Hinduism, though also strongly inflected with Spencerian, evolutionist, and Malthusian themes of population, demography and fertility. The reforms included the abolition of sub-caste, but the symbolic reinstitution of the *varna* system, the education of women, the conversion of 'untouchables' and tribals to Hinduism, the opposition to Hindu orthodoxy and superstition, but the 'reclamation' of syncretic religious and cultural communities into a caste-based Hinduism.

Of importance was the development of a distinct language of Hinduism under social, cultural, political and demographic threat, and the consequent formation of the political languages of separate Hindu rights and interests within the public sphere created under the purview of the national movement. For Hindu nationalists such as Bhai Parmanand and Lala Har Dayal during this period, 'Hindu interests' could be expanded to a series of demands for Hindu *sangathan*, 'Hindu Raj', the *shuddhi* of all Muslims, and the conquest and *shuddhi* of Afghanistan (Brown 1975: 233, Dharamvira 1970, Parmanand 1982).

Equally evident was the birth of 'languages of equivalence' around communities defined communally, the legitimacy of proportional numerical reasoning and the consequent idea of political power as a zero-sum game. By and large, Hinduism was conceived as problematic and in need of strengthening and reform, not principally to remove its injustices or irrationalities, but because Hindus were weak, disorganized and disunited in the face of religious *minorities*. There is indeed a consistent narrative of despair at the perceived state of Hindus in the political tendencies examined above. Political *sangathan* may have been legitimized through the language of internal reform, but its clear purpose was to create, strengthen and consolidate the idea of a distinct nationwide imagined community of Hindus whose interests had to be articulated in the political sphere of Indian nationalism, but which could also be constituted as a distinct communalized public sphere in its own right. This agenda was very different from that of the anti-sectarian tendencies of the national movement, but the two often shared the same public space and sphere of organization. This new 'Hindu community' was idealized not as secular and comprised of individual citizen subjects, but as an organic, ancient Vedic *varnashrama*. The idea of Hindus constituting a 'nation' was now clearly present. However, the claim that Hindus should constitute an exclusive and self-governing nation of the future was to be most powerfully articulated in Vinayak Damodar Savarkar's ideology of Hindutva.

–4–

From Revolutionary Nationalism to *Hindutva*

Not only [do] we own a common Fatherland, a Territorial unity, but what is scarcely found anywhere else in the world we have a common Holyland which is identified with our common Fatherland. This Bharat Bhoomi, this Hindusthan, India is both our [Fatherland] and [Holyland]. Our patriotism [is] therefore doubly sure. Then we have common affinities, cultural, religious, historical, linguistic and racial which through the process of countless centuries of association and assimilation moulded us into a homogeneous and organic Nation and above all induced a will to lead a corporate and common National Life. The Hindus are no treaty Nation – but an organic National Being . . . That is the reason why today we the Hindus from Kashmere to Madras and Sindh to Assam will be a Nation by ourselves – while the Indian Moslems are on the whole more inclined to identify themselves and their interests with Moslems outside India than Hindus who live next door, like the Jews in Germany. (V. D. Savarkar, Presidential Address, 21st Session of the Akhil Bharat Hindu Mahasabha, Calcutta, 1939 in Savarkar 1949: 100–2)

Introduction

The concept of Hindutva, the imputation of a core essence to 'Hinduness', or the 'beingness of a Hindu' that was imagined to be constitutive of Hindu identity is of recent lineage. 'Hindutva', a neo-Sanskrit term, does not have a basis in tradition. (The Sanskrit masculine suffix, '-*tva*', appended to 'Hindu' creates an abstract noun, representing 'Hinduness'.) Popularized in Bengal during the 1890s by Chandranath Basu and used by national figures such as Tilak, its contemporary usage derives largely from Vinayak Damodar Savarkar.

Many of the ideological strands, political demands and forms of mass activity of post-1980s Hindu nationalism are already prefigured in 'Savarkarism', and in the activities of the early movements he influenced, the Hindu Mahasabha (Great Hindu Assembly) and the associated Hindu Sangathan (Hindu Organization) movement. Indeed, the key political ideas of the contemporary Hindutva movement were being articulated by Savarkar and the Hindu Mahasabha (after Savarkar became its president in 1937) some eighty to ninety years ago in virtually identical languages. These included the belief that 'Hindus' constituted in and of themselves, 'a nation', that Hinduism was under siege or threat of 'extermination' in India, that Muslims were the treacherous 'fifth column' in the nation and had 'extra-territorial designs', the fear of the conversions of 'Hindus' to Islam or Christianity, the consequent importance of reconversion campaigns, a critique of 'pseudo-nationalism', a critique of the politics of 'communal vote banks', the idea of 'Hindu nation' as a 'genuinely secular' or authentically nationalist concept, an attack on Hindus who were 'ashamed' of Hinduism, the consequent necessity of declaring with pride that one is a Hindu, the imperative to militarize Hindus, the view of Muslim minorities as constituting a separate nation within but not of India, the idea that India was comprised of 'two nations', the view of the totality of Muslim culture and political ideology as reducible to Quranic injunctions about *jihad, dar-ul Islam*, religious conquest and consequently treachery to 'Hindu nation', and a rejection of the view that communalism was a product of British colonialism in preference for a view of a thousand year war against Muslim (and, secondarily, British) aggression.

The story of Savarkar's revolutionary nationalist and anti-colonial activities and his influence upon early twentieth-century Hindu nationalist movements provides insight into the impact of political Hinduism on several ideological currents within and outside the Indian freedom movement, and which extended well beyond the Gandhian movements that were to become prominent after the 1920s. The example of Savarkar also says much about violent, revolutionary or terroristic anticolonial nationalism and its relation to Hindu nationalism. The argument is not that there was an elementary congruence between Hindu nation-alism and revolutionary anticolonial struggle. For example, and despite the nominal and unconvincing revisionist history of its growth, the Rashtriya Swayamsevak Sangh, the dominant Hindu nationalist organization after the decline of the Hindu Mahasabha, was conspicuously absent from the national movement, though the precise reasons for its disavowal of anti-colonial struggle require careful con-sideration (see next chapter). However, some key Hindu nationalist figures were also activists within various sections of the Indian anti-colonial movement. While revolutionary nationalism and Hindu nationalism were distinct and largely occupied separate spheres of activity, the political and ideological currents of some forms of violent and insurrectionary anti-colonial nationalism in India provide a different understanding of the form, content and aesthetics of Hindu nationalism.

A major strand of Indian anti-colonial activism, certainly the most dramatically influential after the first partition of Bengal in 1905 until the consolidation of Gandhianism in the 1920s, was revolutionary nationalism based on the legitimacy of violent struggle against British rule. Indeed, and despite the popular image of the Indian national movement as primarily non-violent, violent forms of revol-utionary nationalism were dominant within the movement both before and well after Gandhi's emergence as a major political leader. Its key methodologies, which are central to the heroic aura that continues to surround the memory of Savarkar, cannot be understood outside of the period from the late nineteenth century until the inter-war years during which numerous revolutionary nationalist and regional movements, youth groups and secret societies flourished, particularly in Russia and Eastern Europe, but also in Western Europe and in distinctively anti-colonial forms in the colonies. While revolutionary nationalism varied in its ideological content, the emphasis was on the legitimacy of violence, armed and violent insurrection, militarism and its associated masculine aesthetic (itself partly generated by the war situations), self-determination, and an instinctive but often ideologically underdeveloped affective and metaphysical ethno-nationalism informed by diverse nineteenth-century organicist and functionalist ideas. Savarkar's formative importance during his twenties was as an instigator and activist leader within one such revolutionary nationalist network, the Abhinav Bharat.

The Aura of Savarkar

Vinayak Damodar Savarkar was born in May 1883 in Bhagur, a town in the Nasik district of colonial Maharashtra, western India, into a Chitpavan brahmin family. (The material below on Savarkar's life is based on Savarkar 1950, Savarkar and Srivastava 1983, Keer 1988 and the essays by Joglekar and Gupta in Grover 1993.) Colonial and post-colonial Maharashtra has been extremely important in giving rise to a number of Hindu nationalist ideologues and movements, just as the Chitpavan brahmin community of Maharashtra was to become an elitist stronghold of Hindu nationalist activism. The Chitpavan brahmin community of Maharashtra, itself categorized in colonial ethnological taxonomy as often 'Aryan' and 'fair skinned' (Risley 1903, Enthoven 1920: 242–4), has indeed produced a remarkable number of major Hindu nationalist ideologues and leaders.

Savarkar is celebrated in contemporary India as a revolutionary hero ('veer'), a daring and courageous romantic figure who fought British colonial powers within and outside India. However, while the panegyric is a common narrative style in popular Indian writings, even relatively serious studies of Savarkar's social and political thought are often congested with a dense hagiographical tone (Anand 1967, Keer 1988, Trehan 1991, Grover 1993). This is a device in many writings by or about Hindu nationalist founders or ideologues; the semblance to encomiums, to gods, saints and especially medieval Hindu heroes is not accidental. Hence, Savarkar's seditionist activities against the British and his violent 'defence' of Hinduism against Muslims are written as starting virtually from the age of ten or twelve – recounting his politically motivated fights with Muslim schoolboys – and continuing unbroken into political maturity. The overarching themes in his hagiographies are undoubtedly those of uncompromising Hindu militancy, violence, masculine strength and daring, both against British colonial rule and against Indian Muslims.

Savarkar's first serious political involvement began in youth as a founder member of the Mitra Mela (Friend's Group), formed in 1899, a revolutionary nationalist youth group that was transformed by him in 1904 into the Abhinav Bharat ('Young India') a secret revolutionary organization modelled on the Italian republican revolutionary Giuseppe Mazzini's 'Young Italy' unification movement. Mazzini was an extremely important source of inspiration for Savarkar, and indeed for many of the nationalist and revolutionary societies that formed in colonial India well before as well as around the turn of the century. Garibaldi, Mazzini and the *risorgimento* movements were, for example, to variously inspire Ranade, Lajpat Rai, Tilak, and the Nehrus. Savarkar's first influential work was indeed the translation of Mazzini's *Life* into Marathi (Lajpat Rai had also published a translation). The influence of revolutionary and secret societies and conspiracies waned after the Second World War, but they were very much part of the popular imagination in colonial India and within Europe from the latter decades of the nineteenth century and into the inter-war period. It is worth noting here that Mazzini did not provide an internally coherent or completed political philosophy of nationalism. While having strong religious convictions and believing in an abstract godly moral force as the basis for Italian unification that was embodied in the state, Mazzini also considered 'the people', rather than the Pope, Christianity or monarchy as the basis for legitimate authority within his renewed nationalism. Mazzini similarly drew a distinction between ethnic nationalism and the nation state and argued against the view that the two must be congruent. His nationalism was also not based on simple majoritarianism – he viewed minority protection as a foundational concept in his nationalism – but on a federalism that was ostensibly pan-European in spirit and perspective and internally based on devolutionist precepts (see Mack Smith 1994: 52–3, 154–5, 218–19).

The Maharashtrian Abhinav Bharat, like many revolutionary societies such as Bengal's more prominent Anushilan Samiti (as well as the transnationally organized Yugantar group and Ghadar party), was dedicated to violent and revolutionary insurrection against British colonial rule. Its secret lifetime oath included the statement that independence could only be achieved by 'the waging of a bloody and relentless war against the foreigner'. Abhinav Bharat was to significantly expand in influence in the first decade of the twentieth century. Savarkar enlisted at Fergusson College in Poona in 1902. During this time, the activities of Abhinav Bharat included recruitment of 'patriotic' students, the organization of political meetings, and the publication of a political and literary sheet, the handwritten *Aryan Weekly*.

Savarkar studied law in Bombay from 1904 and on graduation earned a 'Shivaji' scholarship for gaining an independent professional qualification in England. He was recommended for the scholarship by Bal Gangadhar Tilak, who wrote Savarkar's reference. Savarkar arrived in England in 1906, aged twenty-three, stayed at India House in Highgate, north London and enlisted at one of the courts at Gray's Inn to become a barrister. While at India House, Savarkar organized the Free India Society, a front organization of Abhinav Bharat that aimed to recruit Indians abroad for the revolutionary nationalist cause. India House had been established as a residence for Indian students by Shyamji Krishnavarma, an Orientalist (and former student and assistant of the Oxford Sanskritist Monier-Williams) and a lawyer with an Arya Samaj background who was active in home rule and revolutionary nationalist networks.

Krishnavarma became close to Savarkar and the two at that time were the most important revolutionary nationalist figures among the Indian expatriate community in London. Krishnavarma was an Indian advocate of Herbert Spencer's evolutionary sociology, primarily through his nationalist monthly, the *Indian Sociologist*. Two Spencerian quotations were part of the masthead of *Indian Sociologist*, and illustrate how Spencerian evolutionary sociology and Spencer's ideas of absolute liberty combined with social engineering became political slogans for revolutionary nationalism: 'Resistance to aggression is not simply justifiable but imperative. Non resistance hurts both altruism and egoism' and 'Every man is free to do that which he wills, provided he infringes not the equal freedom of any other man' (Yajnik 1950). The intellectual influence of Spencerian evolutionism and functionalism was extremely important for the general ideological framework of early Hindu nationalism and how the latter conceived the nature of society, state and colonialism. Colonialism became figured as a competitive 'physiological' struggle between nations. Spencer was certainly directly important for Savarkar's social and political philosophy, particularly for the 'rationalist' and 'scientific' stress Savarkar placed on national evolution and the importance of extreme aggression and military strength for national survival. The first, but significantly only the first, of the above quotations was often referred to by Savarkar in his own writings, and several Spencerian ideas emerged directly as political statements in Savarkar's writings and speeches well into his Hindu Mahasabha period after 1937. It is perhaps intriguing that a statement from British sociological theory could have become a slogan for political action in colonized India. An additional curiosity is that Spencer himself used the tribal and clan wars enunciated in both the Rig Veda and the *Mahabharata* to elaborate his conceptions of aggression and sanguinity (Spencer 1879–1892 [1978]: 374–9).

Abhinav Bharat's political activities in London were wide ranging, and official concerns were frequently raised in Britain about the revolutionary activities of the residents of India House. Indian student activities were subject to intense monitoring by Scotland Yard and the India Office. Abhinav Bharat's strategy was twofold: firstly, propaganda in Britain, Europe and America for Indian independence and the inculcation of a revolutionary and insurrectionary spirit among Indians. Secondly, fundraising for pistols, rifles and bomb-making materials;

smuggling weapons and bombs into India, creating secret networks of bomb-making factories in India; fomenting open revolt at opportune moments (the impending war was thus seen as an important opportunity); undertaking assassin-ations; winning over members of the Indian armed forces to sedition and sabotage; and building alliances with revolutionary nationalist and anti-colonial movements in Ireland, Egypt and Russia (Keer 1988). The beliefs of Abhinav Bharat did not represent a coherent ideological framework of nationalism but comprised a melange of revolutionary anti-colonial and nationalist sentiments, French republicanism, *risorgimento*-type national unification, Spencerian evolutionary and functionalist sociology, and the writings of Kropotkin and Russian anarchist and 'nihilist' groups. Peter Heehs has also highlighted the influence of tracts such as Thomas Frost's *Secret Societies of the European Revolution* and, fascinatingly, the formative influence of the Protestant Irish woman Margaret Noble (Sister Nivedita) and the writings and activism of the Japanese art critic Kakuzo Okakura on Bengal's more important Anushilan Samiti (Heehs 1998: 69, see also Ray 1999).

In the years from 1907–9, following several assassinations and bombings and the discovery of bomb factories in India, colonial authorities had instigated severe repressive measures. These included the banning of public meetings and the mass prosecutions of supporters of numerous nationalist and revolutionary organizations and broadsheets for seditious activities or conspiring to wage war against the King. Among those arrested, deported and imprisoned in the Cellular Jail in the Andaman Islands off the southeastern coast of India, or in Mandalay Prison in Burma, were several formative influences on a characteristically Hindu, rather than specifically Indian nationalism (this included Lala Lajpat Rai). Savarkar's older brother Babarao, an important ideologue and activist in his own right in anti-colonial, and later Hindu Mahasabha and RSS activities, was also transported for life for political activities. There is validity in the assertion that some of the early founders of Hindu nationalism were imprisoned as a result of their revolutionary anti-colonial activities; this may also suggest reasons for their turn toward Hindu supremacism in the 1920s against what they saw as a betrayal by Congress of their efforts.

Savarkar's brother was arrested in connection with a bombing attempt on Lord Minto, the Viceroy of India. Similarly, in 1909 Madan Lal Dhingra, an engineering student at Imperial College and an associate of Savarkar, shot dead, in Kensington, Sir Curzon Wyllie (an aide to Secretary of State for India, Lord Morley) and was himself sentenced to death. Krishnavarma, who had endowed Oxford University with a Herbert Spencer lectureship and several Spencer studentships, was later to establish four 'Martyr Dhingra' scholarships in his memory. As Krishnavarma's political affiliations, articulated in *Indian Sociologist*, became widely known, the university rejected his patronage and he had to flee to Paris in fear of arrest and deportation.

The period of increased revolutionary violence after 1905 (the first Partition of Bengal), and especially 'the Dhingra affair' highlights an important factor about the relationship between violent and non-violent strategies during the early nationalist movement. Abhinav Bharat was explicitly hostile to passive resistance and the kinds of strategies that were to coalesce into non-violent, non-cooperative direct action in the 1920s. Indeed Savarkar's bitter hatred of Gandhi was to become definitive of his subsequent Hindu nationalism.

Gandhi met Savarkar first in 1906, a few times thereafter when he was in London, and then later in India. If Gandhi appeared casually trivializing of the violence of the 'anarchists', as he saw them, at India House, this belied the larger impact on Gandhi's philosophy of the strategy of violence advocated by Savarkar, Krishnavarma and the revolutionary societies in India. Gandhi dismissively labelled Savarkar and his group as 'the moderns' who had embraced fashionable nationalist ideas and political philosophies from the West. Some of Gandhi's formative writings about Indian liberation, especially *Hind Swaraj*, were articulated in opposition to Savarkar and the Dhingra episode (it was widely believed in London that Savarkar had persuaded Dhingra to kill Curzon-Wyllie). Gandhi's main objection to revolutionary nationalism was not simply related to his ethics of non-violence but focused on the innocence that is claimed through an identity of nationalism during a period of colonial victimhood, and the consequent will to power that is indissociable from a strategy of violence. Gandhi, alluding to figures like Savarkar and Dhingra, argued that 'goodness' did not arise automatically from the fact of Indianness or colonial victimhood; similarly, violence as a strategy of liberation would lead to murderers as the future leaders of India (Gandhi 1997: 93–6). It could also be argued that the formative background of Gandhian non-violence was precisely framed in opposition to, and in recognition of the consequences of the strategy of revolutionary violence that Gandhi encountered in London, one strand of which was to consolidate after the 1920s as an explicit ideology of Hindu nationalism backed by a Hindu chauvinist mass movement. One need not concur with Gandhi's distinctive Hindu devotionalism or his nationalist political ethics legitimized through Hinduism to also acknowledge Gandhi's fear about the consequences of a violent revolutionary nationalism inspired by Hindu nationalist precepts.

Savarkar was well known in London for his revolutionary activities and leadership of Abhinav Bharat. His translation of Mazzini's *Life* and his first major and influential nationalist rendering, *The Indian War of Independence, 1857* (Savarkar [1909] 1947) had been proscribed by the British (Shaw and Lloyd 1985: 19). He was also to write a rousing rendition of the Mahratta Confederacy as exemplary of *Hindu Padpadshahi* (Hindu Empire). His uncompromising public defence of Dhingra provoked considerable hostile attention from the British press, the government and moderate Indian nationalists in London. Following the assassination of the Collector of Nasik, A.M.T. Jackson, to avenge his brother, Babarao's transportation for life, Savarkar was accused during the murder trial of supplying from London the Browning pistol with which Jackson was shot. (Savarkar was widely believed to have been a key source for the clandestine supply of guns from Europe to Indian revolutionary societies.) In 1910, a warrant was issued for Savarkar's arrest. He fled to Paris – another important centre for revolutionary Indian nationalists, focused around the figure of Madam Cama – but after a short period returned to London where he was arrested on arrival at Victoria station.

Savarkar was charged with waging war against the King-Emperor of India, obtaining and smuggling arms that were used in both London and India, seditious speeches and conspiring against the sovereignty of the King over India. His transfer to, and short imprisonment in, Brixton prison was accompanied by unsuccessful attempts by Sinn Fein, Indian revolutionaries and British socialists to free him. Savarkar was then shipped to Bombay. During a short stop off near Marseilles, he escaped from a porthole of the ship and presented himself to the *gendarmerie*, but was allegedly illegally rearrested even though under the formal protection of French law. (An international defence committee led by Madam Cama and British socialists was established to protest the illegality of his arrest under international law, and his case was heard, but lost, at the International Tribunal at the Hague.) He underwent three trials in India and was finally transported for life and imprisoned in the Cellular Jail in the Andamans. This particular episode of Savarkar's arrest and his escape attempt ('the daring leap from the ship'), together with the impact on Indian revolutionaries of his personal defence during his trial have been central to the heroic and romantic aura that surrounded him as *swatantraveer* (hero of the independence struggle); he is still widely regarded as a national hero in India. Savarkar was transferred from the Andamans to Ratnagiri Jail and was released in early 1924, after 14 years imprisonment, on condition that he did not leave Ratnagiri (in south-western Maharashtra). When that condition was lifted in 1937, Savarkar became President of the Hindu Mahasabha.

While Savarkar was imprisoned in the Andamans and later in Ratnagiri Jail, he produced writings about Hindu identity that are now more influential than the remembrance of his revolutionary nationalist activities. The production of these writings while under confinement has also acquired a romantic symbolism: they were scribbled on the white walls of his cell with a nail and then committed to memory before the annual prison whitewashing; or they were written in minute writing on bare scraps of paper that were smuggled out by friends (Keer 1988). While Savarkar was well known for his martial history of the 1857 'Mutiny' and for his Marathi nationalist poetry, it was a pamphlet, later published as *Hindutva – Who is a Hindu?* (1923) that was to be of foundational importance in consolidating various strands of Hindu nationalism into a political force from the 1920s.

The Ideology of Hindutva: Territory, Blood, Culture and Religion

Savarkar's ideology of Hindutva was invented in the aftermath of the upheavals following the Partition of Bengal and during the political maelstrom of the 1920s. It is remarkable that *this* particular project was considered important by him during the massive anti-colonial agitations of the early 1920s. It is difficult to provide a precise explanation for Savarkar's ideological movement from violent Indian revolutionary nationalism to the concept of an exclusive Hindu nationalism in a space of about ten years, symbolically indicated by a movement from his celebratory history of the 1857 Indian 'Mutiny' of 1908 to his *Hindutva* published in 1923. His biographer describes his experiences of Muslim prisoners while in internment as important reasons for this change (Keer 1988). However, his published prison letters to his brother during 1918–20, while extolling Hinduism, do not mention Muslims (see Grover ed. 1993: 607–25).

Savarkar's key aim was to provide a comprehensive definition of what constituted 'Hindu identity'. To enable this he attempted to establish what he believed was Hindutva or 'Hinduness', the essence or beingness of a Hindu. Savarkar contrasted his Hindutva with Hinduism, dismissing the latter as a Western '-ism'. However, this was not a rejection of western Orientalist conceptions of an overarching Indian religious tradition, but a displacement of the idea that the Hindu was defined primarily through their personal or collective *religious* beliefs and affiliations. The sectarian doctrines within the main currents of Indian Hinduism were often in stark contradiction with each other in terms of belief, religious practice, caste or worldview. Savarkar was well aware of the rise of the nineteenth Sanatan Dharma movement to defend (brahmin as well as caste) orthodoxy and challenge the modernizing ideology and nominalizing beliefs of the Arya Samaj. 'Hinduism' could not be defined so as to include without contradiction the bitterly, often violently opposing worldviews of Sanatanists or Aryas (as the early Hindu Sabhas had discovered). The Arya Samaj had indeed asked to be classified outside of Hinduism in the colonial census prior to 1911. Indeed, the argument could be made that Savarkar's overarching Hindutva was invented precisely because of his awareness of Arya/Sanatanist conflict.

Hence, religion, religious belief and religious practice had to be displaced by Savarkar as foundational to the identity of a Hindu. This displacement of 'Hinduism' by Hindutva represented a substitutionist logic that strictly demoted religion or religious belief. This was both an essential step in his primarily non-religious, territorial and racial conception of Hindutva and its most contradictory, because at some stage, Muslims and Christians had to be excluded from the Hindu nation precisely because of Savarkar's view of the radically different nature of their *religion* that was seen as coextensive with their identities. Consequently, Savarkar also reintroduced an historically restrictive conception of what he claimed were the foundations of Hindu *dharma* (religion.) There is a sharp tension between the 'non-religious' and 'religious' components of Savarkar's Hindutva.

If Hindutva, rather than 'Hinduism' was to be definitive of Hindu identity, what was the content of Hindutva itself? Savarkar said

> The ideas and ideals, the systems and societies, the thoughts and sentiments which have centred around this name [Hindutva] are so varied and rich, so powerful and so subtle, so elusive and yet so vivid that the term Hindutva defies all attempts at analysis. Forty centuries, if not more, had been at work to mould it as it is. Prophets and poets, lawyers and law-givers, heroes and historians, have thought, lived, fought and died just to have it spelled thus. For indeed, is it not the resultant of countless actions – now conflicting, now commingling, now cooperating – of our whole race? Hindutva is not a word but a history. Not only the spiritual or religious history of our people, but a history in full. (Savarkar [1923] 1989: 3)

This strategic primordialization of Hindu identity was very important and, despite Savarkar's apparent rejection of Western conceptions, drew heavily upon eighteenth- and nineteenth-century European conceptions of Hinduism, its history and its followers. The intellectual conditions of thinkability for Savarkar's 'essence' of Hindu identity were the paradigms of German and British Orientalism. There was, in such views, an essential, ancient, unchanging – or at best processual or gradualist – characteristic to the historicity of India. Time, in this register, was 'pure seriality bereft of consequence' for the immutable essence of Hinduism. Fundamental to these views was that of an unchanging Hinduism, unless it was threatened by *events external to itself*, after which it settled back to an earlier steady state congruent with its primordial content. We should note the concurrence here between Savarkar's and colonial conceptions of Indian history. History comes essentially from outside India, through invasions, wars and conquests directed at Hindus, rather than through any essential historical capacity of Hinduism, which, in the absence of external threat, would continue in its heady, self-absorbed stillness. Savarkar reproduced exactly this historical vision in which there was little content to Indian history (or identity) unless it was rudely interrupted a war against 'invaders'. Similarly, it is instructive that a founding text devoted to explicating Hindu identity barely discusses the actual histories, substantive contents of or beliefs within Hinduisms. Conversely, by linking Hindutva with 'history', Savarkar can be seen to both temporalize and 'secularize' Hindu religions. Similarly, though this requires more detailed and nuanced discussion than can be provided here, Savarkar also rejected the religious metaphysics of non-linear temporality that exists in many Hindu traditions. There is an important epistemic tension here between an unchanging transcendental Hinduism (in the absence of war) and a Hinduism that only changes through temporal, secular processes of migration and war. Arguably, both these conceptions of Hinduism were necessary for the political agendas unleashed in the wake of Savarkarism.

For Savarkar, the Hindu had come into being long before Egyptian and Babylonian civilizations had developed, when 'the foremost band of the intrepid Aryans' crossed the river Indus and entered India. He was much more precise than this – the Aryans first settled in the Punjab and the Sind, although at the time he wrote this was speculative reasoning. Once in India, they spread out to 'the farthest of the seven rivers, the Sapta Sindhus' and had, he claimed, already developed a sense of nationality. Savarkar argued that the name 'Hindu' came from the Aryan name for the Sindhu (Indus river). Rather than designating a term of racial inferiority allegedly used later by Muslims against the inhabitants of India, the name 'Hindu', Savarkar argued, had existed even before the Aryans had arrived and they simply adopted it for themselves, as 'Sindhus'. (The name 'Hindu' was in this sense held by the land itself, prior to the arrival of those who became 'Hindus'.) The Aryans entered lands that were sparsely populated by scattered tribes, with whom, according to Savarkar, they had generally benevolent relations. The land found by the Aryans was, according to Savarkar, of 'a wild and unkempt nature'. However, the civilizing Aryan spirit prevailed and Aryans moved from the north-west across India, creating new colonies (Savarkar's term) in their wake and developing regional identities and empires. This 'colonization' of India concluded with the entry of Rama into Ceylon, 'the real birth day of our Hindu people'. (The colonization of a territory through a geographical movement from the north to the south was also a dominant epistemological component of nineteenth-century European Aryanism.) The human and physical geography known to the Rig Veda is limited to small regions of north-western India; however, Savarkar's view of Aryan colonization reaching across the entire geographical territory that was *colonized* by the British is suggestive.

The idea of fair-skinned Aryans entering India (Savarkar accepted this idea of fair-skinned Aryans (Savarkar 1989: 73)) and civilizing its aboriginal tribes had been a dominant strand of Aryanist thinking in both Britain and Germany since at least the mid-1850s. European Aryanist chronologies of humankind comprised a range of contending speculations, and these contentions were not solely related to where the putative primordial home of the Aryans rested – Europe, India or elsewhere in Asia. However, a common theme in virtually all strands of Aryanist thinking, including those opposed to racism, was the manifestation of an active, vitalist and dynamic masculine principle that was definitive of the Aryan presence. Aryans, whether conceived as pastoral nomadic tribal formations or as technologically advanced precursors to glorious civilizations, were a vigorous, motile, dynamic and active peoples. These spirited qualities of energy, power, mobility, innovation, animation, industriousness, enterprise, genius and daring raised the qualities of the indigenous tribes they encountered and mixed with. This active, vitalist principle was also a supplanting one: the cultures, beliefs and values of the aboriginal populations encountered were insignificant, subsidiary to a dominating Aryan vitalism. This thesis of Aryan (often Indian-Aryan) vigour owed to a number of earlier influences, including Friedrich Schlegel's *On the Language and Wisdom of the Indians* (1808) and his *Philosophy of History* (1828), but was stated in its clearest form by Joseph Arthur de Gobineau in his *Essay on the Inequality of Human Races* published in the mid-nineteenth century. An anti-semitic thrust was exacerbated by Houston Stewart Chamberlain (though this was itself reliant on Arthur Schopenhauer's formidable pro-Hindu but virulently anti-Jewish philosophy). However, even in the strictly anti-racialist writings of Gordon Childe in the early decades of the twentieth century, the active vitalism of the Aryan is fully defended (Childe 1926). A key aspect of many such views was a sharp differentiation between the desirable 'masculine' civilizations and the weak 'feminine' cultures of primordial antiquity. Another common theme in much Aryanist thinking was the idea that once the blood of the Aryans becomes polluted, the civilization that it originally animated commences a process of degeneration.

Savarkar reproduced many of these ideas, including a conception of degeneration during the 'complacent' non-violent Buddhist period and, hence, the necessity of Hindu reinvigoration. Savarkar, unlike Ranade, Tilak or Aurobindo before, and Golwalkar after him, stated his belief, at least in his *Hindutva*, of an Aryan migration into India, with its implication that the originators of Hindutva were not autochthonous to India. However, while Savarkar believed that it was 'the commingling of the blood' of the Aryans and the people they encountered that gave rise to Vedic-Hindu civilization, it is very clear indeed that it was the infusion of Aryan blood, ideas and culture that provided the basis of Hindu nationhood. Savarkar did not discuss any belief systems that may have existed prior to the Aryan migration into India, nor how they may have influenced or changed Aryan-Vedic culture. In his discussions of the *Ramayana* myth, Hanuman, as a representative of the non-Aryan groups, is essentially a subsidiary southern ally of Rama's Aryan mission of national conquest of the Anaryan Rakshas. Even if the Hindu owed its origins to Aryan and Anaryan consanguinity, the definitive influence on Hindu culture, and therefore the Hindu nation, was Aryan.

Savarkar's obsession with taxonomies, definitions and nominal reasoning – his *Hindutva* indeed begins with the subheading 'What's in a name?' – was demonstrated most clearly in his attempt to provide a primordial origin for the word 'Hindu'. However, no clear and definitive origin was proposed – the word indeterminately appeared from (or disappeared into) primordial time as a name pronounced by the 'Vedic fathers', though Savarkar did speculate that it may be been a Sanskritized version of an aboriginal name for the Indus river.

Most interestingly, though, Savarkar also said that the name 'Hindu' was a name that was *given by others*. For Savarkar, the self, in-itself, had no need for a name. 'But when it comes into contact or conflict with a non-self then alone it stands in need of a name if it wants to communicate with others or if others persist in communicating with it' (Savarkar [1923] 1989: 15). This doubling structure to the patronymic is instructive: the name is allegedly pronounced by the 'Vedic fathers', and is pronounced on one by others who, in Savarkar's chronography, are invariably invaders or enemies of Hindus. Indeed, the name 'Hindu' survived against the other names for one's selfhood or land (such as 'Bharat', *Bharatkhanda* or *Aryavarta*) because of 'first close contact, and then into a fierce conflict with the world at large', the 'world' having historically recognized the name 'Hindu' (Savarkar 1989: 16). It is interesting that Savarkar could only conceive 'contact' with others as inevitably resulting in 'conflict'. The primal patronymic, 'Hindu', is therefore both the product of Vedic-Aryan conquest and already foundationally antagonized in history through a conflict with others. The 'Hindu' was conferred his name precisely at the point at which his conflict with others began. This foundational bond between the patronymic and war travelled throughout Savarkar's political career.

Savarkar's Historical Imaginary

The Hindu nation, however, was to degenerate. The first degeneration occurred, according to Savarkar, with the expansion of Buddhism and its propagation of ideals of love, equality, righteousness, toleration – 'the opiates of Universalism and non-violence' (Savarkar 1989: 24). Savarkar considered Buddhist conceptions of love, non-violence, and universal and equal humanity as a *degeneration*. Savarkar claimed that Vedic Hindus were known the world over and India was the holy land for peoples from Cambodia to Mexico. This is a reproduction of an earlier idea of Hindus in sole possession of a divine world historic mission towards the whole of humanity. However, the subsequent Buddhist phase, towards the end of the Maurya period and Ashoka's rule, which is recognized as among the geographically largest in scale and reach of any empire and political-administrative structure in the Indian subcontinent until at least Akbar's reign, if not the modern period, was dismissed in its entirety by Savarkar precisely because of its adoption of non-killing and universal humanism as an ideology. The Ashoka empire is barely registered in *Hindutva*. Under Buddhism, he argued, Indians swapped their swords for a rosary, and disastrously failed to recognize 'the law of nature' – struggle and aggression. It was the formulas of Buddhist universal brotherhood that allowed the invasions of India by 'the Huns and Shakas'. In response, Buddhism declined and the Hindu spirit had to reassert itself.

Nobly did [Buddhist India] try to kill killing by getting killed – and at last found out that palm leaves at times are too fragile for steel! As long as the whole world was red in tooth and claw and the national and racial distinction so strong as to make men brutal, so long as India had a will to live at all a life whether spiritual or political according to the right of her soul, she must not lose the strength born of national and racial cohesion. So the leaders of thought and action grew sick of repeating the mumbos and jumbos of universal brotherhood . . . (Savarkar 1989: 23)

Interestingly enough, Savarkar claimed this was undertaken by severing any links between Hindus and Buddhists, any semblance of common worship with a religion that had 'strangled' India as a nation. Despite its Indian origin, effeminate Buddhism had to be sharply differentiated from the interests of the masculine Hindus whose virility it had sapped: '[Everything] that is common in us with our enemies weakens our power of opposing them' (Savarkar 1989: 24). He also claimed that Buddhists had both attempted to 're-invade' India for religious and political reasons and had created alliances with 'the Huns' to conquer India. Savarkar's abusive disposition to Buddhism is worth noting because Buddhism, after the 1960s, was considered by the Hindu nationalist movement as an integral part of Hindutva and a natural and indigenous offshoot of Vedic Hinduism, an assertion Savarkar also nominally made later in his tract by including Buddhism under his overarching Hindutva. However, Savarkar's main opposition to Buddhism was precisely related to its universalism and its emphasis on non-violence, which he found profoundly emasculating. Savarkar contrasted these ideals with the Spencerian 'natural law' of aggression and competition between nations and races, even while he attempted to enunciate Hinduism as a religion for all humanity.

In his attacks on Buddhism, Savarkar was clearly referring to the themes of non-violent non-cooperative direct action and universal humanism ('the mumbos and jumbos of universal brotherhood') that were by then dominating the national movement, though it should be noted that one could read *Hindutva* without any indication that a genuinely mass, nationwide and militant anti-colonial movement was taking place at exactly the time that this text of Savarkar's was being written. Indeed, the logic of *Hindutva* was to displace British colonialism and instead give prominence to an imagined historical frame of Hindu war and glory against Buddhist, Shaka, Hun and Muslim 'invaders' and usurpers. (In the 1930s, Savarkar vigorously rejected the view that the political strife in his time between Hindus and Muslims was the doing of the British.)

After the fall of Buddhism, Savarkar, using the mythological content of the *Bhavishya Purana*, claimed that King Shalivahana (in the 'Vikramaditya era') reasserted the identity of Hindu nationhood based on a demarcation between Aryans and *mlecchas* (foreigners). This declaration contained a line that Savarkar translated as 'the best country of the Aryans is known as Sindhusthan [the land of the Hindus] whereas the Mlecch [foreigner] country lies beyond the Indus.' This, together with the Puranic declarations that were translated by him as 'from the Himalayas to the

Seas, One Nation!', 'from the Indus to the seas, One Nation!', as well as the phrases 'Hindu Rashtra' ('Hindu Nation') or *'rashtram-rajyam'* ('nation-government') were central to Savarkar's claim that Hindus had since Vedic times conceived of themselves as a nation, and that the territorial nation extended from 'Kashmir to Ceylon', 'from Attock to Cuttack'. In a long footnote about the historical veracity of Shalivahan's decree in the *Bhavishya Purana*, Savarkar argued that it was 'not necessary ... to be very precise either about the date of this Decree or even the King by whom it was issued' (Savarkar 1989: 34); only the salient fact of the content of the decree, interpreted in nationalist terms, was important (ibid: 34–5).

The Puranas, as *itihas* ('thus indeed it was'), are conceived in many caste Hindu religions as the annals of tradition, semi-mythological, religious accounts of the exploits of Gods, Kings and dynasties and the mythological lineages of the latter. Savarkar's strong defence of the Puranas as containing a more reliable record of Hindu history than did 'Western' scholarship, represented an important epistemic and methodological claim, in the tradition of a careless euhemerism (that all myths refer to actual historical events). This method is extremely potent today, especially in the contemporary Hindutva identifications of Hindu cosmology with history. In this view, Puranic mythology is pure reflective history. The methodological importance of marshalling an expansive and open-ended intellectual process of historiographical evidence and interpretation from outside the nominally inferred content of those texts is evaded. Similarly, Savarkar's method, also common in contemporary Hindu nationalism, of allowing the bare fragments of Puranic and Vedic text to speak directly and in an unmediated way to a present consciousness that simply apprehends their content, forcefully elides the active interpretation of those texts from the gaze of a presentist, Hindu nationalism. Hence, Savarkar using Vedic xenologies and differentiations of selves and others, primarily related to language and ritual, interpreted these as the completed nationalism of the Aryans; similarly, the Puranic story of the mythological king Vikramaditya (there are several kings so named in the Hindu religious literature) and the battles of his grandson against others, was transformed into a nationalist war. The territorial boundary of 'Sindhusthan' was made equivalent to the physical geography of the subcontinent, and sharply demarcated against foreigners, Huns and Shakas among them. After these wars of the 'Vikramaditya era', Sindhusthan was left as an undisturbed independent nation of 'peace and plenty' for 'nearly a thousand years', according to Savarkar. In saying this, Savarkar ignored in its entirety a vast historical period of monumental change within pre-Ghaznavid and pre-Mughal India. However, this was congruent with his vision of Hindu history as merely the empty serial passage of time unless and until war with foreigners granted it substantive content.

Savarkar and 'the Medieval Period'

The next sections of *Hindutva*, ostensibly dealing with the raids into Punjab during 1001–1027 by Mahmud of the Ghaznavid dynasty, the rise of the Delhi Sultanate in northern India from the twelfth century, and then the Mughal period (from 1526) decisively supplement the varieties of archaic Vedic-Aryan imagining of Indian history developed by earlier Hindu nationalists and considered in previous chapters. Whereas the latter did present strong anti-Muslim sentiments, Savarkar parcelled the whole period from the eleventh century until the early decades of the nineteenth century through the logic of a single, monumental war between 'indigenous Hindus' and 'Muslim invaders' and 'tyrants'. In important respects, this was Savarkar's *novel* contribution to Hindu nationalist ideology. Savarkar indeed claimed that no one had surveyed 'the whole field of Hindu activities from AD 1300 to 1800', from Ceylon to Kashmir, from Bengal to Sind, from this perspective and as 'an integral whole' based on the defence of Hindutva against Muslims (Savarkar 1989: 45–6.) (In this context, it is noteworthy that wars between or among Hindus was glossed by Savarkar as simply the common history possessed by the Hindu race (Savarkar 1989: 95)). Savarkar hence argued that the invasion by Mahmud signalled the day that

> the conflict of life and death began. Nothing makes Self conscious of itself so much as a conflict with non-self. Nothing can weld peoples into a common nation and nations into a state as the pressure of a common foe. Hatred separates as well as unites. Never had Sindhusthan a better chance and a more powerful stimulus to be herself forged into an indivisible whole as on that dire day, when the great iconoclast crossed the Indus. (Savarkar 1989: 42–3)

It was similarly in this period that Hindus 'were welded into a nation to an extent unknown in our history' (Savarkar 1989: 44–5). Much contemporary theory could be mobilized here to elucidate precisely how Savarkar's politics of integral Hindu identity emerges through an antagonistic constitutive outside that must be its destabilising supplement; that an agonistic presence of Muslims is required before Hindu identity comes to fulfilment discloses the Muslim presence as internal to any imagination of Hindu identity of the kind conceived by Savarkar.

This 'struggle' was 'monstrously unequal' because, according to Savarkar, 'India' was pitted against 'nearly all of Asia', followed by 'nearly all of Europe': 'Day after day, decade after decade, century after century, the ghastly conflict continued and India kept up the fight morally and militarily.' Savarkar used, at length, mainly two examples to illustrate this battle for the defence of Hindutva and Hindu dharma: the early Hindi poem, *Prithviraja-raso* by Chandbardai, which recounted the decisive battles in the early 1190s between Mohammed of

Ghur (who had previously defeated the Ghaznavids) and the Gahadavala ruler Jayachandra in alliance with the Rajput ruler and Cauhan king Prithviraj III; and the battles of the Mahratta king Shivaji against Aurangzeb's general, Afzal Khan after the mid-1600s. Savarkar also marshalled Teg Bahadur's (who became the ninth guru of Sikhism) resistance to and death at the hands of Aurangzeb and Gobind Singh's (who became the tenth guru of Sikhism) battles against Muslim governors, as examples of war for the Hindu race and Hindu dharma. Shivaji was naturally the prominent figure, the Mahratta confederacy symbolizing the flourishing of *Hindupadpadshahi* ('Hindu empire').

These examples, many more of which, Savarkar argued, comprised Hindu history, demonstrated that the struggle to maintain *Hindutva*:

> was being fought out on the hundred fields of battle as well as on the floor of the chambers of diplomacy. This one word Hindutva, ran like a vital spinal chord through our whole body politic and made the Nayars of Malabar weep over the sufferings of the brahmins of Kashmir. Our bards bewailed the fall of Hindus, our seers roused the feelings of Hindus, our saints blessed the efforts of Hindus, our statesmen moulded the fate of Hindus, our mothers wept over the wounds and gloried over the triumph of Hindus. (Savarkar 1989: 46)

With the possible exception of the Mahratta confederacy, which was nevertheless to suffer defeats at the hands of both Rajput and Mughal armies, but which did nominally survive until the advent of the British, each of the examples that Savarkar used *could*, of course, be written from a converse and equally abstracted perspective, as each case he cited was historically a defeat or death of those he celebrated as exemplary of the strength and power of 'Hindus'. However, the salient point is the reconstructive project that Savarkar initiated and that focused its gaze directly on the medieval period as one that could be read reductively in solely religious terms. Later Hindutva writers were to considerably extend Savarkar's imaginary of Muslim invasion, tyranny and persecution to present a predominant vision of Hindu victimhood and suffering during the medieval period. Both these components were based on a periodization of Indian medieval history that had been given in James Mill's *A History of British India* (Mill and Thomas 1975, see Thapar 1996: 4–5). However, Savarkar's project was twofold, both to present a monologic history of the overwhelming innocence and oppression of a monolithic nation of Hindus, and of vitality and power of Hindutva as the grand motor force of history.

Savarkar's euhemeristic conception of 'Hindu history' can be conceived as an attempt to mobilize political identification through an affective dimension based on the cultivation of a 'nostalgic' remembrance of a fiction. It also reproduced an Orientalist vision of the history of Indian Islam that Islamists have also appropriated and wish to celebrate. One regressively logical consequence of Savarkar's *religious* vision of history is that it must necessarily raise an altogether different question for the Hindu religious sensibility: what was the *karma* of 'Hindus'? What must have Hindus done such that they deserved a millennium of uniquely monstrous oppression, violence and genocide? That Savarkar's inventions lead to a further compounding of illusions has been demonstrated by some contemporary Hindutva ideologues who are preoccupied with a 'karmic' understanding of why Hindus faced the 'greatest ever genocide' in history (Gautier 1996).

The Essentials of Hindutva

Those tendencies that view modernist secularism as responsible for the emergence of religious nationalism in India highlight the lack of religious belief of Savarkar and of some of the founders of the Rashtriya Swayamsevak Sangh as evidence of the influence of essentially non-religious, rationalist, secular ideas of nationalism in giving birth to the Hindutva movement. This argument ignores the incongruous influence of the Hindu Mahasabha in the national movement after the mid-1920s. Moreover, it cannot be reconciled with the *religious* definition that Savarkar proposed of the Hindu as one who considered India as their Holyland. This was, however, only one component of Savarkar's Hindu nationalism, because as important were criteria based on blood, race and ethnicity, territory and affect. It is worth examining his argument about the nature of Hindutva in detail.

Savarkar's conception of India's physical geography was a striking image of a landscape of boundaries, the 'natural frontier lines' that both enclose and exclude (the Himalayas, the Bay of Bengal, the Indian Ocean, the Arabian Sea, the Indus and Ganges rivers). According to Savarkar, the first requisite of Hindutva and Hindu identity was citizenship by paternal descent within this physically bounded territory of India. However, this was not, for him, a sufficient condition, since the term 'Hindu' signified more than geographical territory. He posited a second essential requirement for Hindutva, indeed the *most important* one, 'the bond of a common blood'; a 'Hindu' *must* be a descendant of Hindu parents (Savarkar [1923] 1989: 110). Hindus, argued Savarkar were not only a 'Nation' (*rashtra*) but a 'Race' (*jati*), possessing, in their veins, the common blood of 'the mighty race' descended from the Vedic fathers (Savarkar 1989: 85). The term Savarkar used for 'race' was *jati*. This was a novel rendering of a word that usually represents sub-caste typology, classification and endogamous descent, into one which also encapsulated a general view of inherited descent or lineage of larger 'racialized' populations.

Savarkar attacked the racially differentiated conception of caste promulgated by the British while vigorously defending a version of caste that seemed barely different. The very presence of caste, he argued, demonstrated the 'flow of blood *from* a Brahmin *to* a Chandal' (Savarkar 1989: 85, emphasis added). While he argued that both *anuloma* and *pratiloma* marriages (the latter being 'against the hair' or 'unnatural' unions of 'upper' caste women with 'lower' caste men) had taken place historically, and had mixed the 'blood' both within the castes, and that of the four castes with those outside them, his view about the desirable direction of the flow of 'blood' within the castes is unabashedly supremacist:

> the ancient Ganges of our blood has come down from the altitudes of the sublime Vedic heights to the plains of our modern history fertilising much, incorporating many a noble stream and purifying many a lost soul, increasing in volume and richness, defying the danger of being lost in bogs and sands and flows today refreshed and reinvigorated more than ever. *All that the caste system has done is to regulate its noble blood on lines believed – and on the whole rightly believed – by our saintly and patriotic law-givers and kings to contribute most to fertilise and enrich all that was barren and poor*, without famishing and debasing all that was flourishing and nobly endowed. (Savarkar 1989: 86, emphasis added)

Savarkar defended a caste system founded on a hierarchically conceived nobility and purity of 'upper' caste (in essence, Vedic-Aryan) 'blood', while also justifying a view of Hindus as racially undifferentiated and hence entitled to be called a discrete racial unit. Even as he admitted that race was a relative concept, because there was only one human race, Savarkar argued that 'no people in the world can more justly claim to get recognised as a racial unit than the Hindus and perhaps the Jews' (Savarkar 1989: 90). Instead of rejecting the paradigm of race, Savarkar articulated an overintegrated conception of Hindu race formation ostensibly against, but mirroring, the racial supremacism of British colonialism. His objection to colonial race thinking was simply that Hindus were a single race, rather than several races. He indeed repeatedly stated that the racial inheritance of Hindu blood was the most important characteristic of Hindutva (Savarkar 1989: 90, 110).

Moreover Savarkar linked 'blood' integrally with an affective and mysterious dimension of Hindutva:

> We are not only a Nation but a Jati, a born brotherhood. Nothing else counts, it is after all a question of heart. We *feel* that the same ancient blood that coursed through the veins of Ram and Krishna, Buddha and Mahavir, Nanak and Chaitanya, Basava and Madhva, of Rohidas and Tiruvelluvar courses throughout Hindudom from vein to vein, pulsates from heart to heart. We *feel* we are a JATI, a race bound together by the dearest ties of blood and therefore it must be so. (Savarkar 1989: 89–90)

This affective dimension, which recurs at one more point in Savarkar's definition of Hindutva (see below), is also potent in contemporary Hindu nationalism. Its rational inscrutability, and its dependence on the mystery of sentiment and a feeling of attachment is significant and allowed for an epistemic indeterminacy within Savarkar's Hindu nationalism. With some extremely important limitations, whoever *feel* they are Hindu are Hindu; conversely, sentiment and affect become strategic political and disciplinary measures of authentic Hindu identity. This affectivity may be seen analytically as strictly autonomous from his conception of race and blood, but Savarkar's intertwining of both blood and emotion was a paradigmatic example of the necessity of emotional mobilisation as central to any ontology of race formation and racial affiliation. One may lose one's caste, he argued, but never one's Hindutva since, the blood would always out and manifest itself as an affective structure in which Hindus would sense their racial affiliation to their ancestors, and hence to all Hindus.

While Jaffrelot has argued that Savarkar's was essentially a form of ethno-nationalism rather than biological racism (1996: 31–2), this seems to be a restrictive understanding of racism based, strictly speaking, on late nineteenth-century and early twentieth-century 'scientific' or biological racism. Savarkar did deploy a powerful conception of race that was in all respects both hereditarian and caste supremacist but did not rely on the formal resources of disciplinary biology or science. This was akin to anti-egalitarian theories of hierarchical nobility and racial eminence that flourished in Europe in the aftermath of the French Revolution and again during the mid-nineteenth century. These encapsulated a hierarchical paradigm based on both sensibility and heredity that allowed for the transmission and inheritance of the vital impulse, culture, civilization, religious mythology and sublime metaphysical knowledge.

Savarkar's ideology of Hindutva as comprising Vedic-Aryan blood and territorially bounded descent contained, for him, one major obstacle. As he put it:

> The story of [the conversions of Indian Muslims], forcible in millions of cases, is too recent to make them forget, even if they like to do so, that they inherit Hindu blood in their veins. But can we, who here are concerned with investigating into facts as they are and not as they should be, recognise these Mohammedans as Hindus? . . . it is clear that though their original Hindu blood is thus almost unaffected by an alien adulteration, yet they cannot be called Hindus . . . (Savarkar [1923] 1989: 91)

This was because of Savarkar's third criterion for membership of the Hindu nation, the 'common' culture and civilization that he claimed bound all Hindus, whatever their caste or non-caste belonging and regardless of their sectarian religious beliefs. In another deeply hegemonic and substitutionist act, Savarkar insisted that this 'common civilization' was Vedic-based or *sanskriti*, again eliding the brahminic and 'upper' caste purchase of Sanskritism and the early to late medieval *bhakti* movements against it, the latter simply incorporated by Savarkar into the former.

The 'civilizational' methodology Savarkar employed was neither innocent nor 'indigenous' but rested on the diffusion of an eighteenth-century paradigm, contemporaneous with the European Enlightenment period, and reinvigorated in the late nineteenth century in Frederich Max Muller's assertions that Hinduism was not strictly speaking a religion but an archaic if not entirely founding *civilization*. This conception of civilization fundamentally dovetails with upper-caste, Sanskritic and Vedic supremacism and deftly elides those populations in India, the tribals, 'untouchables' and shudras, that were seen in colonial paradigms to have contributed little, if anything, to the greatness of Hindu civilization. As important is the distinction made by Savarkar, and monotonously repeated in today's Hindutva movement, that Hindus share a common *civilization* whereas Christians and Muslims simply have a different *religion* or *ideology*. This civilizational method is patriarchal and, like the blood trope it rests on, depends on an immediacy of identification between the contemporary Hindu man and his ancestral patriarchs and forefathers. Significantly, woman is erased, and reappears as the symbolic territory or ground that allows such an identification to be possible through her unmediated transmission of the patriarchal substance. Conversely, the claim that Islam and Christianity are simply ideologies and hence inferior to Hindu civilization, is also a troubled one, since Savarkar's historical imaginary of India gave considerable power to such 'ideologies' as instrumental in allegedly causing a thousand-year war at the expense of Hindus.

The civilization that Savarkar considered to be shared by all Hindus contained the 'mind of man' and its triumph over matter. The civilization comprised the common thoughts, actions and achievements of Hindus, their history ('the story of the action of our race'), literature ('the story of the thought of our race') and arts, their shared laws, rites, customs, festivals and feasts, all of which were determined by the 'mother tongue', Sanskrit; hence, the common civilization was *sanskriti*. Consequently, Muslims and Christians, despite sharing their territory and 'race' with Hindus, were only in, but not of the Hindu nation

[S]ince their adoption of a new cult they had ceased to own Hindu civilization (Sanskriti) as a whole. They belong, or feel that they belong, to a cultural unit altogether different from the Hindu one (Savarkar 1989: 101)

Even this exclusion of Muslims and Christians was not conclusive for Savarkar since certain *syncretic* communities, such as the Muslim Bohras and Khojas of Gujarat, could also be said to possess as their own, '*sanskriti* culture'. It was in excluding such *syncretic* groups that Savarkar turned for the *first time*, and quite late in his definition of Hindutva, to explicitly religious criteria, namely the meaning of Hindu *dharma* (Hindu religion) itself. The latter, he argued, incorporated all the Vedic and non-Vedic traditions that had originated exclusively from the soil of India: Hinduism, Buddhism, Jainism, Sikhism, the *smriti* and *sruti* traditions, the Puranic traditions, the *bhakti* movements up to the Arya Samaj and the Sanatan

Dharma movements of the nineteenth century (Sikhs, according to Savarkar, were to be classed as Sikhs in religious terms, but as Hindus in both racial and cultural terms). Hence the Bohras had to be excluded from belonging to the Hindu Nation since they and other syncretic Muslim and Christian communities did not view India as their 'Holyland'.

If this religious component arose towards the end of his overweening and taxonomic cultivation of Hindutva, Savarkar gave it considerable importance. Muslims and Christians could not be incorporated into Hindutva:

> For though Hindusthan is to them a Fatherland as to any other Hindu, yet it is not to them a Holyland too. Their holyland is far off in Arabia or Palestine. Their mythology and Godmen, ideas and heroes are not the children of this soil. Consequently their names and their outlook smack of a foreign origin. Their love is divided. Nay, if some of them be really believing what they profess to do, then there can be no choice – they must, to a man, set their holyland above their Fatherland in their love and allegiance. That is but natural. We are not condemning nor are we lamenting. We are simply telling facts as they stand. We have tried to determine the essentials of Hindutva and in doing so we have discovered that the Bohras and such other Mohammedan or Christian communities possess all the essential qualifications of Hindutva but one and that is they do not look upon India as their Holyland. (Savarkar 1989: 113)

In virtually all respects, Muslims and Christians 'fulfilled' Savarkar prescriptive criteria for Hindutva. However, after characteristically outlining that *Hindudharma* (a nationalist Hindutva) was open enough to admit the believer, atheist and agnostic, *Hindudharma* being, he claimed, the religion committed to the greatest possible freedom of belief, it could still not admit Muslims and Christians *unless*

> Ye, who by race, by blood, by culture, by nationality, possess almost all the essentials of Hindutva and had been forcibly snatched out of our ancestral home by the hand of violence – *ye, have only to render whole-hearted love to our common Mother and recognise her not only as Fatherland (Pitribhu) but even as a Holyland (Punyabhu);* and ye would be most welcome to the Hindu fold. (Savarkar 1989: 115, emphasis added)

In these few words, Savarkar initiated a vicious and regressive logic that could *never* reach fulfilment to the satisfaction of the Hindu nationalist imaginary. The mere fact of their existence meant that Indian Muslims and Christians were inherently treacherous and had the overwhelming and perpetually unfinished burden of demonstrating their love and loyalty to the Hindu nation in a manner that could only reach completion, if at all, with the abandonment of their faiths and the adoption of an Hindutva ideology that considered them enemies. In Savarkar's disfigured staging, the rendering of 'love' meant allegiance to Hindutva.

Savarkar's concluding definition of the Hindu was one who 'looks upon' or 'considers' the land that extends from the Indus to the Seas as his Fatherland (*pitribhu*) and Motherland (*matribhu*), who inherits the blood of the race of Vedic-Aryan forefathers, who inherits and claims as his own *sanskriti* culture, and who considers 'Sindhusthan' as his 'Holyland' (*punyabhu*). This characterization of Hindutva was highly motile and each of its components could be differentially mobilised or given prominence The phrase 'looks upon' or 'considers' was his second mobilization of political affect and concealed quite contingent orientations. Parsees, for example, were not considered aversely by Savarkar, though ostensibly the 'holyland' of the Avestans and Zoroastrians was Persia; the Aryan race factor was presumably the predominant one in their affiliation with Hindus. Conversely, Savarkar excluded both the Theosophist and Congress freedom fighter Annie Besant and Margaret Noble (Sister Nivedita) from Hindutva on strictly *racial* grounds. Under Savarkar's schema, the distinctly south Asian *sufi*, Deobandi and Barelwi movements and the Ahmaddhiya sect, all of which arose on Indian soil, would considered inherently 'foreign', as would all manifestations of Islam or Christianity, syncretic or otherwise, despite their presence in India for at least a thousand years.

Savarkar was however keen to include Hindus living on the *far* bank of the Indus river, and hence outside his territorial geography of India; the term 'river', he argued, implied *both* its banks. Similarly, Hindus who had left India were still Hindus because of their 'race' and their 'recognition' of India as their Holyland:

> this definition of Hindutva is compatible with any conceivable expansion of our Hindu people. Let our colonists continue unabated their labours of founding a Greater India, a Mahabharat, to the best of their capacities and contribute all that is best in our civilization to the upbuilding of humanity . . . The only geographical limits to Hindutva are the limits of our earth! (Savarkar 1989: 119)

This expansionist theme, itself dependent on a colonial metaphor, was vigorously taken up by the networks of Rashtriya Swayamsevak Sangh activists who had migrated to countries outside India after the 1950s (on Hindu nationalism in the South Asian diaspora, see Mukta and Bhatt 2000).

Savarkar's Hindu Mahasabha

Despite Savarkar's (often qualified) view that minorities in an independent India would be free to exercise their religious beliefs, practise their religion and have the rights to political representation and citizenship (exemplified as 'one man one vote'), although commensurate with their numerical weight in the population and in proportion to the taxes they paid, Hindutva is definitively not a civic democratic nationalism sovereign over a physical territory but an ethnic and religious majoritarian nationalism sovereign over a racial and sacred conception of physical territory. Notwithstanding its apparent individualism, Hindutva is firmly based on a conception of majoritarian group rights counterposed against the potential rights of what are viewed as 'anti-national' minorities. This Hindutva nationalism was to become profoundly aggressive and militaristic after Savarkar's presidentship of the Hindu Mahasabha from 1937.

The Mahasabha had been revitalized from the period 1922–8 (see previous chapter). Several prominent figures, all of whom had been involved in Congress activities and some of whom had been involved in the Swaraj Party, primarily in factions that had argued for a strategy of 'responsive cooperation' with the British, became important personalities within, or presidents of, the Hindu Mahasabha. They included Lala Lajpat Rai, Madan Mohan Malaviya, N. C. Kelkar, Shyamaprasad Mookherjee, Bhai Parmanand, Swami Shraddhanand, Ashutosh Lahiry, Indra Prakash, L. B. Bhopatkar, N. C. Chatterjee (president after Savarkar and Mookherjee) and Balkrishna Shivram Moonje, the latter a key figure in the founding of the Rashtriya Swayamsevak Sangh.

From 1928, under Kelkar's presidency, the Mahasabha broke with Congress and commenced the process of establishing itself as a political party in direct competition with Congress in provincial council and legislature elections. The key reason for this change was the view of Kelkar and Moonje that Hindus should cooperate with the British in so far as the Muslims did, this fear increasingly turning to a paranoia during the 1930s and 1940s that the British were conspiring with Muslims to establish an 'Islamic theocracy' over India. This theme of Indian Muslims having 'extra-territorial designs' and planning an alliance with Muslim nations to take India over in connivance with the British was to become very prominent in the political language and militarization policies of Savarkar's Hindu Mahasabha.

During the exceedingly politically complex period from the early 1930s and into the Second World War, the 'Pakistan idea' of a self-governing Muslim territory or state had emerged among some Muslim intellectuals. The proposed territory included the Muslim majority areas in the north-west provinces (Punjab and Sind, the latter separated in the early 1930s from the Bombay Presidency) and eastern Bengal, as well as areas within Kashmir, the United Provinces and Hyderabad. Mohammed Ali Jinnah had re-emerged as the leader of the Muslim League and represented it during the Round Table Conferences in London where discussion focused on a constitutional agreement that would not lead to a formal partition but would provide measures of Muslim 'autonomy' and separate electoral representation. Following the 1935 Government of India Act, Congress entered the 1937 elections, intending through its boycott strategy, to destroy the Act, but paradoxically won so many provincial government seats that it could effectively govern India (though under the severe limitations of the Act). Jawaharlal Nehru hence took the decision for Congress ministers to participate in government. The Muslim League had won very few seats in this election and was dismissed as ineffectual by Congress. The League, however, was both to complain of Hindu domination (because of Congress' electoral successes and numerical domination of the provincial ministries) and to grow in popular strength in the Muslim majority provinces from this period.

In 1939, when Britain unilaterally entered India into the Second World War without consulting Congress, the Congress-led provincial governments resigned *en masse*. In contrast, the Muslim League declared support for Britain and celebrated the Congress withdrawal from government as a 'Day of Deliverance'. The next year, the Muslim League declared its demand for an independent Muslim state ('the Pakistan declaration') after the cessation of war. In the meantime, Gandhi launched his anti-war *satyagrahas* (1940) followed by his 'Quit India' movement (1942). This period not only witnessed the mass arrest and internment of Congress leaders and activists throughout India, but the use of British troops against Indian nationalists and revolutionaries (which included several bombing air raids) in a concerted attempt to destroy the national movement by force. India was placed under martial rule from 1943.

Churchill's ingenuous proposal of 1941 (the Cripps Proposal), which ostensibly promised both full dominion status for India after the War and the option for Muslims to opt out of its sovereignty was rejected outright by Gandhi and Nehru. During the war there was deadlock in the negotiations for Indian independence, not least because of the irreconcilable differences between Congress and the Muslim League. The post-war elections of 1945 resulted in the Muslim League winning electoral victories in all its reserved seats in Muslim majority areas. Consequently, the Labour government's Cabinet Mission proposals in 1946 for a federated, three-tier Indian state that included autonomous Muslim provinces were initially accepted by both Congress and the League. However, first Nehru and in retaliation Jinnah withdrew from this agreement. Jinnah declared a 'day of action' for the 'Muslim Nation' and India was plunged into virtual civil war. Finally, under the Indian Independence Act of 1947, rapidly seen through by Mountbatten, India was quickly partitioned and the union of India and the state of Pakistan were born at midnight on 15 August. During Partition, at least 10 million individuals were displaced.

Throughout this tumultuous period, the orientation of the Hindu Mahasabha was decisively preoccupied with Hindu communal interests under the overarching ideology of Hindutva and Hindu Sangathan. It launched numerous campaigns in this period. These included the formation of a 'Pan-Hindu movement' and calls for a 'Pan Hindu-Buddhist alliance' to 'crush' what it viewed as the Pan-Islamic, extra-territorial activities of Indian Muslims; campaigns in support of its self-styled 'Hindu Flag'; Hindu Sangathan (including attempts to form alliances with the

Arya Samaj and Sanatan Dharma organizations and the princely Hindu states for the purposes of political *sangathan*); *shuddhi* campaigns; 'Hindu militarization' campaigns; 'Census' campaigns to ensure all Hindus were enumerated in the decennial census and to ensure Muslims did not 'inflate' their numbers; the so-called 'Nizam Civil Resistance' movement in Hyderabad; and the celebration of 'Hindu Nation Day'.

At best, the Mahasabha's political reasons can be seen as anomalous and at worst direct attempts to disrupt the national movement's campaigns for independence and instead vigorously promote visceral hatred of Muslims. The ideology of the Hindu Mahasabha demonstrated very precisely Pradip Datta's argument that 'Hindu communalism', despite its extraordinarily narrow and limited political programmes, could not name itself as such (Datta 1999), and instead hegemonically claimed a greater identification with and ownership of the whole of Hinduism, the entire Hindu population and its interests, and Indian nationalism.

Congress' claim to represent all Indians was vigorously rejected by the Hindu Mahasabha, which monotonously declared that Congress did not represent Hindu interests, and demanded the Hindu Mahasabha be recognized by the British as the sole legitimate body representing the whole Hindu population of India, Hinduism, in its view also being the genuine national view (All-India Hindu Mahasabha 1942; and see the following in Savarkar 1941: Savarkar's 'Interview with the Viceroy, 15.10.1939', p. 152; 'Resolutions of the Hindu Mahasabha Working Committee 19.11.1939, drafted by V. D. Savarkar', pp. 164–5; and Savarkar's criticisms of the formation of a new 'Hindu League' in the United Provinces, 19.07.1940, p. 224). The Mahasabha was declared to be not a 'Hindu-Dharma-Sabha' but a 'Hindu-Rashtra-Sabha' committed to 'Hindusthan Hinduonka' ('Presidential Address, 19th Session of the Akhil Bharat Hindu Mahasabha, Ahmedabad, 1937' in Savarkar 1949: 9). Congress' strong non-violence and anti-war position, its obstructive and non-cooperative strategy with regard to British rule, its withdrawal of its provincial ministries and its acceptance of constitutional measures for Muslim political representation were similarly rejected by the Hindu Mahasabha (see Prakasha 1942, Bengal Provincial Hindu Mahasabha not dated). The Mahasabha demanded that the League of Nations intervene in deciding the legitimacy of the Communal Award (Hindu Mahasabha 1935). It also attacked the 'anti-Hindu' Cabinet Mission proposals in which, it claimed, 'Hindus had no political existence', were based on 'appeasement' of Muslims by both the Mission and Congress, and would lead to Pakistan (the Mission had rejected the Pakistan idea) and the destruction of the integrity of Hindusthan (All-India Hindu Mahasabha 1946). The Bengal Hindu Sabha, which had undertaken negotiations with the Muslim League after 1936, was denounced and expelled (Bengal Provincial Hindu Sabha 1938). Savarkar's opposition to Congress and other policies regarding measures for Muslim minority representation were informed by his Spencerian view that

Muslims were a minority and Hindus were a majority precisely because Hindus 'have proved themselves fit to the struggle for National existence' (Speech by Savarkar, 14 September 1940 in Savarkar 1941: 233).

The Mahasabha's reasons for supporting the war effort in the late 1930s and 1940s demonstrated Savarkar's and B. S. Moonje's overwhelming fascination and obsession with the aesthetics of aggressive Hindu militarism that were to continue well after Independence. These were enunciated as the following principles and policy of the Mahasabha under Savarkar:

- Hinduise all politics and Militarise Hindudom
- Enemy of our enemy is our best friend
- Enlightened national self-interest must be the guiding principle of foreign policy
- So long as the whole world is unjust, we must be unjust, so long as the whole world is aggressive, we must be aggressive
- Military strength behind your nation is the only criterion of greatness in the present day world
- He wins half the war who takes the offensive – who is aggressive
- Only those who are strong enough to protect not only themselves but also create fear in the minds of the enemies can talk of peace, non-aggression and non-violence. (Savarkar not dated)

Aside from the Mahasabha's determined policy of 'responsible co-operation' with colonial rule in order to secure 'Hindu interests' under Dominion status, it is unusual that the above should be chosen as its key principles during the war period. In particular, Savarkar's slogan to 'Hinduise all Politics and Militarise all of Hindudom!' was frequently reiterated in his speeches, his meetings with the Viceroy and in Mahasabha resolutions and policy documents. The emphasis on the aesthetics of violence within both the Mahasabha and the RSS was one of the key reasons for their exclusion from a Congress committed to non-violence.

For Savarkar and Moonje, the practical 'militarization' of all Hindus from high school age (from 14 years of age) and in adulthood (those aged 18 to 40) was foundational to their conception of Hindu Rashtra and of their belief that India was under the threat of Muslim conquest from Afghanistan and other Muslim-populated countries. The Mahasabha's policy of Hindu militarization pre-existed the start of war. In 1938, the Mahasabha submitted a demand to central and provincial Indian governments and legislatures that compulsory military training be provided to Hindus in all high schools and colleges (Savarkar 1941: 33–4). This included pressure on schools to immediately adopt rifle training and initiate rifle clubs throughout India (Savarkar 1941: 29, 33). The second component of this strategy was to use the conditions of war to encourage the widest possible military training of Hindus by urging all Hindus (not just those deemed by the British to be 'martial castes') to join the army, navy and air forces to become trained and skilled in methods and techniques of modern warfare. The ultimate aim of these intended activities was to raise a 'Hindu National Militia' in all Indian provinces that could defend Hindus from perceived external *and internal* threats ('Interview with the Viceroy, 15.10.39', p. 151; see the resolutions drafted by Savarkar regarding the war, p. 156; on the idea of a Sikh National Militia, see Savarkar's speech to the Khalsa Youngmen's Union Sikh Conference, 5 June 1940, p. 201–2; all references to Savarkar 1941) The Mahasabha consequently started several regional 'militarization boards' under Savarkar, his brother Babarao and its later president, N. C. Chatterjee. These were ineffectual policies but illustrated the gratuitous personal fascination with war, violence and militarism that was definitive of Savarkar's and Moonje's world view.

Savarkar's hatred of Gandhian non-violent direct action was based on his view, stated in 1941 and unchanged since the early 1900s, that 'resistance to aggression in all possible and practicable ways is not only justifiable but imperative. As Herbert Spencer puts it absolute non-resistance or absolute non-violence hurts both altruism and egoism' (Speech on 'direct action', 24 June 1941 in Savarkar 1941: 433). Non-violence was, for Savarkar, not simply wrong but *actively immoral*, whereas 'justifiable aggression' defined individual or collective morality. This active reworking of Spencer with the ethical premise of 'disinterested violence' from (his reading at least of) the *Bhagavad Gita* was not a rhetorical flourish but demonstrated what he believed to be a conscientious equivalence between 'morality' conceived in elementary terms of Hindu survival and existence, and violence conceived in terms of dynamic hostility and aggression towards non-Hindus. This violent vision was foundationally anti-democratic and was to be promoted by Savarkar well after Independence, in 1961, when he was approaching his eighties. Claiming that military strength was the only criterion of greatness, and that it was the religious duty of Hindus to die while killing the 'enemy', Savarkar stated that against 'useless, impotent and coward' rulers who represented democracy in India, he would prefer the 'great leader' Hitler (Speech in Poona, 15 January 1961, p. 13; speech of May 1952, p. 28, in Savarkar not dated).

While Savarkar's admiration for Fascism and Nazism remains to be examined, of salience here is the direction of this aggressive orientation towards Muslims during the 1930s and 1940s, including an open threat of civil war against Muslims (Speech, 25 April 1941 in Savarkar 1941: 368). The Hindu Mahasabha's stated aims during this period, enshrined in its constitution, were 'the maintenance, protection and promotion of the Hindu race, culture and civilization for the advancement and glory of Hindu Rashtra (Hindu Nation)'. Indian Muslims were, conversely, said to be cherishing extra-territorial ambitions and dominion over Hindus, with whom they had no allegiances and instead wished to humiliate and annihilate. Self-rule '*at the humiliation and cost of Hindutva* itself is for us Hindus as good as suicide' ('Presidential Address, 19th Session of Akhil Bharat Hindu

Mahasabha, Ahmedabad, 1937' in Savarkar 1949: 14, 19–24, emphasis added). Savarkar claimed that the Mahasabha's policy of 'one man one vote irrespective of caste, creed, race or religion' demonstrated its genuine nationalism, in comparison with the 'Pseudo-Nationalism' of Congress; nevertheless, 'we Hindus aim to be masters in our own house' (Savarkar 1949: 24). Hence, Savarkar's admonition to Muslims regarding self-rule: if you come, with you; if you don't without you; and if you oppose, in spite of you' (Savarkar 1949). This binary, communalizing logic was iterated most fully in Savarkar's claim, made in 1937, that:

> As it is, there are two antagonistic nations living side by side in India. Several infantile politicians commit the serious mistake in supposing that India is already welded into a harmonious nation . . . That is why they are impatient of communal tangles and attribute them to communal organizations. But the solid fact is that the so-called communal questions are a legacy handed down to us by centuries of a cultural, religious and national antagonism between the Hindus and the Moslems . . . Let us bravely face unpleasant facts as they are. India cannot assumed today to be a unitarian and homogeneous nation, but on the contrary there are two nations in the main: the Hindus and the Moslems, in India. (Savarkar 1949: 26).

Savarkar also said in 1941 that he had no intellectual disagreement with Jinnah's two-nation theory, since Hindus and Muslims did constitute two separate nations. However, Savarkar, while promulgating an inherently antagonistic 'two-nation' theory and explicitly dismissing the view that communalist ideology and political administration was a consequence of British rule, rejected an equivalence between Hindu and Muslim antagonism. The 'Hindu nation' had no problems with identifying with Indian nationality, because these were congruent once the latter was conceived as more than a territorial concept. It was solely Muslim 'fanatical hatred, enmity and distrust' of the Hindu Nation that was problematic. Muslims, he claimed, remained 'Muslims first, Muslims last, Indians never!'; hence what he called 'the non-Indian Moslem nation' was pitted against the legitimate 'Hindu Nation' ('Presidential Address, 20th Session of Akhil Bharat Hindu Mahasabha, Nagpur, 1938' in Savarkar 1949: 49, 53). Savarkar's view that Hindutva was 'genuine' rather than 'pseudo-nationalism' was to be supplemented by a later discourse that Hindutva alone guaranteed 'genuine secularism', though in both cases 'genuineness' meant an elementary Hindu majoritarianism.

Savarkar, Nazism and Fascism

A definitively altered and much stronger conception of Hindutva emerged in Savarkar's writings and speeches in the late 1930s and under the influence of far-right wing nationalist ideologies emanating from Eastern and Western Europe.

Savarkar's displacement of a civic-territorial conception of Indian nationality was directly and intimately related by him to his view of the nationality of both the Sudeten Germans and the German Jews. In 1938, Savarkar drew comparisons between Hindus and ethnic Germans, and between Indian Muslims and German Jews. These can be said to have critically transformed his conception of Hindutva. Whereas his *Hindutva* of 1923 barely mentioned Europe, and was more concerned to define Hindu identity through the parameters of 'history', land, civilization, race and religion, his Hindu nationalism of the 1930s is strikingly fixated on war, militarism and minorities and draws consistently and heavily upon European examples, especially Nazi Germany. It is also of considerable interest that whereas *Hindutva* did not refer directly to British colonialism, his 1930s writings and speeches consistently did so, but in a manner that attacked both British colonialism and Congress anti-colonialism while valorizing Nazi designs on Eastern Europe. These particular themes also travelled into Madhav Golwalkar's definition of Hindu nationality. They certainly inspired Savarkar's far more militant conception of Hindu Nation, unequivocal, active and militant opposition to Congress and his declaration of a 'Hindu Nationalist Front' (Savarkar 1949: 69–83).

For Savarkar, the Sudeten Germans had been made 'a mess of' by being artificially parcelled with Czechs, Slovaks, Poles and Hungarians under the 'patchwork' territorial nation of Czechoslovakia, despite having linguistic, cultural, racial and historical affinities with the German people and 'glorying' in being part of Germany. Conversely, the German Jews had been bound unnaturally as a territorial unit with the ethnic Germans of Germany (Savarkar 1949: 56–7). Savarkar rejected the view that nationalism based on racial and religious affiliations was 'a thing of the past'. These existing nationalities of Sudeten Germans and German Jews were, he claimed, artificial 'mappings' against which existed the real 'affinities' of race and religion that had 'roots deep down in human or even animal nature' (Savarkar 1949: 58). Savarkar's support for the extension of the Nazi *Anschluss* to Czechoslovakia was supplemented with his threat to the Muslim League. He claimed in 1938 that like the Sudeten Germans, they had threatened to call upon their co-religionists outside India for assistance.

> If they grow stronger they can play the part of Sudeten Germans alright. But if we Hindus in India grow stronger in time these Muslim friends of the league type will have to play the part of German-Jews instead. We Hindus have taught the Shakas and the Huns already to play that part pretty well [sic]. So it is no use bandying words till the test comes. The taste of the pudding is in its eating. (Savarkar 1949: 65)

These comments were not stray infelicities. In the same year (1938) during a Hindu Mahasabha mass meeting in Poona, Savarkar demonstrated uncritical admiration for both Nazism and fascism, instead reserving his venom for Nehru's and Congress' denunciations of Nazism. Savarkar said that 'Germany had every right to resort to Nazism, and Italy to Fascism', the only 'sound principle' being that no form of government or political ideology was 'absolutely good or bad' for all people alike in all circumstances.

> Hitler knows better than Pandit Nehru does what suits Germany best. The very fact that Germany or Italy has so wonderfully recovered and grown as powerful as never before at the touch of the Nazi or Fascist magical wand is enough to prove that those political 'isms' were the most congenial tonics their health demanded . . . Pandit Nehru went out of his way when he took sides in the name of all Indians against Germany and Italy. Pandit Nehru might claim to express the Congress section in India at the most. But is should be made clear to the German, Italian or Japanese public that crores of Hindu Sangathanists in India who neither Pandit Nehru nor Congress represents cherish no ill-will towards Germany or Italy or Japan or any other country in the world simply because they had chosen [sic] a form of Government or constitutional policy which they thought suited best and contributed most to their national solidarity and strength ('Speech on India's Foreign Policy', Poona, 3 November 1938 in Savarkar 1941: 51–2)

The Hindu Sangathan movement, he said, held that 'Germany was perfectly justified in uniting the Austrian and Sudeten Germans under the German Flag'. It was the Czechs, he stated, who were acting against democracy by holding the Germans 'under foreign sway and against their will'.

> The fact is that when Germany was weak, they [the British] partitioned [her] piecemeal. Now that Germany is strong, why should she not *strike* to unite all Germans and consolidate them into a pan-German State and realise the political dream which generations of German people cherished. ('Speech', Poona, 3 November 1938, Savarkar 1941: 53, emphasis added)

Against the anti-Nazism of Congress, Savarkar urged a policy of 'neutrality' that barely disguised his sympathies. These continued well into the 1960s (after the full horrors of the Holocaust were known) when Savarkar favourably compared Hitlerism with the 'cowardly' democracy of Nehru (Speech, Poona, 15 January 1961, in Savarkar not dated: 13). In this context, it is also worth noting that the Hindu Mahasabha's proposal in 1935 for a 'common Hindu Flag', which was investigated by a committee that included Savarkar's brother, resulted in a 'Hindu National Flag' that in 1938 did not include the swastika, but by 1941 did (Hindu Mahasabha 1935, Savarkar 1930, 'The Congressite Charkha Flag and the Pan-Hindu Flag', 22 September 1941 in Savarkar 1941: 469).

In an excellent and fascinating recent assessment, Marzia Casolari (2000) has drawn attention to Savarkar's and the Hindu Mahasabha's approval of Nazism. In 1939, Savarkar made further comparisons between Indian Muslims and German

Jews, both the latter seen as an illegitimate presence in an organic nation and harbouring extra-national loyalties. In 1939, the Hindu Mahasabha also celebrated Germany's 'solemn revival of Aryan culture, the glorification of the Swastika, her patronage of Vedic learning, and the ardent championship of the tradition of Indo-Germanic civilization' (Casolari 2000: 224). Casolari has also demonstrated the active links between Nazi representatives in India and Savarkar and the Mahasabha. Similarly, as Christophe Jaffrelot has highlighted (1996: 51–2), the Nazi newspaper *Volkischer Beobachter* reported on Savarkar's speeches in exchange for the promotion of Germany's anti-semitic policies in Marathi periodicals. Apparently, this exchange resulted in Savarkar receiving a copy of *Mein Kampf* from Germany (Casolari 2000: 224). In 1941, Savarkar also called for a 'Pan-Hindu-Buddhistic alliance' with Japan 'to crush' what he, in a characteristically paranoid vein, believed was a 'Pan-Islamic alliance' that was to invade India (Speech on the 'Front of a Hindu-Buddhistic alliance from Jammu to Kashmir', 25 April 1941, in Savarkar 1941: 369–70). Savarkar's support for Jewish settlement in Palestine was also congruent with his view of Germany's Jews, since Palestine was their 'Fatherland and Holyland', and a militarily strong Israel was conceived by him as an anti-Islamic fortification against the Arab world ('A statement on the Jewish International Question', not dated, in Savarkar 1941: 70). In 1943 the Hindu Mahasabha under the presidentship of N. C. Chatterjee declared itself opposed to fascism and Nazism (All-India Hindu Mahasabha 1943). However, it is not clear that Savarkar repudiated Nazism or fascism in the aftermath of the full knowledge of the Holocaust.

The dismal associations between Savarkar's Hindu Mahasabha and German Nazism and Italian fascism were not unique, but were pursued by other Indian nationalist leaders and movements. They are evident, for example, in Subhas Chandra Bose's visits to Fascist Italy and Nazi Germany, his call for India to become 'fascist', and in the Indian National Liberation Army he mobilized in Burma under Japanese patronage (on Subhas Chandra Bose, see Gordon 1990, Bose 1997a, Bose 1997b, Bose 1998); in the activities and ideology of the Rashtriya Swayamsevak Sangh from the 1930s (see Chapter 5); and in various other minor currents of racial supremacist Aryanism in India that heralded Nazism as the coming to fruition of a primordial Aryan-Vedic civilization that had been born on Indian soil (Goodrick Clarke 1998).

After Independence

While Savarkar attempted to resign as president of the Mahasabha several times after 1940, he was repeatedly returned as president, with (variously) L. B. Bhopatkar, Shyamaprasad Mookherjee and then N. C. Chatterjee occupying this role during Savarkar's illnesses in the early 1940s and after his final resignation in 1944 (All-India Hindu Mahasabha 1944). However, both Savarkar's influence and his ideology remained dominant in the Hindu Mahasabha until well into the late-1950s. In the period leading up to, as well as after Independence, the Mahasabha directly contested elections on a platform of uniform opposition to Congress (Prakasha 1942). It performed very poorly in all elections. Mahasabha activists were instrumental in promoting Congress as representing a 'Gandhi-Muslim conspiracy' against Hindus, aimed at 'vivisecting' India, though both Gandhi and Congress opposed Partition (Hindu Nationalist 1941, Anonymous not dated, Mehta 1941, Bharti 1992). While continuing its Sangathanist and 'Hindu Rashtra' policy it considered itself as the only representative of Hindus and opposed the independent formation of other Hindu nationalist political organizations.

Under president N. C. Chatterjee, the ideology of Aryan culture, Hindu Rashtra, Hindu militarization, 'economic socialism' and a visceral anti-Muslim orientation continued well after Independence in 1947 and into the 1950s (Akhil Bharat (All-India) Hindu Mahasabha 1948a, 1949b, 1950a, 1951). It also claimed to have '[saved] Western Bengal and Eastern Punjab' from alleged Pakistani encroachments during Partition. The Mahasabha narrative of internal and external Muslim threats to 'Hindu Rashtra' and the view of Indian Muslims as 'fifth columnists' remained unchanged (All India Hindu Mahasabha 1947). In November 1948 (the year following Independence) the Mahasabha outlined the placed of Indian Muslims in 'Hindu Rashtra'. Ashutosh Lahiry, the Mahasabha's general secretary, declared that Indian Muslims had to demonstrate acceptance of India as their homeland, and adopt its 'past history', 'language', 'traditions' and 'national dress'. All 'non-Hindus', he said ominously, were 'non-national'.

> [The Hindu Mahasabha] believe all the Muslims now living in India are not true nationals of India. Those who have not been able to approximate themselves to the standard of nationalism as conceived by the Hindu Mahasabha . . . shall remain in India as aliens . . . The Muslims who still owe allegiance to Pakistan will be treated as aliens. (All India Hindu Mahasabha 1948a: 7–8)

The Mahasabha, in alliance with the Ram Rajya Parishad vigorously opposed Nehru's Hindu Code and Hindu Marriage Bills which sought to replace Hindu personal law with a civil code, make polygamy illegal and created other provisions for the regulation of marriage, divorce, caste, inheritance and family relations and obligations (Jaffrelot 1996: 102–3). Muslim personal law was excluded from these provisions. However, it is necessary to recognize that, while couched in a language that attacked Nehru's alleged 'favouritism' (or Nehru's 'fear') of Muslim constituencies, the Mahasabha opposed in principle *any* interference in Hindu personal law, the latter seen as a threat to Hinduism – 'the crushing of the Hindu social system' and its traditional regulation of caste, gender and family relations (All

India Hindu Mahasabha 1949a; see also All India Varnashrama Swarajya Sangh not dated). In 1950, the Mahasabha also continued to campaign against what it saw as the harassment of Maharashtra brahmins following Gandhi's murder (All India Hindu Mahasabha 1950b). The Mahasabha political orientation throughout the 1950s was similarly determined by opposition to Nehruvianism and what it saw as the 'evil' of secularism, the necessity of inculcating an 'aggressive Hinduism' against 'internal enemies', the militarization of Hindu youth, *shuddhi*, and the consolidation of all Hindu nationalist forces against Congress policies (All India Hindu Mahasabha 1952, 1953, not dated, 1959). One of its earlier leaders, Shyamaprasad Mookherjee was to call for a new political party in 1950. From September 1949, resolutions were made by the Mahasabha's working committee and during its annual sessions which concerned the alleged destruction during the medieval period by Muslims of Hindu temples in Uttar Pradesh (All India Hindu Mahasabha 1949a, 1949c).

Conclusion

Savarkar's *Hindutva* was to have considerable and definitive influence on the burgeoning Hindu nationalist movements of the mid-1920s. Hence, contemporary Hindu nationalism is aptly referred to as 'the Hindutva movement' working in the service of what is conceived to be the 'Hindu nation'. It is however striking, especially given the momentous discussions of Indian constitutionality occurring contemporaneously, that the content of 'Hindu nation' in Savarkarite and Mahasabha ideology was narrowly and obsessively preoccupied with the themes of race, culture and militarism. It should not be surprising that Gandhi's murder on 30 January 1948 was undertaken by Nathuram Godse, a major activist in the Hindu Mahasabha and formerly a member of the RSS who also came from Maharashtra's Chitpavan brahmin community. Godse was a close colleague and friend of Savarkar, and Savarkar, although acquitted, was also to stand trial for allegedly conspiring in Gandhi's murder.

The Hindu violence that Savarkar, the Hindu Mahasabha and the Rashtriya Swayamsevak Sangh had sought to cultivate did not arise in the way they had foreseen. Instead Hindu wrath at the murder of Gandhi was turned against the Mahasabha and the RSS whose representatives attacked and offices destroyed in the nationwide violence that followed the murder. The Mahasabha's Working Committee (New Delhi, 14–15 February 1948) said 'it was a matter of shame and humiliation that the alleged assassin was connected with the Hindu Mahasabha' and 'unequivocally condemned this foul act', but went on to deplore the attacks on Mahasabha workers and property and the 'virulent campaign' against the Maharashtra brahmins, the latter popularly viewed as collectively responsible for Gandhi's murder (Akhil Bharat Hindu Mahasabha 1948b, 1950b).

Sumit Sarkar has said that both Godse and Gandhi were devotees of Ram and pious Hindus, and both could be called nationalists (Ludden 1996: 271). Sarkar is alluding to the dominant Hindu religious strands (such as Gandhianism) within what was ostensibly intended to be a secular, nationalist movement. It is at this point that the Hindu nationalism of Tilak, Bankimchandra, Lajpat Rai, Munshi Ram among others described in previous chapters, and believed by them to be congruent with their activities in the national movement, can be distinguished from the neo-Hinduism of Gandhi. Gandhi was not only a devotee of Ram and Krishna, but referred to a future independent India as 'Ram Rajya' (the rule or government of Rama); he was also a consistent and vocal supporter of cow protection. However, the distinction between Gandhi's Hinduism and the Hindu nationalists within and outside the national movement has to be seen as definitive. With one crucial exception, every major campaign that Gandhi launched from his period in South Africa through the non-cooperation movement, the salt tax and anti-Rowlatt *satyagraha*s, the anti-landlordism campaigns, and the anti-war and Quit India campaigns were directed to secular matters and not to any distinctly or exclusively Hindu concerns. This was in contrast to many of the campaigns and activities of Tilak, Lajpat Rai, Munshi Ram, Malaviya, Savarkar and the Hindu Mahasabha. The one exception in which Gandhi's Hinduism was definitively brought to bear related to caste. Gandhi was a strong believer in *varnashramadharma*. His attempted 'upliftment' of untouchables, however humanistically conceived, was undertaken by interpellating them as descendants of Hari, itself an act of 'upper'-caste Hindu hegemony. His attempted 'fast unto death' at the prospect of separate electoral representation for the scheduled castes was exactly related to his view that 'untouchables' would be separated from 'a Hindu fold', even though the latter had in actuality long rejected them. Scheduled caste and non-brahmin movements were perceived by Hindu nationalists in Maharashtra as a major political threat during the 1920s. It was in response to the upsurge of such movements that some Maharashtrian Hindu nationalists launched the Rashtriya Swayamsevak Sangh.

–5–

The Rashtriya Swayamsevak Sangh's
Ordered Society

The idea was spread that for the first time the people were going to live a National Life, the nation in the land naturally composed of all those who happened to reside therein and that all these people were to unite on a common 'National' platform and win back 'freedom' by 'constitutional means.' Wrong notions of democracy strengthened the view and we began to class ourselves with our old invaders and foes [the Muslims] under the outlandish name 'Indian' . . . We have allowed ourselves to be duped into believing our foes to be our friends, and with our own hands are undermining true Nationality . . . In our self-deception, we go on seceding more and more, in hopes of 'Nationalising' the foreigners and succeed merely in increasing their all-devouring appetite. (Golwalkar 1944: 14)

Introduction: the RSS and its Parivar

The Rashtriya Swayamsevak Sangh (RSS, the 'National Volunteer Corps' or the 'National Volunteers' Self-Service Society') became the most important and politically successful Hindu nationalist organization following the independence of India. Even leaving aside its main offshoot organizations, the RSS is one of the largest organizations in northern Indian civil society. Although the RSS's numerical membership is difficult to discern precisely, because it claims not to keep membership records, it has about 20,000 regular branches (*shakhas*) and has a regular membership of several million *swayamsevaks* in India (estimates range from 2.5 to six million followers). The RSS claims to be the largest voluntary organization in the world, although its detractors might legitimately view it as the largest voluntary, private paramilitary body existing in any nation, with the consequences this implies for a secular state and civil society. The RSS considers itself the basic or foundational organization of the 'family' of affiliated organizations and movements (*sangh parivar*) that it either directly initiated or assisted in forming with the political labour of its own *pracharaks* (on the RSS and its *parivar* see Curran 1951, Goyal 1979, Andersen and Damle 1987, Basu et al 1993, Jayaprasad 1995, Jaffrelot 1996; on RSS's or sympathizers' renditions of its history, see Malkani 1980, Deshpande and Ramaswamy 1981, Rashtriya Swayamsevak Sangh 1985, Seshadri 1988, Madhok 1996, Chitkara 1997, Pattanaik 1998, Hingle

1999; recent information given below on RSS projects is from the *Seva Disha* 1995 and 1997 reports published by its all-India welfare department (*seva vibhag*)).

The RSS's first affiliate, the Rashtra Sevika Samiti (Organization of Indian Women) was formed in 1936 and claims about 3,500 branches in India. In 1948, the RSS formed its student wing, the Akhil Bharatiya Vidyarthi Parishad (ABVP – the All-India Students Council) to combat 'leftist' or 'polluting' influences in education. By 1996, it had some 800,000 members. In 1952, the Vanavasi Kalyan Ashram was formed with RSS support and by 1980 had become a nationwide organization working among 'tribal' communities in order 'to integrate them into the Hindu mainstream', launch 'reconversion' campaigns and combat the influence of 'foreign' Christian missions. The name of the organization is significant: *vanavasi* means forest dweller and substitutes the accepted term *adivasi*, meaning the original (aboriginal) inhabitants of India; *ashram* denotes a Hindu religious instruction centre. The organization reported over 7,600 projects in 1997 which, significantly, had 'crossed the 25,000 mark' by the end of 1998. The Vanabhandu Parishad ('Friends of Tribal People') was established in Calcutta in 1989 and organizes educational visits of urban Hindus to *adivasi* areas, the aim being to 'integrate' *adivasis* into 'mainstream' Hindu society and prevent them affiliating to 'anti-social, anti-national forces or separatist tendencies'. The RSS's labour affiliate, the Bharatiya Mazdoor Sangh, formed in 1955 to defeat communist influences in industry, is the largest unofficial body of organized workers in India; this was followed by its farmers affiliate, the Bharatiya Kisan Sabha, formed in 1979. The Bharat Vikas Parishad was established in 1963 to work among poor communities and in health-related areas. The Bharatiya Sikshan Mandal, created in 1969, works within education and among teachers to promote the RSS's aim of introducing 'eternal Bharatiya values' throughout the educational system, rewriting school and university textbooks to provide a 'history of the Indian Freedom Struggle' against 'foreign invaders [over] the last 2,500 years', and making Sanskrit teaching compulsory. The Rashtravadi Sikshak Parishad (Nationalist Teachers Council), established in 1993, works against 'communist bias' among teachers. In 1976, the RSS established the extremely important Vidya Bharati, its educational wing providing education to toddlers and running primary and secondary schools in line with RSS Hindutva ideology and in opposition to Christian-run schools. Its *vidyalayas* emphasize Hindu education and sports and it claims 13,500 educational projects in India. The RSS has a nationwide welfare network, organized under its Seva Bharati, formed in 1989, and which claimed almost 23,000 *sevakarya* (welfare and charity) projects in India in 1997. The RSS also has an international wing, Sewa International, which organizes welfare work outside India and raises funds for *parivar* projects in India. The Deendayal Research Institute, formed in 1991, and its journal *Manthan*, act as a focus for the intellectual dissemination of Hindutva ideology. There are a number of other organizations belonging to the

RSS *parivar*, including its Sikh offshoot, the Rashtriya Sikh Sangat, as well as forums for youth, lawyers, 'self-reliance', and 'social integration' (*samarajik samarashtha*). The most successful organizations created by the RSS are the Vishwa Hindu Parishad, formed in 1964 and the Bharatiya Janata Party created in 1980 out of the RSS remnants of the previous Bharatiya Jana Sangh political party.

The Origins of the RSS

The RSS arose in Nagpur (then incorporated in the Central Provinces and now part of Maharashtra state) in the period from 1924 to 1926 from within the town's brahmin community. The RSS's version of its early history and that of one of its founders, Keshav Baliram Hedgewar (1889–1940), is characterized by a dense hagiographical orientation in which Hedgewar, together with Madhav Sadashiv Golwalkar its second supreme leader (*sarsanghchalak*) after Hedgewar's death in 1940, are virtually 'sanctified' and described only in effulgent and effusive tones (Malkani 1980, Deshpande and Ramaswamy 1981, Seshadri 1988). Hedgewar, in particular, is represented as a major activist in the national movement and a vigorous and indefatigable fighter for India's freedom from colonial rule, indeed at the 'forefront of the freedom movement' (Seshadri 1991: 7). Hedgewar was an activist in Congress' 1920 Nagpur Session and was allegedly associated with the revolutionary Anushilan Samiti centred in Bengal. He was imprisoned for sedition in 1921 for one year and again for nine months during the Jungle Satyagraha in 1930, although his involvement in the latter campaign cannot be detached from his desire to propagate and recruit for the RSS. The founding mythology, ceaselessly iterated today, of Hedgewar and the early RSS as an important anti-colonial force requires substantial modification, if not complete rejection (Goyal 1979). The RSS's phantasmatic conception of its origins, inspiration and history requires careful disentanglement from its actual history. For example, whereas Congress and allied movements and activists were variously violently repressed, banned or imprisoned in huge numbers, the RSS was not considered an adversary by the British. On the contrary, it gave loyal consent to the British to be part of the Civic Guard (Chandra 1987: 118). The RSS was not proscribed by the British, but was banned three times by Indian governments. Both Hedgewar and Golwalkar (its second leader) actively opposed joining the anti-colonial movement in favour of 'character-building' work in the service of the Hindu Nation (Deshpande and Ramaswamy 1981: 119). Similarly, the RSS, as a matter of explicit organizational policy, refused to join the non-cooperation movement and anti-colonial *satyagrahas* in the 1920s and 1940s, including the anti-Rowlatt agitations, the Civil Disobedience and Quit India movements, and the Naval mutiny in Bombay. This is at considerable variance from the RSS's depiction of Hedgewar who, while primarily associated with Nagpur Congress, was to definitively abandon the anti-colonial movement from the early 1920s and dedicate himself to his different vision of what India required.

There are other reasons for caution about RSS presentations of its history. The RSS's organizational structures promote an authoritarian institutional secrecy that conceals the internal workings of the organization and conflict and dissension within it, particularly conflict among its leaders, and between the (regional) cadre and leadership. This is primarily to project a symbolic unity of the 'Hindu nation' at the core of which the RSS believes that it alone can be. The RSS's literature is also deeply imbued with a dense, carefully cultivated ideological language that inscribes its own political imaginary onto the realities it is ostensibly claiming to describe. One other factor relates to the RSS's description of itself as a 'non-political' organization, an appellation that has permeated relatively objective studies of the RSS. Its allegedly 'non-political' stance is related to its early reasons for not officially participating in the anti-colonial movement and the conditions related to the lifting of the ban on the organization in the immediate post-independence period. This claim was also related to its alleged rejection of the 'party politics' or 'power politics' between Congress and the opposition parties in the 1940s and 1950s. While (although with significant qualifications) it remained outside formal party politics, and indeed demonstrated a disastrous understanding of the political situation in the period just before independence, the RSS has not refrained from active political interventions from its inception.

The RSS's view of its origins is usually articulated as the result of an original, founding vision of Keshav Baliram Hedgewar, a 'Deshashta' brahmin from Nagpur who had trained to become a doctor. This is often described in the language of a religious vision that led to the invention of a novel organizational method by Hedgewar after the early 1920s. However, its actual organizational development in the 1920s and 1930s is located in several different political events both in Maharashtra and nationally, as well as the formative impact of distinctly European influences.

The politically tense period of the 1920s saw the rise of the Non-Brahman movement, influenced by the earlier ideology of Jotiba Phule. The peaking of the Non-Brahman movement during the early 1920s and the influence of non-brahmin candidates in the government of Bombay was considered a major threat to Maharashtrian brahmin power within the legislatures, and was indeed one of the key reasons for the cooperation strategy pursued by regional Hindu Mahasabha leaders and candidates in the region in the early 1920s. Mahasabha leaders from Poona, such as N. C. Kelkar, argued against non-cooperation precisely because otherwise they could not safeguard the interests of brahmins in the public services that were being challenged by Non-Brahman ministers (Gordon 1975: 183). 'Lower' caste and 'untouchable' political ascendancy in Maharashtra was also powerfully represented by the political emergence of Bhimrao Ramji Ambedkar during a conference on the depressed classes held at Nagpur in 1920. The early RSS certainly viewed the rise of the 'depressed castes' as a threat to its ideal of an organic and unified 'Hindu society'. It also abhorred the anti-brahmin ideology of 'lower' caste and 'untouchable' movements. However, of salience was the palpable threat to Maharashtrian, and particularly Chitpavan brahmin political and caste hegemony, which the RSS articulated as a 'division' within Hinduism. Virtually all the founders of the RSS in the period 1924–6 were from the brahmin castes of Maharashtra.

In Nagpur during the same period, conflicts had emerged between Hindus and Muslims following complaints about the playing of music in front of mosques during the annual public Ganesh immersion processions, the latter re-emerging from a period of dormancy in forms previously organized by Tilak in the late nineteenth century. In 1923, both Hedgewar and Moonje were instrumental in inaugurating a Nagpur branch of the Hindu Mahasabha in protest at restrictions on music in front of mosques. This resulted in militant Hindu campaigns to popularize the public singing of Ganesh *bhajans* in the city, and Hedgewar's biography describes how:

> Because of the in-built fear of the Muslims among the Hindus, the band troupes sometimes shirked to play before the Masjid. On such occasions, Doctorji [Hedgewar] himself would take over the drums and rouse the dormant manliness of the Hindus. (Deshpande and Ramaswamy 1981: 71)

This masculinist celebration of intentional Hindu provocation of Muslims is characteristic of the RSS, as is the view that Indian Muslims were a force that was ceaselessly and secretly conspiring and plotting its 'murderous designs' against the 'Hindu nation'. The RSS's vision of perpetual conspiracies against the 'Hindu nation' by internal but anti-national forces in alliance with external enemies ('Muslim', 'Christian' and communist states) to foment disorder and chaos as a prelude to bringing down and then taking over the nation was characteristic of its paranoid style of politics.

The RSS is quite explicit that one of the reasons for its formation was Hedgewar's view that whereas Muslims were organized and strong, Hindus were disaggregated and weak and hence had to be consolidated into a militant, unified and aggressive force (Malkani 1980). Hedgewar's diagnosis of the political situation in the early 1920s was as follows:

> The upsurge witnessed during the days of non-cooperation movement has died down. The various *evils accompanying the movement* are now having a heyday. Mutual distrust and ill-will, personal and caste rivalries, Brahmin and non-Brahmin controversy have all raised their ugly heads. No institution or organization seems to be free from these *internal squabbles and utter lack of discipline*. The snake of Muslim fanaticism, *having*

!n fed on the milk of non-cooperation, is now baring its poisonous fangs and spreading *? venom* of violence and riots all over the country. (Deshpande and Ramaswamy 1981: 75, emphases added)

It is instructive that Hedgewar viewed the political rise of the non-brahmin, 'lower' caste movements and Hindu-Muslim joint political action during the non-cooperation movement as 'evil', and the dissension and debate within a democratic Congress and the non-cooperation movement as a matter of *non-discipline*. The visceral imaginary of Muslims as poisonous snakes both elided the considerable violence exercised against Muslim communities during this period and attempted to instil a dehumanizing characterization of Indian Muslims. Like the *sangathan* movement that was reinvigorated at this time, Hedgewar also believed that it was the 'lack of cohesion and self-respect' among Hindus that was the key problem facing Hindu society during this 'dark night of self-oblivion', which, for him, characterized Gandhi's non-cooperation movement.

For Hedgewar, the fundamental reason for 'foreign domination of Hindus' (by which he primarily referred to the Muslim presence in India as well as British colonialism, the latter also conceived as primarily 'Christian') was the result of 'Hindu failings', of which 'Hindu disunity' was the prime example. Consequently, 'Hindu consciousness' had to be moulded and disciplined into one of 'self-respect, unity and courage' so that the 'inner brilliance' of the 'Hindu nation' would 'burst forth' (Deshpande and Ramaswamy 1981: 75). The same 'diagnosis' is presented by the RSS today, but extended to account for the presence of secularists within India.

It was the native chieftains who facilitated the repeated destruction of the sacred Somnath shrine. Wasn't it Raja Mansingh who, by becoming a kingpin of Akbar's regime, betrayed the interests of the Hindus . . . considerable sections of the so-called academia and the elite even today display a singular lack of national consciousness even after witnessing such horrendous insult to nationhood as partition of the country. The fact that such a breed continues to exist even after so much historical and recent experience provides the strongest raison d'etre for intense and continuous propagation of the ideal of [Hindu] nationalism and the recognition of Hindu national identity as *a fundamental fact transcending corroboration and discussion*. (Seshadri 1988, 'Antidote to Self-Oblivion', emphasis added)

Hedgewar had organized volunteers during the 1920 annual Indian National Congress session held at Nagpur and in 1922, as joint secretary of the provincial Congress, started 'a disciplined volunteer corps'. The uniform of these volunteers, based on that of the colonial police force, was adopted by the RSS from 1926, a black cap being added a few years later. In 1923, N. S. Hardikar had started a similar volunteer organization, the Hindusthani (or Rashtriya) Seva Dal during the Congress session at Kakinada. The semi-paramilitary style of such volunteer bodies was anathema to a Congress committed to non-violence and they were to be prohibited. (Congress' Hindusthani Seva Dal was later to vigorously oppose the RSS.) Hedgewar's biographers also mention his involvement in both sports associations and Moonje's rifle clubs in this period, many of the latter formed under the auspices of the Hindu Mahasabha (Deshpande and Ramaswamy 1981: 67). In 1927, under the direct influence of Moonje, Hedgewar's fledgling RSS was invited to present a demonstration of callisthenics at the annual meeting in Ahmedabad of the pre-Savarkarite Hindu Mahasabha (Deshpande and Ramaswamy 1981: 97). After the mid-1920s, the Mahasabha had also organized several volunteer youth associations that emphasized physical and military training and its own Tarun Hindu Mahasabha was to merge with the RSS in the early 1930s under the impetus of Babarao Savarkar (Deshpande and Ramaswamy 1981: 130). The relationship between the RSS and the Hindu Mahasabha was later overdetermined by what the RSS styled as its 'non-political orientation'. This relationship was to become greatly strained after, firstly, Savarkar's presidentship of the Mahasabha and after Golwalkar's assumption of the leadership of the RSS in 1940. (Savarkar, referring to the RSS's narcissistic self-absorption, was moved to say that the epitaph of an RSS member would be of one who was born, joined the RSS and died having achieved nothing.) However, Mahasabha models of Hindu youth organization existed prior to the formation of the RSS, and were not Hedgewar's unique invention (Goyal 1979: 60).

The RSS was ostensibly formed during a meeting in 1925 said to be held on Vijaya Dashmi (the day that celebrates the mythological Rama's conquest of Lanka) and attended by Hedgewar, B. S. Moonje, Babarao Savarkar (the brother of V. D. Savarkar), L. V. Paranjpe and B. B. Thalkar. This group consisted entirely of Hindu Mahasabha activists. Goyal has argued that a key purpose of the meeting was to discuss how middle-class Hindus should organize to combat what was seen as 'Muslim rowdyism' (Curran 1951: 12, Goyal 1979: 60). Hedgewar was delegated the task of recruiting teenage boys.

In 1926, the Rashtriya Swayamsevak Sangh acquired its name and, from May of that year, instituted a daily routine of physical exercise, military drills and marches, weapons training, ideological inculcation, and Hindu nationalist prayers to 'the Motherland and Holyland' and to the RSS's new saffron flag (*bhagwa dhwaj*). The RSS's *shakhas* included *danda* (weapons training with *lathi* or a wooden staff), *khadga* (sword training), *vetracharma* (fighting with canes), precision drill marching and *yogchap* (callisthenic exercises such as with a *lezim* – metal plates wound together around a wooden bar and played with the hands). Its training today extends to non-Indian martial arts. Its distinctive salute (*pranam*) to the saffron flag, although also common among other youth groups in the 1920s and 1930s (including those of Congress), today cannot but evoke the period of

1930s Europe. The RSS's prayer was initially in Marathi and Hindi, but was changed at the end of 1939 into a 'neo-Sanskrit' version. The prayer (composed by N. N. Bhide, a schoolteacher) glorified 'Hindubhumi' and 'Hindu Rashtra' while eliciting a declaration of Hindu 'heroism', and was to be later supplemented by the RSS's *Ekata Mantra* and its *Ekatmata Stotra*, among a range of distinctive Hindu nationalist 'unity' hymns and songs. The *swayamsevaks* – RSS members working in the service of the Hindu Nation – were obliged to wear the RSS's uniform from 1926. The next year the RSS's annual Officer Training Camp (OTC) was started and in 1928, the RSS undertook its first mass initiation of *sway-amsevaks*, the latter swearing a lifelong oath of service and sacrifice that involved 'offering himself entirely – body, mind and wealth – for the preservation and progress of the Hindu Nation' (Deshpande and Ramaswamy 1981: 99). From this point, *swayamsevaks* were also to view the RSS flag as their only 'guru' or 'true preceptor', and offer monetary donations to it (in the manner of *guru dakshina*). The RSS transformed some Hindu traditions in which a disciple selects and follows a guru, ideally for life, into one in which the 'guru' is the Hindu nationalist flag. From 1930, the RSS began to institute the *pracharak* (full-time organizer) system whereby trained *swayamsevak* cadres were sent to other provinces to initiate branches (*shakhas*) and undertake the propagation of its ideology; it had trained about a hundred active *pracharaks* by the early 1940s. The RSS *shakha* network expanded and one *shakha* was started at Madan Mohan Malaviya's Benares Hindu University at which Madhav Sadashiv Golwalkar was teaching. The latter became first the RSS Sarkaryavah (General Secretary) and in 1940 the *sarsanghchalak*.

In November 1929, the RSS inaugurated the office of *sarsanghchalak* (Supreme Leader or the 'Guide and Philosopher' of the RSS), the practice of *pranam* (a gesture of prayer) to the leader and the overriding organizational principle of *eka chalak anuvartitva* or subservience to the one 'Supreme Leader'. Also of importance was the characterization of the *sarsanghchalak* as *parampoojaniya* – the principal one who is to be venerated. The narcissistic *parampoojaniya* status of the Supreme Leader is at considerable variance from RSS assertions that its leaders do not promote a cult of personality. The RSS also claimed that the inspiration for its hierarchical leadership principle was not derived from any 'perverted foreign model' such as Mussolini's fascism, but was based on the traditional idea of a 'model Hindu family' (Curran 1951: 11, Deshpande and Ramaswamy 1981: 112). However, as problematic in numerous ways, is the claim to 'Hindu family tradition' to justify a secretive all-male organization, led by older men and recruiting young boys, founded on the institutional absence of women and in which one leader holds absolute patriarchal authority and requires uncritical and *devotional* reverence from members. This can lend credence to the argument that the RSS is in essence a cultish organization (Goyal 1979, Jaffrelot 1996).

In 1927, RSS held one of its first public, and political, interventions during the communal disturbances in Nagpur surrounding both the Hindu Mahalakshmi festival and Muslim religious processions. It is worth noting the differential communal language used by the RSS in its description of the rising communal tension in Nagpur during 1926–7. Muslims, it said, 'were making hectic preparations for assaulting Hindus', 'had secretly planned to revolt', 'planned to loot' rich Hindus, had a 'murderous design' on and adopted a 'warlike posture' against Hindus. Hindus, on the other hand, 'were in a festive mood', 'subject to frequent harassment and humiliation', lacking morale, and too preoccupied with the festival to help other Hindus under Muslim attack. Hedgewar's RSS, however, 'was determined to protect Hindus' and 'repelled the attacks instantly', made Hindus 'emboldened', 'fought back Muslim aggression', while the Muslims 'were totally taken aback' and 'given a fitting reply' (Deshpande and Ramaswamy 1981: 94–6). The RSS viewed its interventions in this event as evidence of its growing strength. Subsequently, RSS branches emerged in other Marathi-speaking parts of Maharashtra (the Central Provinces). Under the organization of Babarao Savarkar, RSS *shakhas* were started in Delhi, and reflected the organizational importance of existing Hindu Mahasabha networks in the RSS's early growth. By 1940, the RSS had spread into all the provinces of northern India as well as Bangalore, Karnataka and Tamil Nadu (Goyal 1979: 73). Its paper, the *Organiser* was published from 1947. Towards the end of 1948, the RSS was well-established in the Marathi and Hindi speaking areas of the former Central Provinces and Madhya Pradesh, Uttar Pradesh (then the United Provinces) and parts of Punjab and north-central India.

There was a noticeable difference, which the British had observed from 1927, between the RSS's organizational presence in violence against Muslim communities, and the circuitous and convoluted nature of its involvement, or lack of, in the national movement. In 1930, Gandhi launched his anti-salt tax *satyagraha* and civil disobedience campaign, as part of the Congress strategy of 'Complete Independence', the latter demand curiously viewed by the RSS as one which Congress had appropriated from it. Hedgewar wrote to RSS branches stating that RSS members could join the *satyagraha* in an individual capacity and if given permission by RSS organizers, but that the RSS as an organization 'had not resolved' to participate in the movement (Deshpande and Ramaswamy 1981: 117). Hedgewar was involved in the related Jungle Satyagraha of 1930, and it is claimed that a contingent of medically trained *swayamsevaks* 'wearing Swastika symbols on their shoulders' was also sent to assist those on *satyagraha*. It has been suggested that the reason for Hedgewar's participation in the *satyagraha* was to prove his patriotic credentials during a period when tens of thousands of Indians were being imprisoned for active opposition to British rule, while the RSS remained self-preoccupied (Goyal 1979: 48). However, the explicit reasons given by the RSS for Hedgewar's participation are important to note, because they gave him:

> an opportunity to get acquainted with the patriotic youth from many places who would throng prisons; and he could expound to them the need for the positive work of building up a disciplined nation-wide organization. That would greatly help in expanding Sangh [RSS] activities in future. (Deshpande and Ramaswamy 1981: 118)

It is significant that Hedgewar resigned as *sarsanghchalak* before joining the *satyagraha*, since this would have *formally* associated the RSS with political, militant non-cooperation with British rule. He said:

> All of us are participating in this movement in our personal capacity. There has been *no change either in our policy or in our way of working, nor has our faith in the Sangh suffered in the least because of these developments* [i.e. Gandhi's *satyagraha*] (Deshpande and Ramaswamy 1981: 119, emphasis added)

The RSS's refusal to officially partake in the national movement, Hedgewar's resignation as its leader during the *satyagraha*, his interested reasons for participation, as well as the strictures on *swayamsevaks* wishing to involve themselves in the then largest anti-colonial mass movement since the 1920s, are frequently glossed in the RSS literature. The explanations usually given are that the nation (meaning the 'Hindu nation') would not have arisen from what were seen as the 'short-term' activities of Gandhi, Congress and the national movement, but required long-term work within Hindu society, taking individuals one by one, disciplining them for an 'organized national life' and 'moulding' their character. The implication of such narratives is that this work was somehow both necessary and complementary to what the national movement was undertaking. Another frequently iterated reason is that the RSS wished to remain outside what it viewed as the limited and polluting nature of 'politics' and concentrate instead on slow, patient work in civil society. It should, however, be noted that neither its allegedly nonpolitical orientation nor its 'man-moulding' activities prevented the RSS's formal participation in organized violence against Muslim communities.

There are other explanations for the RSS's reticence about joining the national movement and the peculiar construal of its early history. Of considerable importance in the early formation of the RSS was the role not of Hedgewar but of Balkrishna Shivram Moonje (1872–1948), a doctor from Maharashtra's brahmin community. While he is now celebrated by the RSS as 'Dharamveer' ('a hero in the religious struggle'), his role in the formation of the RSS has been distinctly minimized in favour of Hedgewar's. Aside from being one of Hedgewar's closest and intimate associates, during the 1920s and 1930s Moonje was, unlike Hedgewar, a clearly recognizable national figure in India through his prominent role in one faction of the national movement and in Hindu communal organizations. Indeed he is one of a number of sources of influence that include Savarkar's *Hindutva* and the work of Bhai Parmanand, Babarao Savarkar and Malaviya's Hindu Mahasabha, who were instrumental in fostering the development of the incipient RSS but have been mostly disavowed in its histories of its origin and its eulogizing of Hedgewar. Des Raj Goyal, a former *swayamsevak*, has argued that this 'smacks of a deep-seated inferiority complex' such that members' faith and loyalty to the founder would weaken if other sources of inspiration were acknowledged (1979: 50).

As seen in previous chapters, Moonje was an important anti-Gandhite figure in the 'responsive cooperation' factions within Congress and, from the early to late 1920s, he was a key figure in Malaviya's Hindu Mahasabha. Moonje remained within the Mahasabha under Savarkar and in many respects his practical promotion of aggressive Hindu militarism was to better that of Savarkar. Moonje was not only a member of the Mahasabha's 'Hindu Militarization Boards' but also founded the Central Hindu Military Education Society in Nasik, north-western Maharashtra in 1935, followed by the Bhonsala Military School in 1937. The latter exists today as the Bhonsala Military Academy, dedicated to instilling in its cadets a 'brahmin-kshatriya' ideology that celebrates 'the power of knowledge and the knowledge of power'.

Moonje and the Organizational Influence of Italian Fascism

In her recent reassessment of the relationship between early Hindu nationalism and fascism, Marzia Casolari (2000) has highlighted the direct, barely mediated relation between the organizational structure and ideology of the early RSS after the mid-1920s and Italian fascism, in particular the Fascist Balilla and Avanguardisti movements and fascist military academies and training schools. Fascist Italy was already a source of inspiration for Hindu nationalist movements in the 1920s and (with Nazi Germany) 1930s, especially in their desire to demonstrate organized Hindu strength and militarize the Hindu nation. British reports had highlighted how, from 1927, Moonje, who had key responsibility for organizing RSS branches in Maharashtra and in the central Provinces, was inspired to model the RSS on the Fascist and Nazi movements (Casolari 2000).

In 1931, Moonje visited Fascist Italy and met with Mussolini, who impressed him greatly. Of the Fascist Balilla movement, which organized military training and fascist indoctrination of boys from the ages of six to eighteen years in forms similar to those used by the RSS, Moonje said in his diary:

> The Balilla institutions and the conception of the whole organization have appealed to me the most . . . The whole organization is conceived by Mussolini for the military

regeneration of Italy, Italians, by nature, appear ease-loving and non-martial, like the Indians generally. They have cultivated, like Indians, the work of peace and neglected the cultivation of the art of war. Mussolini saw the essential weakness of his country and conceived the idea of the Balilla organization . . . India and particularly Hindu India need some such institution for the military regeneration of the Hindus . . . Our institution, the Rashtriya Swayamsevak Sangh of Nagpur under Dr Hedgewar is of this kind, though quite independently conceived. I shall spend the rest of my life developing and extending this institution of Dr Hedgewar all throughout Maharashtra and other provinces. (Moonje quoted in Casolari 2000: 220)

Casolari has shown how this visit inspired Moonje to immediately promote these ideas among Hindus in Maharashtra and begin the organization of Hindu youth movements based on this fascist model. This included a conference on fascism and Mussolini's political thought in 1934, presided by Hedgewar, at which Moonje spoke, together with further organizational meetings in that year, the belief being that Hindus could not be united

unless we have our own swaraj with a Hindu as a dictator like Shivaji of old or Mussolini or Hitler of present day Italy and Germany . . . But this does not mean that we have to sit with folded hands until some such dictator arises in India. We should formulate a scientific scheme and carry on propaganda for it. (Moonje quoted in Casolari 2000: 221)

Hence, aside from the methodological and organizational similarities between fascist youth organizations and the RSS, there was also an ideological commitment among RSS leaders in which an equivalence was created between self-rule and a dictatorial fascism moulded to Indian circumstances, even extending the dictatorial metaphor to Shivaji.

While some writers have described the *sangh parivar* as 'fascist' (Sarkar 1993, Raychaudhuri 1995), the dominant view of the RSS in the literature on Hindu nationalism is that the RSS cannot be strictly conceived as 'fascist' because of its declaration of its 'non-political' orientation and because of its alleged aversion to the seizure of state power – at best it is 'proto-fascistic' (Anderson and Damle 1987, Jaffrelot 1996, Laqueur 1996, Vanaik 1997). An additional argument relates to the political views of RSS (Jana Sangh) cadres, discerned through questionnaire interviews, which broadly demonstrated an authoritarianism regarding social and moral issues but an 'egalitarian' or 'socialist' orientation towards economic issues (Curran 1951: 51, Andersen and Damle 1987: 195). The burgeoning field of 'fascism studies' has tended to be preoccupied with a combination of taxonomic categorization and the belief that a definitive 'fascist minimum' can be discerned, primarily through a consideration of European fascist and Nazi states and neo-Nazi movements. Within such ventures, non-Western examples of possible fascism are either elided or dismissed.

However, it is useful to employ an analytical distinction between fascist political ideologies, social movements, organizational and institutional forms, and cultural aesthetics and between all these and fascism as an exceptional form of state power. Of additional importance here is the conception of both state and civil society and their forms of ordering within fascist political ideologies. A corporatist orientation to economic issues, economic nationalism or an organicist economic 'egalitarianism' has not been incongruent with classical fascism; indeed a corporately governed and qualified economic redistributivist ideal has been a key characteristic of fascist states. In ideological, aesthetic, social movement and organizational terms, characterising the RSS as fascist is by no means unwarranted. However, disclosing the fascism of the RSS and its family of affiliated organization by demonstrating historical connections with the fascist and Nazi regimes is not politically sufficient because contemporary fascisms can be precisely predicated on the widespread memory of the past existence of those regimes from the 1920s to the mid-1940s. In other words, the possibility is there that movements can come into being for which no historical, ideological or inspirational relation to past fascism or Nazism can be demonstrated, but which can share many of the definitive social and political characteristics of the latter.

Golwalkar's Philosophy of 'Hindu Race', Nation and Minorities

Hedgewar is characterized as having supreme organizational skills. Indeed *sangathan*, or the strategic organization of Hindu society in order to achieve 'Hindu unity', is the RSS's quotidian philosophy. However, it was under its second leader, Madhav Sadashiv Golwalkar (1906–73), that the RSS extended the ideological content of its Hindu nationalism. Golwalkar was also a Maharashtrian brahmin, and was born near Nagpur. He was both a student and tutor of zoology at Malaviya's Benares Hindu University and later a lawyer at Nagpur. Unlike Hedgewar, he was inclined towards Hindu spiritualism (he left the RSS for a short period to become a follower of Swami Akhandananda in Bengal, the latter a former disciple of Ramakrishna). Golwalkar joined the RSS in 1931 while a teacher at the University and became an RSS worker from 1933. Following Hedgewar's request, and after his death in 1940, Golwalkar became the second *sarsanghchalak* of the RSS until his own death in 1973.

RSS writings about Golwalkar are suffused with the same eulogistic tone that accompanies their renditions of Hedgewar's life and thought and Golwalkar occupies an importance in RSS hagiography second only to the founder. He is portrayed in RSS tracts (especially during childhood and youth) as having excelled in, if not superseded, the personality, qualities and dispositions of mere humans. A couple of examples are illustrative:

Principal Gardiner, who frequently quoted from the Bible, made an incorrect reference. Madhu sprang to his feet and boldly told the Principal that the reference was wrong. He gave the correct Biblical expression from memory . . . Principal Gardiner was surprised at the marvellous memory of this youth. (Golwalkar 1956: 9)

The Examination was drawing near. One night when he was completely absorbed in studies a scorpion stung him in the leg. But nothing would distract his attention. He went on with his reading – as if nothing had happened! To astonished friends he simply remarked: 'the scorpion has stung my leg not my brain.' (Golwalkar 1956: 10)

The effusive exaltation of quotidian events, such as answering a question in class – another rendition of the scorpion story has Golwalkar dressing the wound and placing his foot in a bath of potassium permanganate (Malkani 1980: 40) – has a precedent. It draws on the hagiographic prose style in which the lives of Hindu Gods, kings, saints and gurus was written following the broad spread of the print media in nineteenth century India, especially among younger people. In this particular case, it is employed to elicit reverence from RSS followers, especially in its valorization of education (important for the age, gender and class sections from which the RSS recruits) and in the demonstration of the supreme intellect and wisdom of its leadership, whose guidance followers are required to accept.

Organic Culture and 'Artificial' State

In the period 1938–9, Golwalkar wrote his definitive treatise on Hindu nationalism, *We, Or Our Nationhood defined* (1939) (hereafter, *We*). This tract was republished four times, including towards the end of 1944 (the second edition) and after the Second World War (in 1947) and was followed by another major work, *Hindu Vichaar (Bunch of Thoughts)* published in 1966. In 1956, *We* was considered by the RSS to be 'an unassailable exposition of the doctrine of nationhood' (Golwalkar 1956: 13). In *We*, Golwalkar's distinctive contribution was to link Savarkar's conceptions of Hindutva, Hindu nation and Hindu war with both a 'political sociology' of the nation state, democracy, rights, citizenship and minorities, and an ideology of xenophobic racism. The political context surrounding the writing of *We* was the nationwide success of Congress in the provincial elections of 1937, followed by the Congress resignation of its ministries at the declaration of war in 1939.

For Golwalkar (for whom there is no evidence of participation in the anti-colonial struggle – for example, he forbade *swayamsevaks* to participate in the Bombay naval mutiny in 1947) this period signified 'strange times' when 'we do not live but merely exist', and in which 'traitors should sit enthroned as national heroes and patriots heaped with ignominy' (Golwalkar 1944: 14). Hindus, he argued, should be 'at war at once with the British on the one hand and the Moslems on the other', Muslims conceived by him as both 'foreigners' and 'foes'. Golwalkar vehemently rejected 'the amazing doctrine' that a nation comprised all its citizens living within a given territory. He conceived this as a 'betrayal', 'the wild goose chase after the phantasm of founding a "really" democratic state'. Instead he contrasted 'nation' with 'state', the latter identified as a 'haphazard bundle of political rights' (Golwalkar 1944: 3). Given the considerable importance of Golwalkar's ideology for the contemporary Hindutva movement, it is worth considering his conceptions of both 'nation' and 'state' in some detail.

'Nation', for Golwalkar, was a cultural entity whereas the 'state' was a political one and, although they overlapped, they were fundamentally distinguishable such that the form of state had to be subsidiary to and determined by the national concept (Golwalkar 1944: 51). This particular 'Herderian' idea (the qualification being that Herder was frequently dismissive of the importance of the state and of any concentration of power within it, and it is by no means clear that this is the *sangh parivar* view) was to travel through to the post-Independence 'Integral Humanist' ideology of Deendayal Upadhyaya. Golwalkar's 'nation', like that of Savarkar's, started with the Aryans in the 'Vedic period', the latter conceived by him to be far older than any other civilization. However, he rejected the view (held for example by Savarkar) that the Hindus-Aryans were exogenous to India: 'Undoubtedly . . . we Hindus have been in undisputed and undisturbed possession of this land for over 8 or even 10 thousand years before the land was invaded by any foreign race' (Golwalkar 1944: 6). Hence, he opposed the 'western hypotheses' that Aryans came from outside India, and instead argued that:

> we Hindus came into this land from nowhere, but are indigenous children of the soil always, from time immemorial and are natural masters of the country . . . And we were one nation – 'Over all the land from sea to sea one Nation!' is the trumpet cry of the ancient Vedas!' (Golwalkar 1944: 8)

But, as in Savarkar's *Hindutva*, this 'Hindu nation' started to degenerate into small principalities, consciousness of 'Hindu Race' and 'Nationhood' waned, and Buddhism caused 'over-individualization'. The 'Hindu nation', he argued, became too secure in its glory, 'careless' and divided against itself. It was hence unable to resist 'the first real invasions of murdering hordes of Mussalman free-booters' (Golwalkar 1944: 10).

But 'the race spirit did not wholly die out. The Race Spirit is too tenacious to be dead so easily.' Hindus were 'an immortal race with perennial youth'. Knowledge of this 'immortality' (*mritunjaya*, related to the idea of rebirth or metempsychosis) was the sole possession of Hindus and they therefore had a world mission towards the whole of humanity. Golwalkar reiterated the familiar Hindu nationalist historical narrative of an Hindu empire or nation, followed by an '800 year war' following the arrival of Muslims, which demonstrated Hindu heroism, strength and martyrdom. The vast geographical territory of Golwalkar's 'Hindu nation' included not only the borders of contemporary India, Pakistan, Kashmir, Bangladesh and Sri Lanka but also Nepal, Tibet, Afghanistan, Burma ('Brahmadesh'), Indonesia and parts of Laos, Thailand and Kampuchea. Indeed, the symbolic geography of 'Akhand Bharat' in the contemporary Hindutva movement can represent both pre-Partition India and this much larger territory.

For Golwalkar the history of the Hindu Nation was

> the story of our flourishing Hindu National life for thousands of years and of a long unflinching war continuing for the last ten centuries, which has not yet come to a decisive close . . . And Race Spirit calls, national consciousness blazes forth and we Hindus rally to the Hindu standard, the Bhagawa Dhwaja [saffron flag], set our teeth in grim determination to wipe out the opposing forces. (Golwalkar 1944: 13)

As a result of this war, the 'Hindu nation' was 'exhausted' and unable to fight the British, who had invaded India 'with the help of the Mussalmans'. However

> The Race spirit has been awakening. The lion was not dead, only sleeping. He is rousing himself up again and the world has to see the might of the regenerated Hindu Nation strike down the enemy's [the British] hosts [the Muslims] with its mighty arm. (Golwalkar 1944: 12)

Nation, for Golwalkar, was composed of what he called the 'unassailable' and 'scientific' 'famous five unities': Country, Race, Religion, Culture and Language. 'Race'(*jati*), for Golwalkar, was a foundational component of nation:

> It is superfluous to emphasise the importance of Racial Unity in the Nation state. A Race is a hereditary Society having common customs, common language, common memories of glory and disaster; in short it is a population with a common origin under one culture. Such a race is by far the most important ingredient of a Nation . . . We will not seek to prove this axiomatic truth, that the Race is the body of the Nation, and that with its fall, the Nation ceases to exist. (Golwalkar 1944: 21)

Nation, Citizenship and Minorities

Despite Golwalkar's claim of the generosity and the tolerant spirit of 'broad Catholicism' that he said was the essence of Hinduism, his organic Hindu-Racial totality was inherently xenophobic.

in Hindusthan exists and must needs exist [sic] the ancient Hindu nation and nougnt else but the Hindu Nation. All those not belonging to the national i.e. Hindu Race, Religion, Culture and Language, naturally fall out of the pale of real 'National' life . . . All others posing to be patriots and wilfully indulging in a course of action detrimental to the Hindu Nation are traitors and enemies to the National Cause . . . all those who fall outside the five-fold limits of that idea can have no place in the national life, unless they abandon their differences, and completely merge themselves in the National Race. So long, however, as they maintain their racial, religious and cultural differences, they cannot but be only foreigners, who may either be friendly or inimical to the Nation. (Golwalkar 1944: 45–6)

Golwalkar similarly proposed unanimist conceptions of culture and religion. Culture, for Golwalkar, was indistinguishable from religion. Religion for Golwalkar was not private faith or individual belief, but instead (as *dharma*) regulated all the functions of society. Both religion and culture created 'the peculiar Race Spirit' and 'Race consciousness' that animated the 'Hindu nation'. Religion, he said, was 'eternally interwoven' into every aspect of the life of the Race: 'every action in life, individual, social, or political is a command of Religion'. Golwalkar hence combined an avowedly theocratic conception of state and civil society with a racial philosophy of 'nation'.

Golwalkar bemoaned the post-First World War settlement that created new states 'composed of the original race with an incorporation in its body politic of a people racially, culturally and linguistically different' (Golwalkar 1944: 30) and which led to the rights of and protection treaties for national minorities that were negotiated under the former League of Nations. Like Savarkar, he sympathized with Nazi Germany's territorial claims regarding the Sudeten ethnic Germans. He did not conceive of 'minority treaties' as other than 'preferential treatment.' Minorities should not, he argued, 'tax the generosity' of the nation by 'demanding privileges'. In discussing 'minority rights' in India, he said that for a 'foreign race' to have 'preferential treatment, it should not be an upstart, a new, voluntary settlement, and it should not be below 20% of the total population of the state' (Golwalkar 1944: 31), a stipulation which Muslims, at just under twenty percent of the population, failed. Similarly, he argued that the 'National Race' had

the indisputable right of excommunicating from its Nationality all those who, having been of the Nation, for ends of their own, turned traitors and entertained aspirations contravening or differing from those of the National Race as a whole. (Golwalkar 1944: 34)

For Golwalkar, no minority was deserving of any 'right what-so-ever' or 'any obligations from the National race'. Minorities could:

live only as outsiders, bound by all the codes and conventions of the Nation, at the sufferance of the Nation and deserving of no special protection, far less any privilege or rights. There are only two courses open to the foreign elements, either to merge themselves in the national race and adopt its culture, or to live at the sweet will of the national race. That is the only logical and correct solution. That alone keeps the national life healthy and undisturbed. That alone keeps the Nation safe from the danger of a cancer developing into its body politic of the creation of a state within a state. From this standpoint, sanctioned [by] the experiences of shrewd old nations, the non-Hindu peoples of Hindusthan must either adopt the Hindu culture and language, must learn to respect and hold in reverence Hindu religion, must entertain no ideas but those of the glorification of the Hindu race and culture i.e. they must not only give up their attitude of intolerance and ungratefulness towards this land and its age-long traditions but must also cultivate a positive attitude of love and devotion instead – in a word they must cease to be foreigners, or may stay in the country wholly subordinated to the Hindu nation, claiming nothing, deserving no privileges, far less any preferential treatment – not even citizen's rights. We are an old nation; and let us deal as old nations ought to and do deal with the foreign races who have chosen to live in our country. (Golwalkar 1944: 48–9)

Golwalkar's use of somatic metaphors – the healthy body of the 'Hindu nation' threatened by a minority 'cancer' – supplemented his ideological double binds in which minorities could not be other than 'foreign', but nor should they exist in the Hindu nation unless they became Hindus. Similarly, citizenship is made conditional on Hindu racial, cultural and religious affiliation. Conversely, disenfranchisement and, indeed, an explicit policy of subjugation was to be coextensive with non-Hindu affiliations.

The thorough abandonment of civic nationalism commenced by Savarkar was taken to its logical conclusion by Golwalkar. In Hindu Mahasabha ideology under Savarkar, there was an explicit rejection of a civic nationalism comprised of individuals living within a territory who in principle could spontaneously have varying and contingent political affiliations. Instead the Mahasabha proposed a religiously and racially defined conception of collective political affiliation – in essence the cultivation of a permanent Hindu 'vote bank'. But, and leaving aside the definitive Hindu majoritarianism that would have necessarily accompanied its combination of 'one man one vote' with Hindu communalism, even Savarkar's Hindu Mahasabha in the late 1930s stated that it stood for the right of religious minorities to practise their religion and for minorities to have the formal rights of citizenship, such as those related to political enfranchisement. Under Golwalkar's RSS this was rejected in its entirety until after Independence.

Golwalkar's severe nationalism was Western both in content and origin, and its thinkability is inconceivable outside the formation of nationalism and the idea of 'the people' that emerged in Europe during the nineteenth century (Bhatt 1997).

While reserving some sympathy for Deendayal Upadhyaya's ideology of integral humanism, Chaturvedi Badrinath (1993) has consummately refuted Golwalkar's indigenist claims about the 'Hindu nation' and the relation of the latter to dharmic concepts. 'Nation' neither existed within nor can be conceived as part of *dharma*; indeed in Golwalkar's conception it is a 'grievous wounding' to actual Hindu, Islamic and Christian religion. Golwalkar's exclusivist Hindu nationalism also mobilized a distinct idea of the 'chosen people', itself foreign to Hindu *dharma*. It must also be compelled to support the justice of Partition since Muslims could not possibly be conceived by Golwalkar as sharing land with Hindus. One important point made by Badrinath (1993: 298–303) is that in emphasizing devotion to the nation (*rashtra-bhakti*) rather than God, and in propagating the 'man-making' ideology of the RSS, Golwalkar paradoxically instituted a definitively Western conception of 'Man' and 'nation', rather than God, at the centre of the universe. One need not affiliate with the dharmic ideals of Badrinath to recognize that for conscientious and interested believers, Hindu nationalism poses a grim challenge to '*dharma*', rather than anything like its fulfilment. Indeed, a vivid characteristic of Hindu nationalism is its reduction of the dense and sophisticated metaphysical content of Hindu and Buddhist philosophy to bare Hindu nationalist political slogans and mottos that are incapable either of conveying the vast range of speculative metaphysics within the different schools of Indian philosophical thought or of challenging Western or Eurocentric philosophical hegemony, aspects of which they uncritically reproduce. This idea of 'Man' as at the core of Hindu nationalist political epistemology was to be made even more explicit in Deendayal Upadhyaya's ideology of 'Integral Humanism' (see next chapter).

Of additional importance is Golwalkar conception of 'Hinduism'. Golwalkar proposed that all minorities had to become Hindus not through a conscientious and voluntary choice that accompanies religious affiliation but against their will and conviction and under an explicit and palpable threat of violence. Indeed, Golwalkar articulated the expansion of his imagined ancient Aryan-Hindu empire not as a mission of religious education or even persuasion, but as one of military conquest: 'Obviously we did not expand into Central Asia and South-East Asia by sermons alone. It is significant that every Hindu god is armed' (Malkani 1980: 42). While such sentiments have been read as reflecting a Hindu nationalist attempt to emulate what is conceived to be the aggressive nature of Islam, this can lead to a view that Hinduism does not have its own histories of and resources for institutional religious violence. However, M. K. Gandhi's articulation of religion as a moral force dependent on conscientious conviction that faces the considerable test of one's inherent personal disbelief or disavowal, while conceivably problematic for other reasons, illustrated the profound difference between these two reconstructive projects that attempted to hegemonize Hinduism. Of significance is that Golwalkar was instrumental in forming the Vishwa Hindu Parishad (World

Hindu Council) in the mid-1960s, a body committed to organizing religious Hinduism under an overarching and violent Hindutva ideology. Golwalkar's articulation of compulsion as central to Hindu religious belief was to travel directly into the VHP's ideology and political programme.

Golwalkar and Nazism

In *We*, Golwalkar employed distinctly metaphysical, rather than strictly biological or simply hereditarian, conceptions of 'race'. This emerged most forcefully in his comparisons between India and fascist Italy and Nazi Germany. Both Italian fascism and German National Socialism were conceived by him as the legitimate 'awakening' of the 'desires and aspirations' of 'racial consciousness'. Such aspirations of the race, he argued, were historic and embedded in a primordial past of ancient tradition. A nation was compelled to 'tread the road' that the traditional past had 'opened out for it'. Conversely, if a nation abandoned its 'fixed groove' of tradition and 'race spirit', it seriously endangered its 'life soul' and hence 'the whole fabric of its existence.' Both an individual and the race had its 'mental frame' conditioned and shaped by the historic awakening of the 'race spirit of today' (Golwalkar 1944: 31). Hence, for Golwalkar, the emergence of fascist Italy demonstrated the 'rousing' of the 'old Roman Race consciousness of conquering the whole territory round the Mediterranean Sea' (Golwalkar 1944: 33). Similarly with Nazi Germany, where the 'ancient Race spirit which prompted the Germanic tribes to over-run the whole of Europe has re-risen' (Golwalkar 1944: 31). Golwalkar claimed that in Nazi Germany, each of his five constituents of the 'nation idea' had been 'boldly vindicated'. The 'national spirit' in Nazi Germany, he claimed, was logical, and merely sought to bring into its ownership what was 'originally' German land, namely the territories of Poland, and those of Czechoslovakia in which ethnic Germans lived.

> German pride in their Fatherland for a definite home country, for which the race has certain traditional attachments as a necessary concomitant of the true Nation concept, awoke and ran the risk of starting a fresh world-conflagration, in order to establish one, unparalleled, undisputed, German Empire over all this 'hereditary territory'. This *natural and logical aspiration* has almost been fulfilled and the great importance of the 'country factor' has been once again *vindicated* in the living present. (Golwalkar 1944: 36, emphases added)

Golwalkar articulated not simply a spiritual nationalism, but a spiritual racism, while combining both these concepts. Leaving aside the 'Herderian' and Fichtean themes, or Ernest Renan's proposition of a nation as a 'soul' or 'spiritual principle', Golwalkar's distinctly spiritual racial nationalism, encapsulating both degeneration and palingenesis, is reminiscent of other nineteenth-century European philosophical strands, especially prominent in the anti-semitism of Schopenhauer, Wagner and the Bayreuth Circle, the latter indeed reliant on marshalling a sharp polarization between the Hindu-Buddhist and the Judeo-Christian-Islamic traditions. As suggestive are semblances to both pre-Nazi and Nazi Germany (in the writings of Walther Darré, Dietrich Eckhart and, in a cruder fashion, Alfred Rosenberg, among others) and influences on pre-fascist and fascist Italy (in both René Guenon's and especially Julius Evola's projects, both again dependent on Hindu-Buddhist metaphors).

For Golwalkar, Nazi Germany also validated the 'scientific' prescription that a 'nation' should comprise a pure 'Race' having no contaminants, a model he believed India should emulate. This is often illustrated by the following quotation, a frequent source of embarrassment for the RSS, and eminently worth repeating:

> German race pride has now become the topic of the day. To keep up the purity of the Race and its culture, Germany shocked the world by her purging the country of the semitic Races – the Jews. Race pride at its highest has been manifested here. Germany has shown how well nigh impossible it is for Races and cultures, having differences going to the root, to be assimilated into one united whole, a good lesson for us in Hindusthan to learn and profit by. (Golwalkar 1944: 37)

If Golwalkar's sympathies for Nazism and fascism were shared by the earlier founders of the RSS and by Savarkar during the same period, of importance is that there has been no explicit and unconditional disavowal of such doctrines by the RSS but only a modulated defensiveness, more concerned to avoid public criticism of Golwalkar's Nazi-like philosophy than to reject it. This is also demonstrated by the RSS's ceaseless promotion of Golwalkar's *Bunch of Thoughts* (1966). The latter text however in essence espouses the philosophy of *We* but without explicit reference to Nazism, fascism or racial doctrines.

Christophe Jaffrelot has importantly and usefully highlighted one direct influence on Golwalkar's (and Savarkar's) political philosophy, the *Theory of the State*, written by an German exponent of formative political science, Johann Kaspar Bluntschli and first published in 1895 (Jaffrelot 1996: 53, Bluntschli [1895] 1971). Bluntschli valorized a hierarchical concept of 'race', discussed a racial conception of 'nation' and discussed nationhood in Herderian terms as reflecting the *Volksgeist* of a people. There is significant ambiguity in his political philosophy between conceptions of 'nation', 'people' and 'state'. However, while Bluntschli argued that there were advantages for a nation based on a single dominant nationality (*Hauptnation*) and in which other populations were an insignificant proportion, he also rejected the idea that political rights be apportioned differentially on the basis of nationality, instead arguing that political community and equality of rights must be shared by all members of the nation alike (Bluntschli [1895] 1971: 105–6). Bluntschli was also critical, though with reservations, of conceptions of a religious state. Moreover, aspects of his *Theory of the State* reiterate a racial-dynamic idea of Aryanism that is distinctly based on white supremacy, and contains fairly disparaging remarks about non-white populations, both of which might have troubled Golwalkar. It is therefore difficult to ascertain what precisely Bluntschli's political theory meant for Golwalkar and whether the inspiration of fascism and Nazism was more directly formative.

Golwalkar and varnashramadharma

The systematic forms of technical-rational organization and algorithmic inculcation of the RSS are central to its aim of ordering the social formation in accordance with its vanguardist imagination. This technical rationalism commenced with the need to 'create the proper type of man', who was to be assigned a place in an integrated social order based on caste. Instructively, it was here that Golwalkar explicitly marshalled religious texts to defend caste. While the RSS ostensibly champions its opposition to caste, this has to be considered very carefully indeed. The RSS is primarily opposed to *jati* (sub-caste), which is seen as an unnecessary division of the 'Hindu nation' based on material and economic factors and selfish extrapolation of family or endogamous ties, but it is not opposed to *varnashrama* (the system of four castes) which is seen simply as a reflection of 'natural law' (*dharma*), indeed 'a supreme and scientific social order based on the division of labour' (Golwalkar 1956: 63). Golwalkar's defence of *varna* and the RSS's rejection of sub-caste as equivalent to *jati* can also be considered from a different perspective. For Golwalkar (as for Savarkar, who wrote relatively little on caste in his *Hindutva*), *jati* was equivalent to the 'Hindu race'. Hence one can view the rejection of sub-caste as the criticism of an *inappropriate* use of the concept of *jati* as an irrelevant hereditarianism of family and community that diminished the power of *jati* for a larger racial-hereditarian conception of the Hindu.

Golwalkar was explicit that the ideal social order should be *varnashrama*, 'the best order for achieving human happiness', and argued that '[e]ven those who loudly trumpeted individual liberty had to accept collectivism and the doctrine of heredity.' What he termed the 'feeling of inequality' had, he claimed, 'crept' into the caste system and was not 'proper'. Despite this nominal admission of the injustices of caste, he argued that 'the Geeta tells us that the individual who does his assigned duties in life only worships God through such performance':

> If a Brahmana becomes great by imparting knowledge, a Kshatriya is hailed as equally great by *destruction of the enemy*. No less important is the Vaishya who feeds and sustains the community through agriculture and trade, or the Shudra who *services society* through

his art and craft [sic]. Together, and by their mutual interdependence, they constitute the social order. That, indeed, is the spirit of our land. (Golwalkar 1956: 50, emphases added)

While it *may* be possible to conceive of Golwalkar's vision of an organic caste-based social order as largely symbolic, it nevertheless strongly legitimated existing caste structures. It is also illustrated a hierarchically differential promotion by the RSS of an apparently anti-caste ideology to new recruits and outsiders, while retaining a strong caste ideology at its core. A version of caste ideology still exists today in the RSS and is apparent even when the RSS is ostensibly describing its anti-caste projects. Two characteristics are apparent in RSS accounts of its projects against untouchability. Such accounts describe, in tones of overwhelming joy and delight, the views of 'untouchables' that *sangh* workers are contented to sit, dine and converse with them, or invite them to their homes. On occasion, there is description of *dharmacharyas* who may partake of these activities. The need to banish *the word* 'untouchability' is frequently iterated. If these examples are intended to demonstrate an aversion to untouchability, the overwhelming thrust is about how 'untouchables', ostensibly prey to 'foreign' missionaries, are instead being integrated into the 'national (Hindu) mainstream'. There is no critical scrutiny, condemnation, even mild disapproval of *caste itself*, its hierarchies or injustices, or brahmin or 'upper' caste domination or propagation of caste ideology. The onus is upon the 'untouchable' communities to enter 'the Hindu mainstream'. Where non-'untouchable' groups are mentioned, this is to encourage them to undertake personal encounters with 'untouchable' groups, such as interdining. There is a foundational difference between criticizing untouchability or *jati* from within the context of building a 'Hindu nation' and undertaking a systematic critique of the legitimating system of *varna*, the latter explicitly based on the religious texts, such as the *Manudharmashastra*, that the RSS valorizes.

Caste was also central to Golwalkar's imagination of nation and state. He brazenly claimed that 'history does not record a single instance of one *Varna* or caste attacking another *Varna* or caste. Nor did any *Varna* ever run counter to the national interest' (Golwalkar 1956: 63). The role of the state was, he argued, subsidiary to and important only for maintaining the ideal *varna*-based social order. Each aspect of the social order – caste, economy, state and civil society – were to be integrated, and economic differences, such as class conflict, suppressed. (Such a functionalist conception of the social order was also central to Deendayal Upadhyaya's 'Integral Humanism.') The form of government Golwalkar proposed was both idealized and undemocratic. For example, he valorized the village council or *panchayat* system not because it led to greater local decision-making power but because it led to an organically interconnected nation in which *panchayat* would lead to 'a reinforcement of the centre'. In the mid-1950s, Golwalkar was to argue that the ideal form of state was not specifiable and had to be determined by the 'national idea'.

> If the basic structure of society is strong and enduring, any form of Government, from monarchy to democracy, will be workable. None of them will be able to shake off the basic structure. This is why there is no insistence on any particular form of Government in our way of thinking. (Golwalkar 1956: 56)

Golwalkar's xenophobic nationalism, as well as his inclement attitude towards the religious minorities in India was demonstrated during the war with Pakistan in 1965 and earlier with China following the latter's border conflicts with and invasion of India in 1962. Golwalkar was frustrated with the limited nature of these wars and called instead for 'a total war'. Such a war 'would involve every one of our countrymen in active participation in an all out war effort and would have been a great chastener of the national mind' (Golwalkar 1966: 312). According to Golwalkar, the centuries had bred vice and weakness, indolence, selfishness and parochialism among Indian men.

> It is therefore that a bigger and total war is welcome in spite of the temporary hardships it may entail us. In fact, we should heartily pray for such a war, though we are traditionally incurable lovers of peace and not war-mongers; for that is the price we have to pay for peace with freedom and honour and the sooner we pay the price the better. (Golwalkar 1956: 12)

This logic was reflected in the advocation by the RSS of a strong nuclearization policy for India (see Kendriya Karyakari Mandal resolution of October 1965 in Rashtriya Swayamsevak Sangh 1983: 47). It is similarly significant that the RSS Central Executive Committee referred to the conflict with China as a *dharma yuddha* (holy war) (Rashtriya Swayamsevak Sangh 1983: 32, 35).

The RSS and Gender

Hindu nationalist ideologies have from their inception been deeply gendered and obsessively focused on the imagined potency – or weakness – of the 'Hindu man'. Nevertheless, Hindutva women's organizations have also existed since at least the 1930s. The first formal affiliate of the RSS was its women's wing, the Rashtra Sevika Samiti, formed in October 1936 by Laxmi Kelkar (1905–78) (known as 'Mausiji') the first *pramukh sanchalika* of the Samiti (on the Samiti see Bacchetta 'Hindu Nationalist Women as Ideologues' in Jayawardena and Alwis 1996, Sarkar and Butalia 1995). The difference in the names of the Samiti and the RSS are instructive: 'rash*tra*sevika' connoting servant *to* the Hindu nation, whereas 'rashtr*iya* swayamsevak' signifying a volunteer server *of* the Hindu nation. The organization was subsequently headed by its second *sanchalika*, Saraswati Apte (known as 'Taiji'), whose husband was the Poona RSS *sanghchalak*, Vinayakrao Apte. Kelkar, who was born in Nagpur, formed the Samiti after discussions with Hedgewar, who wished the RSS to remain a strictly male organization and wanted to establish a formal, institutional distance between the two organizations. While attempting to present Kelkar as an anti-colonial freedom fighter, based on the evidence of her reading of *Kesari* (a Tilakite periodical), the Samiti's formation is described as resulting from Kelkar's view that:

> the defiance of law which was used to harass the foreign power, may take an unwarranted turn to lawlessness in free Bharat and may lead to chaos if not controlled sternly. Obtaining political freedom was a must, but a proper channel inspiring the people to devote themselves to social and national duties and to abide by the laws and rules of a free country was also utterly essential. Then only the long cherished ideal of Ramraj could be a reality. (Rashtra Sevika Samiti, not dated, chapter 2)

This acknowledgment that the non-cooperation and civil disobedience movements were problematic precisely because they would allegedly lead to an undisciplined Hindu society clearly characterized the RSS's different aims during the anti-colonial period. Tapan Basu et al. (1993) have also said that one of the founding myths for the formation of the Samiti was the harassment of Hindu women by Muslim *goondas* (thugs). However, of significance in the founding of the organization was the Samiti's concern that, during the 1930s:

> Due to western impact women were struggling for equal rights and economic freedom. This was leading to individual progress only, inviting self-centredness. There was every risk of women being non-committed to love, sacrifice, service and other inborn qualities glorifying Hindu women . . . Many women were attracted to the new easy going and showy way of western life. Forgetting their own self, they were fascinated by the idea of equal rights and economic freedom. This *unnatural* change in the attitude of women might have led to disintegration of family, the primary and most important unit for imparting good Sanskaras. This was worrying Laxmibai. (Rashtra Sevika Samiti, not dated, chapter 2, emphasis added)

The Samiti was explicitly formed in opposition to agitations for women's social and political equality, rights and economic independence, the latter contrasted with what it claimed were the natural qualities of Hindu women – devotion to and sacrifice for the Hindu family.

However, a modification of such views was also required if Hindu women were to participate in defence of Hindutva. The Samiti's founding ideology, like that of the RSS, was militant Hindutva. Similarly, its organizational structure, which included women's *shakhas*, was modelled on that of the RSS and, like the RSS, it was to build an all-India organization. However, the RSS's view of itself as a 'family' for its male members, and of its offshoot organizations as part of the RSS 'family', did not explicitly address gender relations. It is apparent that the key texts of the Hindu nationalist movement, from Savarkar's *Hindutva* through to Hedgewar's pronouncements and Golwalkar's tracts, celebrate only Hindu masculinity, especially in its distinctly violent forms, and ignore, virtually in their entirety, women and girls, personal and familial relationships.

Hence, the Samiti's function can be seen as the development of a distinctive Hindutva gender ideology within an overarching patriarchal configuration established by the RSS. The formal characteristic of Samiti gender ideology is a characteristic elision of any criticisms, duties or obligations of *Hindu* men and instead a dense and exclusive focus of the roles, duties, obligations and limitations of Hindu women regarding both the actual family and the 'greater family', namely the 'Hindu nation'. The Samiti's gender ideology commences with the patriarchal premise of *matruvat paradareshu* – that all women except one's wife are to be regarded as one's mothers. The significance of this statement is that both its subject and its intended object or addressee is male – woman is present only as a wife or mother. The Samiti's daily *shakha* prayer also stipulated the four stages of the life of a woman as 'daughter, sister, wife and mother'. The domicile is where a women's character, emotions, duties and aspirations are designed and moulded. Home is where the woman becomes happy, not in her own happiness, which the Samiti considers 'selfish', but by getting 'trained to seek happiness in the happiness of others'. The Samiti's ideology of domesticity focuses overwhelmingly on personal sacrifice, forbearance and sensitivity to the needs of others in the home.

It is significant that it is precisely in the section of the Samiti's discussion of *the home* that the following lines are present:

> Every home is like a fortress. Admitting or refusing entrance there is left to the sole discretion of the commander of the fortress. Similarly, the mistress of the house has to resolve what to patronise and what not thereby to keep away the evils. It is not enough not to be a party to evil acts. It is equally essential to encourage to do good things. Eradication of malpractices and promotion of morality requires a lot of strength, mental as well as physical. A Hindu woman has performed excellently in this respect by her forbearance, affection and dedication. It is quite natural to get wounded during a battle but it requires boldness, steadfastness, bravery and tenacity to sustain injuries. These qualities are to be acquired by a Hindu woman to deal efficiently with problems of all sorts. She must be bold enough to stand for what is right and condemn what is wrong, with reference to national interests. (Rashtra Sevika Samiti, not dated: chapter 5)

The allusions seem glaring. The Hindu man is granted absolute power over the home, the latter described using a military metaphor. However, there appears to be acknowledgement of the conspicuous potential for both his 'evil' and his violence, the responsibility for bearing with both resting with the woman; it is otherwise unclear in this context what other meanings the references to battles, wounding and injury have. They do not emerge anywhere else in the Samiti's elaboration of its ideology, even in the sections elaborating militant Hindutva.

The RSS's and Samiti's ideology of passive and all-sacrificing homemaking and motherhood is supplemented by its conceptualization of the Goddess, the latter symbolically identified with the sacralized topography of 'India' as Bharatmata (Motherland). This religious-territorial identification serves several encompassing functions in the Samiti's gender ideology that illustrates both its patriarchal nature and opens up the possibility of a more active and militant conception of Hindu womanhood. In Samiti ideology, the Motherland has given rise to her children, the Hindus, whom she loves selflessly and with unbounded affection, demanding nothing of them in return except their happiness and prosperity. According to the Samiti, 'the Motherland's' unqualified love for her children exists, despite her agony and suffering, the torment she has endured over centuries of 'foreign aggression' and 'mutilation' which persists in the separatist and fissiparous tendencies that exist today; yet 'the Motherland' endures, sacrificing herself for her Hindu children thinking of nothing else but their welfare, her forgiveness arising from her suffering.

While this is a stark mobilization of political affect in order to cultivate a religious-territorial nationalism, its key intention is to function as pedagogy for an idealized Hindu womanhood: if Bharatmata has suffered so much and so selflessly and for so long for her children, so should you. It should be noted that while the aggressor against the Motherland is 'the foreigner', the aggressor against the Hindu woman is not symbolized as such, indeed is not named. Here, there is an acknowledgement of and a legitimation for the suffering that Hindu women have to endure as a result of a patriarchal Hindu society that cannot, however, be so designated. The other function of the Motherland is its characterization as 'Durgadevi'. In the Samiti's ideology, the Goddess Durga is articulated as the strength of the Hindu woman in facing the (unarticulated) problems of her life. Suggestively, Durga is *not* simply symbolized as the power of the 'Hindu nation' facing aggression, but instead as the resilience the Hindu woman must cultivate to be strong in the face of adversities, to remain chaste, pure and virtuous, to serve and to sacrifice. While Durga in the contemporary period has acquired great importance in symbolizing the power and strength of the 'Hindu nation' against its putative 'enemies', this is not the exclusive way she is used.

The Samiti's ideology is not, however, completed by the Hindu woman's selfless sacrifice and suffering (Sarkar and Butalia ed. 1995, Agnes 1995, Banerjee 1995, Basu 1995, Bacchetta 1996). The Samiti's founding ideology of militant Hindutva, and its organizational form dedicated to 'character-building' have the aim of actively and militantly fighting for the Hindu nation and against those tendencies which are viewed as 'anti-national', 'separatist' or 'foreign'. For this task, Hindu women have to be trained 'physically, intellectually and mentally'. Hence, within the Hindutva ideal, Hindu women have a dual role that is not simply confined to motherhood and homemaking, because the greater 'family' in RSS ideology is fundamentally the nation.

> A Hindu woman is an eternal mother a symbol of love, sacrifice, dedication, fearlessness, sanctity and devotion. The tenderhearted woman becomes bold and aggressive if time demands. (Rashtra Sevika Samiti, not dated)

A Vision of Similitude in Action

The RSS's idealized vision of Hindu nation is of an organic, disciplined, integrated, ordered social formation based the consolidation of a strong, collective Hindu majoritarianism. Discipline and organization (*sangathan*) are at the core of RSS social and political philosophy. This reflects the technocratic and rationalizing sensibility of a mechanistically conceived natural science rather than any religious sensibilities (It is of interest that Hedgewar was medically trained and Golwalkar was a biologist, and that a significant number of Hindutva ideologues have backgrounds in physics, chemistry, engineering, mathematics, computing, medicine and other natural science disciplines.) In Hedgewar's and Golwalkar's philosophy, the RSS *was* 'the society' (*sangh*) against which the existing 'Hindu society' had to be measured, and that disclosed the latter's lack of discipline, disorder and disunity (*asangathan*). Consequently, the Indian social formation had to be recreated into the shape of the RSS: 'Right from its inception the Sangh has clearly marked out as its goal the moulding of the whole of society, and not merely any one part of it, into an organised entity' (Golwalkar 1966: 341).

Hence, the RSS disowns the actually existing social formation and the existing beliefs and practices of Hinduism as fundamentally deficient and defective in comparison with its own form of organization. Consequently, the RSS has emphasized slow, patient, long-term work in civil society, a method of political labour that is at variance with those traditionally employed by left movements. This work is literally the creation or moulding of a new Hindu man whose influence would cascade into the existing institutions of civil society, which would in turn become increasingly organized.

> The ultimate vision of our work, which has been the living inspiration for all our organizational efforts, is *a perfectly organised state of our society wherein each individual has been moulded into a model of ideal Hindu manhood and made into a living limb of the corporate personality of society.* (Golwalkar 1966: 61, emphasis added)

This functionalist, organicist and authoritarian conception of an ideal social order may be viewed as the 'utopian' vision of a movement that sought to entirely regulate the social formation. It is neither credible nor reflected in the tangible practices or histories of the RSS or its *swayamsevaks*. However, the salient point is that this vision was comprehensively different from, and had foundationally different concerns from, not just the national movement in the midst of anti-colonial struggle, but also virtually all other Hindu nationalist movements with which it was contemporaneous. This was a fundamental displacement of the discourses of Indian anti-imperialism and their distinctive themes of freedom, liberty, struggle, disobediance, obstruction, resistance, equality, diversity and independence for another narrative peculiarly and obsessively focused on the fetishization of discipline, order, obligation, organization, regulation, compliance, uniformity, obedience and hierarchy. It is not simply that the latter themes reflected precisely the British view of the qualities that Indians lacked, or the British desire for how subjugated Indians should have behaved. They signalled a novel project with aims that were radically distanced from those occupying the national movement. The RSS and its discourses of order and obedience emerged from an aversion and in precise opposition to the freedom movement's strategies of disruption and disobedience.

'Man Moulding' and the Shakha

The RSS method for 'creating' new Hindu men was the technique of organization, discipline and *shakha* apparently developed by Hedgewar and based on 'taking individual after individual and moulding him for an organized national life' (Golwalkar 1966: 332). This 'technique' of engineering Hindu bodies and personalities is disingenuously claimed to be inherently 'Hindu', the RSS asserting that it has 'eschewed [all] self-defeating alien types of organization' (Golwalkar 1966: 342). While both the RSS and some of its critics have described the *shakha* as falling within the Hindu (and Buddhist) *akhara* or gymnasium tradition, this view has also been rejected (Alter 1992: 261–3). There is nothing 'traditional' about the RSS's forms of organization and discipline, its 'man-moulding' mission or its mechanical-algorithmic view of the human personality. It is also at variance from Spencerian historical sociology. For Spencer, society was an organic 'growth', not a 'manufacture', whereas for the RSS, the 'society' has to be painstakingly fashioned anew through its *shakha* regime. Similarly, there is an epistemological rift between Golwalkar's rejection of all social contract approaches, and a belief in originary, fully formed nation having its unique 'national soul', and the irreducible, if hierarchical, 'social contract' at the core of the *shakha* method.

The RSS *shakha*, held for one hour every day, was described by Golwalkar thus:

There is an open playground. Under a saffron flag groups of youths and boys are absorbed in a variety of Bharatiya games. Resounding shouts of joyous enthusiasm often fill the air . . . The leader's whistle or order has a magical effect on them; there is instant perfect order and silence. Then exercises follow – wielding the *lathi*, Suryanamaskar, marching etc. The spirit of collective effort and spontaneous discipline pervades every programme. Then they sit down and sing in chorus songs charged with patriotism. Discussions follow. They delve deep into the problems affecting the national life. And finally, they stand in rows before the flag and recite the prayer: Many salutations to Thee, O loving Motherland! whose echoes fill the air and stir the soul. 'Bharat Mata ki jai' [Long Live the Motherland!] uttered in utmost earnest furnishes the finishing and inspiring touch to the entire programme. (Golwalkar 1966: 333–4)

Regular discipline and the training of 'mind, body and intellect' were seen by the RSS as necessary for ideological inculcation and 'character-building' so that the successful *swayamsevak*, after a lengthy and indeterminate period of *shakha*, was considered to have acquired the correct disposition, 'appearance' or 'face'. Golwalkar revealingly said:

It is a common experience that if a particular idea is repeated at a fixed hour regularly it goes deep into our being and becomes an inseparable part of our character. Hence the untiring stress on regularity and punctuality in the Sangh. (Golwalkar 1966: 347–8)

Despite the ancient, powerful call of the Hindu race, *swayamsevaks* nevertheless had to be ideologically indoctrinated *from childhood* into a Hindu identity that only the RSS considered appropriate. The function of adult men recruiting young boys, the organizational absence and distancing of women, the emphasis on the bodily aesthetics of physical and virile masculinity, and the valorization of affective and cosy brotherhood has undertones of concupiscence that cannot be discussed here. But they do require a fuller, careful and politically nuanced elaboration that does not recklessly reduce fascism to certain narratives of desire nor works against the political goals of India's progressive liberation movements against intense oppression and for social acceptance. However, the recruitment of young children, who are not fully socialized nor in possession of determined social or political worldviews, is emblematic of the RSS's careful strategy, the latter reliant on attracting and retaining children by combining enjoyment with responsibility, and amusements (games such as *kho kho* and *kabbadi*) with ideological inculcation of Hindutva (Sarkar 1996).

One key aspect of 'man-moulding' and 'character-building' in the *shakha* was to 'imprint' the correct *samskars* ('impressions' or the RSS world-view). Psychologists, according to Golwalkar, claimed three factors were essential to permanently 'imprint' ideas into minds, to 'fashion' new persons, to 'make men out of dust':

firstly, constant meditation of the ideal that is to be formed into a samskar; secondly constant company of persons devoted to the same ideal; and finally engaging the body in activities congenial to that ideal . . . (Golwalkar 1966: 350)

In the corporeal and somatic activities of the *shakha* aimed at making the modern Hindutva body, 'all the various apparently little things like games, wielding of lathi, singing, marching' had 'the potency of instilling deep *samskars*'. Golwalkar considered this as an urgent necessity since 'the bad habits and tendencies of centuries', especially indiscipline, could not be 'washed off in a single day'.

Golwalkar employed the metaphor of cellular destruction to describe the *shakha* regime. He claimed that in the human body, every cell not only feels its identity with the entire body, but more importantly is 'ever ready to sacrifice itself for the sake of the health and growth of the body.' This 'self-immolation' of millions of cells, he claimed, released the energy available to the human body. The cells in the human body were compared to RSS members. They had to undergo this process of self-annihilation and sacrifice for the *sangh*, and eventually, the Hindu society. Notwithstanding the biological inaccuracies, of which Golwalkar would have been aware, of significance is his rather hostile and dismissive characterization of the Hindu personality and body which had not achieved the requisite level of *sangh* training (though Golwalkar, like many RSS senior leaders, also barely, if ever, participated in *shakha*). The strong narrative, which also pervades contemporary RSS literature, is that ordinary Hindus were not 'men' but 'dust', undisciplined, riddled with 'bad' and disagreeable habits, effeminate, weak, unhealthy, possessing undeveloped personalities, lacking character, indolent, selfish, disorganized, and unreliable.

The strict training of the *shakha*, Golwalkar said, gave the individual 'the necessary incentive to rub away his angularities.' This included emotions that Golwalkar considered to be detrimental to the 'moulding' of character:

all our great authorities on mental discipline have ordained us not to succumb to overflow of emotions and weep in the name of God but to apply ourselves to a strict discipline of day-to-day penance. Effusion of emotions will only shatter the nerves and make the person weaker than before leaving him a moral wreck. It is just like a liquor-addict who is left imbecile after the effects of liquor subside. (Golwalkar 1966: 349)

This aversion to individual variation and diversity in the human personality is emblematic of the RSS's vanguardist project. The RSS's trope of 'character building' is occasionally considered by others as a positive benefit to the Hindu boys who are socialized into it. However, 'character building' is not a neutral description of socialization, and is certainly not preoccupied with civic citizenship-building. The RSS's view of what constitutes a desirable character is the 'imbibing' of the moral, cultural and spiritual *samskars* in the 'tradition of the highest human virtues that made the Hindu Nation the cultural and spiritual mother of the entire humanity for millennia' (Seshadri 1991: 10). The explicit qualities valorized as conducive to 'character building' include 'selflessness'; 'dedication to the social good'; 'highest life-values'; 'the values of the Nations Life-Force'; 'the noblest of social and spiritual urges'; 'selfless dedication to the national cause without expecting anything in return', as well as 'discipline'; 'chaste national ideals', 'obedience', 'confidence' and strength. These qualities can be interpreted either in the tradition of social service to Hindus or as the ideological formation of Hindu nationalist loyalties. Certainly, since 1989 the RSS has taken its social welfare (*seva*) work seriously. But these qualities also represent empty signifiers in the strictest sense and which are practically filled with the content of the RSS's ideology of organization and commitment to Hindutva.

For an ostensibly ethical character formation process, they do not address the central imperative for any ethical system – one's ethical obligation to the person who is radically disaffiliated from oneself or one's beliefs. The radically other emerges consistently as an enemy, traitor, or 'the fallen' of Hinduism who has to be reclaimed. One can contrast this with other ethical systems within or outside Hinduism, including Gandhian ethics, which are predicated on an *existential obligation* to the other, based firmly on an avowal of the existence of radical alterity, diversity and difference in the human condition. The RSS's moral and ethical system does recognize alterity, but fundamentally through a compulsion premised on the erasure of difference in favour of vanguardist unanimism. Even where the RSS may rhetorically claim to celebrate diversity within Hinduism (though only in Hinduism, Islam and Christianity never accorded their full, complex and diverse histories or philosophies), the latter is both couched in the rhetoric of the variety of paths to God-realization and underpinned by the overarching RSS need to organize the whole of Hindu society in its image of sameness and homogeneity.

The ideological loathing of individualism was also manifested in Golwalkar's views about what he believed to be the destructive nature of sexuality, effeminacy and 'unmanliness' and the consequent need to suppress them.

> The 'modern fashion' of young men is to appear more and more feminine. In dress, in habits, in literature and in every aspect of our day-to-day life 'modernism' has come to mean effeminacy. 'Sex' has become the one dominating theme of all our 'modern' literature. History of countries the world over has time and time again shown that sex-dominated literature has been an unfailing precursor to the ruin of nations and civilizations. (Golwalkar 1966: 230)

There is an important divergence here between the individuality of emotional being that Golwalkar said had to be suppressed and the intense emotional, one is tempted to say libidinal, passion that needed to be 'roused' for the goal of creating the 'Hindu nation'. Golwalkar argued that in repressing their sexual and emotional being, the *swayamsevaks* behave in the spirit of oneness with their brethren 'and fall in line with the organised and disciplined way of life. Discipline enters their blood.' During Golwalkar's leadership, *pracharaks* were indeed expected to remain celibate and unmarried. Golwalkar was indifferent to the loss of individuality among the *swayamsevaks*, and was scornful towards detractors who made this criticism, in a manner that perhaps only confirmed their anxieties about the RSS:

> [A] gentleman charged the Sangh as being 'fascist' because according to him all persons in the Sangh from Kashmir to Kanyakumari whether aged or in their teens gave the same kind of reply to a question, which indicated there was no freedom of thought in the Sangh! . . . It is natural that the persons in the Sangh imbued with the correct national perspective react spontaneously to the various national problems that arise from time to time in the same manner. To mistake it for mental regimentation is to call the spirit of nationalism itself as an instrument of regimentation! It is the undigested modern ideas like 'freedom of thought', 'freedom of speech' etc., that are playing havoc in the minds of our young men who look upon freedom as licence and self-restraint as mental regimentation! (Golwalkar 1966: 355–6)

After Independence

The RSS achieved a degree of respect among some Hindus, including some senior members of Congress and members of the Indian Liberal Federation, for the work it undertook among Hindu refugees, mainly in Punjab, during the Partition period. However, the RSS and its *shakhas* were banned by the Indian government following Gandhi's assassination in 1948 and the RSS, like the Mahasabha, was to face the wrath of Indians in the form of attacks on its members, *shakhas*, offices and properties throughout India. The RSS reported that some 20,000 of its members were imprisoned for various periods during this time. Golwalkar was detained (under the allegation that he had been involved in the conspiracy to murder M. K. Gandhi) first for six months from early February until his conditional release in early August 1948. He was again detained towards the end of 1948 for breaking the conditions of his release. The government initially attempted to get the RSS disbanded. However, following what the RSS called its *satyagraha* (the holding of *shakhas* in contravention of the ban) the strictures against the RSS were lifted and Golwalkar was released, although the organization remained banned for a period. Mainly through negotiations between government Home Minister Vallabhbhai Patel, the RSS was required to have a written Constitution that committed it to internal democratic procedures, especially in the nomination and selection of its leader; recruited only adults (those aged over 18); renounced violence; accepted the constitution of India and the Indian flag; and accepted India as a secular state, among other stipulations. It is alleged that Patel also urged the RSS to join Congress and work towards the development of its organizational base (Andersen and Damle 1987: 53). The RSS only partially or ambiguously accepted some of these conditions, rejecting entirely the ones related to democratic procedures in the selection of *sarsanghchalak*, recruitment of pre-adolescents, and acceptance of India's constitution (see Appendix in Golwalkar 1958).

In the crucial stipulations relating to India's democratic and secular nature and the renunciation of the concept of a Hindu state, the ambiguities in Golwalkar's response to Patel were significant. He argued that 'To a Hindu, the State is and has always been secular' (see also RSS resolution, October 1961 in Rashtriya Swayamsevak Sangh 1983: 26) Golwalkar fashioned an equivalence between 'secularism' and his view that Hinduism had tolerated a wide range of Hindu religious beliefs and sects. This is also the basis of a dominant, although not exclusive, contemporary Hindutva ruse that Hinduism cannot be other than inherently 'secular'. Of considerable interest is that Golwalkar highlighted the eventually non-violent and Buddhist Ashoka empire together with the Mughal states as examples of theocracy and departures from Hindu secularism, whereas the Mahratta confederacy 'founded a secular state in conformity with Hindu heritage' (Golwalkar 1958: 79). Similarly, Golwalkar argued that 'The RSS does not advocate a Hindu Raj *to the exclusion* of non-Hindu citizens of the country' (Golwalkar 1958: 79–80, emphasis added). Golwalkar said that an exclusive Hindu state that denied citizenship to minorities was 'a phantasm created by over-strained nerves and too lively a imagination, deserving only to be ignored as not worthy of consideration' (Golwalkar 1958: 80). However, Golwalkar did not abandon the concept of Hindu rashtra, but had seemingly only modified his earlier more aggressive views on the citizenship status of non-Hindus.

The RSS was nevertheless unconditionally unbanned on 11 July 1949 and Golwalkar immediately stated both in July and August that the RSS had given up 'nothing' of its original principles and had made no compromises with the government (Golwalkar 1958: 101). Aside from vehemently reiterating this point two decades later in a conference with newspaper editors and journalists, Golwalkar also elaborated on his views of India's Muslims and how they were to live in post-Independence India. Indian Muslims, he said, 'think separately, act separately and plan separately. It is the Muslim who thinks that non-Muslims will go to hell.' Similarly, 'the Muslim does not look upon partition as a final solution. He regards it only as a step forward.' We must, he said, make Hindusthan one by consolidating only the Hindus. The latter he claimed can only ever be 'secular'. Hence, for 'genuine secularism', Muslims must be taught to revere the 'Hindu nation' and its Gods as their heroes. In response to an editor's question about whether Muslims should be so taught by 'beating them', Golwalkar stated:

Beating is of two kinds. A mother beating her child and an enemy striking a man. We have not done any beating. But if and when we do teach by beating, it will be like the mother's out of love and solicitude for the child's welfare. (Golwalkar 1970: 26)

Golwalkar put forward several disingenuous equivalences in the 1970s which are very much the ideological planks of contemporary Hindutva: that a state that embodied Hindu religion or a 'Hindu cultural ethos' is inherently 'secular'; that Hindu numerical majoritarianism was equivalent to both 'secularism' and 'democracy'; that Indian Muslims (and Christians and leftists) were internal enemies determined to destroy the integrity of the Hindu nation; and that Indian Muslims had the permanent burden, under a barely veiled threat, of demonstrating their 'love', loyalty and obeisance to the 'Hindu nation' by, in essence, giving up their religious beliefs, affiliations and identities.

However, a democratic ideal necessarily means that, in principle, there cannot exist a permanent or fixed constituency of the 'majority' or its view, or the possibility of the enshrinement of the latter in the state. A permanent majority or view is exactly contrary to the ideal of democracy. Democracy also necessarily implies that a minority view, including what one might conceive as a 'Muslim' or 'Christian' minority view, has the determinate possibility of emergence as a dominant but impermanent elected power. Conversely, a democratically pluralist ideal cannot be predicated on the protection of (the rights of) a 'religious majority'; but it is foundationally based on the protection of the civil and citizenship rights of cultural, ethnic and religious minorities. Similarly, notwithstanding the perverse rendition of 'love' by Savarkar and Golwalkar, democratic rights cannot be conditional upon whatever is meant by 'love' for a majoritarian ideology or, indeed, for a nation. None of these conditions for democracy can *in principle* be satisfied by the Hindu majoritarian views expounded by Savarkar or Golwalkar. The claim that Hindutva guarantees democracy is simply duplicitous.

The experience of the Partition of India, the impact of the ban on RSS members and organizers, as well as the status of the RSS in the Nehruvian period as an organization that was reviled by most other political parties, the press and within popular sentiment was to be significant. There is a curious episode, now part of RSS organizational mythology, in which the RSS believed that, during the immediate period leading up to Independence, it had foiled a coup attempt orchestrated by the Muslim League in Delhi which had the intention of killing all the Hindu members of government and seizing India for Pakistan. The RSS claimed to have warned Nehru and Patel of it 'in the nick of time' and foiled the plot (Golwalkar 1958: 106). This indicated how the RSS viewed its own importance, but was quite unprepared for and had misread both Independence and Partition; it also could not believe or accept the nation-wide ignominy it faced after Independence.

The RSS had important individual supporters within government, such as Shyamaprasad Mookherjee, who became a minister in Nehru's Cabinet, as well as from sections of Congress, but its ideological stance and peculiar form of organization and discipline was not amenable to the project of Nehruvian nation-building in the 1950s. However, an indication of its post-Independence political role was intimated in a letter written by Golwalkar in September 1948 to Nehru pleading for the ban on the organization to be revoked. Golwalkar argued that:

> During this period the RSS having been disbanded the intelligent youth are rapidly falling into the snares of Communism. With the alarming happenings in Burma, Indo-China, Java and other neighbouring states, we can envisage the nature of the menace. The one effective check of the RSS no longer exists. The Communists had always considered the RSS as their main obstacle . . . News of their progress is alarming. ('Letter to Nehru', 24 September 1948 in Golwalkar 1958: 8–9)

Golwalkar attempted to convince Nehru both that the RSS was a non-political, cultural organization and that it had a crucial, nation-saving and explicitly political role in preventing Hindu youths from affiliating with India's legal communist parties. Despite his earlier valorization of fascism and Nazism, Golwalkar nevertheless considered communism to be 'foreign', 'anti-national' and on a par with what he considered to be the 'anti-national' designs of Muslims and Christians. This vigorous anti-communism was a key component of RSS ideology in the post-independence period.

It has been argued that the experience of the year-and-a-half ban during 1948–9 resulted in an important internal change in the RSS, reflected in the tension between the leadership and the regional *pracharaks* and cadres who had acquired a degree of political autonomy, and a desire among sections of the cadre and leadership for an explicitly political, rather than simply 'character-building' orientation for the organization (Andersen and Damle 1987: 110). (The constitutional model for the regional and national structure adopted by the RSS was broadly based on that of Congress, but was to evolve its own distinctive style.) The organizational and ideological tensions between and within the cadre and leadership are paramount in considering the evolution of RSS strategy in the post-Independence period. While the formation of various offshoot organizations can be characterized as responses to such tensions, of importance has been the divergence of goals and accompanying strategy within the RSS and its *parivar* organizations. The RSS's first ever written constitution had stated that 'the Sangh, *as such*, has no politics and is devoted purely to cultural work'. The qualification was to prove to be as misleading as it was significant in the coming decades.

-6-

The Sangh Parivar in Politics

The BJP is committed to the concept of 'One Nation, One People and One Culture' . . . Our nationalist vision is not merely bound by the geographical or political identity of Bharat but is referred by our timeless cultural heritage. This cultural heritage which is central to all regions, religions and languages, is a civilizational identity and constitutes the cultural nationalism of India which is the core of Hindutva. This we believe is the identity of our ancient nation 'Bharatvarsha' . . . The evolution of Hindutva in politics is the antidote to the creation of vote banks and appeasement of sectional interests. Hindutva means justice for all. (Bharatiya Janata Party 1998)

We are committed to establishing a civilised, humane and just civil order that which does not discriminate on grounds of caste, religion, class, colour, race or sex. We will truly and genuinely uphold and practise the concept of secularism consistent with the Indian tradition of [equal respect for all faiths] and on the basis of equality for all. We are committed to the economic, social and educational development of the minorities and will take effective steps in this regard. (*For a Proud, Prosperous India*, [the BJP-led] National Democratic Alliance Manifesto 1999)

Introduction

Within barely four years after Independence, RSS officers and cadres were instrumental in organizationally creating and occupying key political positions in the Bharatiya Jana Sangh (BJS) political party initiated by Shyamaprasad Mookherjee and launched in 1951. In the period from 1949–1965, the RSS launched several national organizations, including the BJS and the Vishwa Hindu Parishad (VHP, World Hindu Council). This process accelerated after the late 1970s as new organizations and projects belonging to the RSS 'family' (*sangh parivar*) proliferated at national and local (state) levels. During the 1980s and 1990s, there was a massive expansion of the *parivar* into an extraordinarily wide range of fields (*kshetra*), reflecting a sociologically differentiated strategy of political labour in the party political process, civil society, social movements, and latterly the institutions of the national and local state. The RSS front organizations, while relatively autonomous, share the RSS's core ideology, and their existence emphasizes the wide-ranging transformations in the political cultures of Indian civil society that the RSS wishes to induce and manage. The RSS ostensibly retains a strong distinction between its *parivar* (family) and other organizations that the *parivar* may undertake joint projects with or help establish. However, in recent years, the ideological distinctions between some non-RSS organizations and members of the *parivar* (especially the Vishwa Hindu Parishad) have diminished. Conversely, several of the RSS's offshoot organizations, in particular the Bharatiya Janata Party (BJP) and the VHP, have exhibited significant distance from the core RSS ideological and organizational backbone. For example, the orientation of the BJP to national economic liberalization and to economic and technological globalization can be seen as a dramatic movement away from the parochial religious concerns of the VHP and the broadly protectionist *swadeshi* orientation of the RSS. Similarly, the vast number of projects that the VHP has initiated across India and internationally, while affiliated to the Hindutva ideology of the RSS, demonstrate the emergence of a new Hindutva social and political movement in its own right, separate from and differently organized from RSS, and capable of unleashing both a sophisticated, branded 'Hinduism' for popular consumption and ferocious violence against minority groups.

A culturally and politically aggressive Hindutva can be seen as both a product of and a response to the new period of global capitalism characterized by the collapse of communism, the proliferation of general and niche consumption economies, information technology, deregulated, globalized and unevenly contiguous economies, and a global cultural hegemony centred on the West. Hindutva represents an amalgamation of the archaic and the obscurantist with the high-tech and the late modern, reflecting the innovatory and modernizing characteristics of cultural nationalism. Under its slogan of 'Resurgent India' the BJP can certainly *rhetorically* suture the Vedas and Ramjanmabhoomi with a thrusting vision of an informatics revolution, the Internet, deregulation and economic liberalization, foreign investment and globalization, all guaranteed by a militarily strong, nuclear India. Conversely, and not least because of its parochial political sociology of a hermetic Hindu nation-state and civil society, the RSS remains, in the main, deeply suspicious of globalization, especially its cultural impact, although with additional concern for the economic competitiveness of north Indian middle classes, small businesses and urban and rural industries. It is therefore unclear how the different organizational strands and ideological configurations of new Hindutva in an unprecedented period of 'globalization' can hold together in a unitary way, though since the mid-1990s what has been apparent is how rapidly, if differentially, Hindutva strands have proliferated at state and local, and at national and international levels.

Precursors: the Bharatiya Jana Sangh

In the aftermath of Independence and the period of its banning during 1948 and 1949, the senior leaders of the RSS conducted several re-evaluations of its relationship to the formal party politics that it had often disowned as detracting from its main mission of 'character-building' for the 'Hindu nation'. Several senior RSS *pracharaks*, who had established a degree of regional and national organizational independence during the ban, argued for the RSS to acquire a direct role in the political environment of the Lok Sabha, which, at the time was dominated by Nehru's Congress but also included Communist, Socialist and Hindu Mahasabha deputies as representatives (Baxter 1971: 55). Aside from the Mahasabha, which had withered in the intervening period, the RSS considered each of the other main parties as vigorously opposed to its Hindu nationalist aims; conversely, the RSS was strongly attacked by Nehru, Congress, and the left parties. Key proponents of an increasingly political orientation for the RSS included Balraj Madhok, Dadarao Paramarth, Vasantrao Oke and Keval R. Malkani.

Golwalkar opposed the transformation of the RSS into a political party, but apparently considered the involvement of RSS *pracharaks* in the formal political process as both problematic and politically expedient. This particular orientation of Golwalkar's is difficult to explain. It has often been argued that Golwalkar had to agree to the political participation in an individual capacity of senior RSS members in order to offset organizational and ideological tensions among sections of the senior RSS leadership while also retaining his different 'non-political' vision of the RSS (Jaffrelot 1996). However, Golwalkar's evasive orientation regarding the political involvement of RSS *pracharaks* and his decision to loan RSS workers for Jana Sangh activities shoud be noted (Golwalkar 1970). Of additional relevance are two related issues: whether Hindu nationalist ideology proffered a coherent theory of political power, and whether the substantive content of Hindu nationalist ideology betrayed a considerable intellectual paucity from which no philosophical or transcendental vision, let alone a political theory of government, governance and administration, could be realized. With some exceptions noted below, Hindu nationalism has, perhaps until recently, been unable to articulate a coherent theory of political power or 'Hindu government' which moves beyond an eclectic melange of militant religious-nationalist symbolism and an inexperienced politics of expediency and pragmatism.

From a broader perspective, other factors also seem important in explaining the RSS's entry into politics. The decline of the Mahasabha (and Savarkar's unpopularity) during the 1940s had created a political vacuum for Hindu communalist tendencies during a critical period when Nehruvianism represented not just a non-communal orientation but one determined to 'secularize' the Indian state and make India's post-Partition Muslim minorities feel secure and integrated into Indian civil society. The 1950s represented a period of secular nation building and an attempt to forge a nationalist ideology reliant on the memory of the anti-colonial struggle and leaning towards distinctly programmatic, socialist directions. It has been argued that during this formative period, Nehruvianism failed to instigate a nationwide, deep-seated cultural policy that supplemented, and hegemonically articulated, its vision of secular nationalism for Hindus, Muslims and other groups (Rajagopal 1996). A cultural politics of secularism was hence radically underdeveloped. The importance of cultural politics in civil society, seen from a Nehruvian perspective as potentially capable of stirring Hindu communal interests, was elided in favour of a belief that a strong secularism of a federal state and an 'equal', benevolent orientation to India's religious traditions would suffice. In Nehru, one can perhaps see an attempt at merging a federated civic nationalism with a hesitant religious pluralism under a broader framework of planned, democratic, 'secular', socialist governance. What the ideological inculcation from the centre of an Indian nationalism reliant on anti-colonialism could have meant for the plurality of Indian civil societies that were not simply suffused with religious sentiment but deeply organized through divergent religious affiliations, was therefore unclear. Of importance were not Nehruvian techniques of governance, but the elision of the public and private institutions of a potentially differentiable civil society in the making, and of the alternative communitarian, religious-public spheres that were arising from the latter.

During the 1950s, the institutionalization of the political power of nationalist elites was also underway, the latter process both reflecting as well as creating new centres of regional and national Congress power during a period of invigorated nationalism building. Congress foreign policy leaned towards, and later allied itself with the communist Soviet Union. Conversely, the US had forged links with Pakistan, its main anti-communist ally in south Asia during the Cold War period. Nehru also referred the settlement of the Kashmir issue to the United Nations, whereas Hindu nationalists demanded its immediate occupation, the expulsion of Pakistani forces (and Muslims), and the integration of Kashmir with India. Later border clashes with China and Pakistan (in the early and mid-1960s respectively), combined with what was seen by Hindu nationalists as Nehruvian foreign policy based on amicable settlement rather than war, fuelled Hindu nationalist visions of post-Independence India, their new 'Hindu Rashtra', as under military threat; hence their calls for the aggressive militarization, including the nuclearization of India. The various sweeping social and political changes in the Nehruvian period, reflecting the heyday of Indian nationalism and social reform, were each characteristically grating for Hindu nationalist sensibilities. In this respect, some form of Hindu nationalist political emergence can be seen as inevitable, though not necessarily pre-given in form or content, especially after the death of Nehru in 1964.

During the period of the RSS ban, Golwalkar had indicated strongly to Nehru the potential 'non-political' role of the RSS in forming a bulwark against communist influence among India's youth. This was to be a central ideological plank during the initial stages of the formation of the Bharatiya Jana Sangh (on the Jana Sangh, see Jhangiani 1967, Baxter 1971, Puri 1980, Graham 1993, Jaffrelot 1996; the latter sources have been drawn on below). In his 'programme for a new political party', formulated in 1950 by RSS activist, K. R. Malkani, the RSS's political role was pitted against the threat of communism to India, a threat that could only be countered by Hindus through the mobilization of Hindutva (Baxter 1971: 60). The early discussions within RSS *pracharak* networks about the basis for a new political party were to dovetail into attempts by Shyamaprasad Mookherjee to establish initially a regional and then a national political platform outside and in opposition to the ruling Congress Party (Baxter 1971).

Mookherjee had been president of the Hindu Mahasabha (after Savarkar) but was given a Cabinet post as Minister of Industries and Supplies in Nehru's government. However, he resigned his Cabinet position following the agreement between Liaquat Ali (Pakistan's Prime Minister) and Nehru regarding procedures for addressing the grievances of minorities and provisions for the return of refugees to their respective countries. The 'Liaquat-Nehru pact' stipulated that neither country could make 'extraterritorial claims' on behalf of minorities in the other country. Mookherjee viewed this as a betrayal of the Hindus of East Bengal, many of whom had arrived in India claiming persecution by the Muslim majority. Nehru's granting of limited autonomy to Kashmir was similarly opposed by Mookherjee. In the following year, while senior RSS activists were creating Jana Sangh political groupings in various regional centres, Mookherjee, although supporting the latter, launched first his own 'People's Party', centred in Bengal, and subsequently (in 1952) the National Democratic Party, aimed as a federation of various smaller parties. In October 1951, Mookherjee was elected president of the Bharatiya Jana Sangh at its founding convention held in Delhi, which launched it as a national party (Baxter 1971: 77). The general secretary of the Bharatiya Jana Sangh was Deendayal Upadhyaya, an RSS pracharak (depicted as an 'ideal swayamsevak') whose ideology of 'integralism' and 'Integral Humanism' became considerably influential within the RSS, the Jana Sangh and, later, the Bharatiya Janata Party. The Jana Sangh contested the 1951–2 elections and secured just over three per cent of the votes for the Lok Sabha and 2.76 percent of the votes in the state legislative elections. This was to rise to almost 9.5 per cent by the 1967 general elections, and almost 9 per cent in the state legislative elections. However, it was not until the critical period of the mid-to-late-1970s that the Jana Sangh emerged as a major national political force, nor can one understand the emergence and the political direction of the BJP without consideration of the political experience gained by the Jana Sangh and the RSS during and in the aftermath of Indira Gandhi's Emergency period (Puri 1980).

From its inception, the Jana Sangh advocated its fundamental principle of 'one nation, one culture, one people', a political sentiment that continues to be strongly articulated by the contemporary BJP. The Jana Sangh mobilized this view both in opposition to the partition of India, which it believed should be 're-united', and in its vision of post-Independence nationalism, the latter based on the consolidation of 'Bharat' through *sanskriti* culture and *maryada* ('political rectitude', or 'righteousness' as conceived in Hindu tradition). Similarly, the Jana Sangh opposed the idea that India constituted a composite nationality, the latter conceived as a policy of 'appeasement' or 'special treatment' of India's religious or regional minorities (Graham 1993: 50). Consequently, the Jana Sangh robustly opposed Nehruvian secularism, the latter seen as equivalent to a policy of 'appeasement' of Indian Muslims. The application of the war metaphor of 'appeasement' to describe both Nehruvian foreign policy towards Pakistan and domestic secular policy towards India's Muslims is instructive and continues to resonate in both senses today. The Jana Sangh initially conceived of post-Independence India as 'Bharatiya Rashtra' (or 'Indian nation', as conceived in Hindu usage.) This was to change to 'Hindu Rashtra' in 1956, the Jana Sangh claiming that the two were equivalent and coextensive with 'Indian' nationalism (Baxter 1971: 133).

Upadhyaya's 'Integral Humanism'

From 1947 until the late 1950s, Deendayal Upadhyaya, an RSS *pracharak* and general secretary of the Bharatiya Jana Sangh had published articles in RSS periodicals on the medieval Indian *advaita* theologian, Shankaracharya, and on Tilak's and Dayananda's political philosophies (on Upadhyaya, see Baxter 1971, Deodhar 1991, Jog 1991, Upadhyaya 1992; on 'Integral Humanism', see Golwalkar, Upadhyaya and Thengadi 1991, Nene 1991, Thengadi 1991, Bhishikar 1991, Kelkar 1991, Kulkarni 1991). From these writings, he developed a political ideology of 'Integral Humanism', which he expounded in four lectures in April 1965 (Golwalkar, Upadhyaya and Thengadi 1991). 'Integral Humanism' was accepted as central to the new political philosophy, principles and policies of the Jana Sangh from January 1965, and was formulated in direct opposition to Nehruvian, Marxist, communist, capitalist free enterprise and possessive indiv-idualist political philosophies (Kelkar 1991). 'Integral Humanism' was also based on a rejection of large-scale technology and mechanized industrial development, as well as Western economic and cultural 'imperialism' (Nene 1991). In its vision of 'Bharatiya nationalism', Upadhyaya rejected (as had Golwalkar) all social contract theories as erroneous 'western' impositions.

Upadhyaya claimed that 'Integral Humanism' followed the tradition of *advaita* ('non-dualism' or spiritual 'monism') developed by Sankara. Upadhyaya's conception of *advaita* was important less for its theological veracity than the purpose for which it was used by him. 'Non-dualism' represented the unifying principle (*ekatmata*) of every object in the universe, and of which humankind was a part. This, claimed Upadhyaya, was the essence and unique contribution of 'Bharatiya culture'. Leaving aside his simplification of *advaita* and his dismissal of the diversity of Indian philosophical traditions that owed to (what are called) 'dualist' and 'non-dualist' philosophies, or to neither, of importance was his strongly rationalist rendering of the relation between 'Man', 'Society' and 'Universe'.

Humankind, according to Upadhyaya, had four hierarchically organized attributes of body, mind, intellect and soul. These corresponded to four universal objectives, *kama* (desire or satisfaction), *artha* (wealth), *dharma* (moral duties under 'natural law') and *moksha* (total liberation or 'salvation'). These objectives were also hierarchically valorized: while none could be neglected, *dharma* was the 'basic', and *moksha* the 'ultimate' objective of humankind and society. For Upadhyaya, the problem with both capitalist and socialist (including welfare statist) ideologies was that they only considered the needs of body and mind, and were hence based on the materialist objectives of desire and wealth. An ideal social system would take into account, and balance, all four of 'Man's needs' while simultaneously realizing the four universal objectives. The principle of *ekatmata* also meant that an individual existed only in so far as he or she was social. Upadhyaya hence rejected social systems in which individualism 'reigned supreme', the latter leading, he claimed, to selfish self-centeredness. Conversely, however, he also rejected sociologies (such as communism) in which individualism was 'crushed' as part of a 'large heartless machine'.

Society, according to Upadhyaya, also had these four needs and had to accomplish the four objectives if perfect order and happiness was to be achieved. Society, rather than arising from a social contract between individuals, was fully born at its inception as a natural living organism with a definitive 'national soul' or 'ethos' (*chiti*), as well as the 'unified fighting strength' (*virat*) that 'accompanied' and 'protected' the 'national soul'. The needs of the social organism paralleled those of the individual. These needs were, according to Upadhyaya, the *dharma*, *artha*, *kama* and *moksha* of society.

It was at this point that the nation idea emerged in Upadhyaya's philosophy. *Dharma* for Upadhyaya was neither religion nor any particular sect or path towards God. Instead the *dharma* of society was 'innate law', 'that which sustains, which upholds' the subjects of a society (Golwalkar, Upadhyaya and Thengadi 1991: 48). This included 'natural tendencies', rules and regulations, sanctions and liberties that allowed for the smooth, harmonious functioning of a society comprised of different individuals and groups having different dispositions and at 'different stages of development'. Under the 'unifying principle', *dharma* imparted mutual understanding and cooperation between these various sectors, nurtured the citizens of a society and instilled cooperation while avoiding conflicts and 'perversions'.

Upadhyaya considered the power of *dharma* as best exemplified in the ideal of the family. He claimed it was in the family that *dharma* infused a feeling of belonging and love. Similarly, the power of *dharma* was reflected in society through a deep love and affinity for the motherland, its common history, culture, traditions, values and ideals. The direction and form of *dharma*, he argued, could be read through the *emotions* that were evoked by the ideas of Akhand Bharat and Hindu Rashtra. Social *dharma* (*samashti dharma*) also implied that India as a constitutional federation (union) of states was in opposition to *dharma*. *Dharma* meant an 'undivided India', or 'Akhand Bharat' in which Pakistan 'realizing its mistake' would reunite with India. Similarly, the constitutional separation of states in the Indian Union would have to be negated under a national unity in line with the aspirations of the 'national soul' or 'ethos' (Nene 1991, Golwalkar, Upadhyaya and Thengadi 1991).

In Upadhyaya's rather derivative and mechanically holistic 'third way' philosophy, there is also the continuation of a strand of 'religious' nationalism (similar to Ernest Renan's nineteenth century proclamation of 'national soul') that travelled from Aurobindo and Savarkar, and into Golwalkar's writings. Upadhyaya's '*dharma*' was in all its essential aspects nationalism, though it should be noted that at its core is the idea of 'Man'. Upadhyaya's assertion that his '*dharma*' was based on Hindu precepts is highly problematic. Leaving aside the caste and gender supremacist strictures of *varnashramadharma* or *stri-dharma*, for solemn devotees, the *dharma* within Hindu metaphysics is nothing less than the universal arrangement of the cosmos (!), whereas for Upadhyaya *dharma* is redacted to the soul (*chiti*) of the densely parochial Hindu Rashtra. This also reflects the unsophisticated curtailment, diminishing and simplification of Hinduism and Buddhism in Hindu nationalism. Upadhyaya's 'integralism' was an elementary reduction, legitimised through *advaitin* language, of the totality of Hinduism and the diversity of its philosophies and beliefs into a *materialist* concern with 'man', 'society' and exclusive nationalism. Religious commitment becomes a matter of nationalist affiliation (or conversely, nationalism becomes the sole measurement for religious commitment). *Dharma* is arguably productive for Hindu metaphysics because it is an empty transcendental signified. In Upadhyaya's philosophy, it was instead filled with material, temporal concerns of land and nation.

For Upadhyaya, the *artha* of society similarly had to reflect its 'Bharatiya' economic ethos. This meant rejecting Western mass industrial and technological development, unbridled free enterprise, Nehruvian state planning, and welfarism, the latter promoting 'parasites' on society (Nene 1991: 59). Instead an 'integrated' economic approach was to be promoted:

> based on our cultural tradition, social values and material needs. Blind adoption of foreign technique will neither solve our problems nor will it help in creating a self-reliant and

self-sufficient economic system. Jana Sangh would recognise family as being the basis of production-system and would try and decentralise the system. While every effort will be made to maximise the production, provision shall also be made for a fair distribution of production as well as property. (Kelkar 1991: 112)

It is difficult to ascertain what Upadhyaya's and the Jana Sangh's *swadeshi* and 'decentralization' approach would have meant in practice. Upadhyaya put forward several principles for an economic policy that was suited to 'our national genius' and which included: production that would both guarantee a minimum standard of living for every individual, and military defence of the nation; increasing the minimum standard of living so that 'the individual and the nation acquire the means to contribute to the world progress on the basis of their own *Chiti*'; meaningful employment to each individual while avoiding 'extravagance in utilising natural resources'; and development of 'Bharatiya Technology'. National or private ownership of the means of industrial production would be decided on a pragmatic basis. Moreover, the 'Bharatiya' economic system 'must protect cultural and other values of life' – not doing so would risk 'great peril' (Golwalkar, Upadhyaya and Thengadi 1991: 69–71). While much of this was already completed in a far-reaching Nehruvian economic policy, the distinctiveness of the Jana Sangh's economic doctrine was its reactiveness to Nehruvianism, rather than the creation of a concrete and viable national policy of its own. Hence, the Jana Sangh opposed 'command' forms of state planning, cooperative farming and associated land reforms, and generally aimed to protect the economic interests of the rural and urban middle classes.

The neo-romantic thrust of Upadhyaya's philosophy was reflected in his conception of the *kama* and the *moksha* of society. Both arose from and were completed within *dharma*. Central to his conception of state was an idea already encountered in Golwalkar's philosophy. This was like a 'Herderian' conception in which absolute ontological priority was placed on the social formation in accordance with its 'national soul' and inherent cultural attributes, rather than the state. The state was conceived as subsidiary to and an overseer of the 'nation's soul' in accordance with the principle of *Rashtra-dharma* ('the innate law of nationalism'). However, in Upadhyaya's view, the state could not assume authority or powers over the people in contravention of '*dharma*'. In such cases, the people, in so far as they acted in accordance with '*dharma*', had an obligation to oppose the state. He argued that a well-organized society with an 'awakened *chiti*' and organized resistance and power (*virat*) would not tolerate an 'unnatural' government acting against the direction of *dharma*.

While Upadhyaya's philosophy employed a modernist conception of 'the people', he did not privilege the majority will of the people. He argued that *dharma* could not be guaranteed simply by the resolve, motivation or desires of the mass of people:

Of the 450 million people of India, even if 449,999,999 opt for something which is against *Dharma*, this does not become truth. One the other hand, even if one person stands for something which is according to *Dharma*, that constitutes truth because truth resides in *Dharma*. It is the duty of this one person that he tread the path of truth and change people. It is from this basis that a person derives the right to proceed according to *Dharma*. Let us understand very clearly that *Dharma* is not necessarily with the majority or with the people. *Dharma* is eternal. Therefore, it is not enough to say, while defining democracy, that it is the government of the people. It has to be a government for the good of the people. What constitutes the good of the people? It is *Dharma* alone which can decide. Therefore, a democratic government, *Jana Rajya*, must also be rooted in *Dharma*, i.e. must be a *Dharma-Rajya* . . . the true democracy is only where there is freedom as well as *Dharma*. *Dharma-Rajya* encompasses all these concepts. (Golwalkar, Upadhyaya and Thengadi 1991: 54)

Upadhyaya's drastically circular and tautological argument contained a revealing vagueness regarding democracy. While the Jana Sangh was formally committed to democracy, it is precisely in these words of Upadhyaya that many of the ambiguities and problems of what can be termed 'Hindu nationalist theories of governmentality' and their possible forms of political governance are exposed. If democracy is apparently necessary, but must depend on *dharmic* precepts, and if *dharma* necessarily oscillates between 'natural law', 'national soul' and 'Hindu Rashtra', then the democratic process must perpetually be subsidiary to whatever is decided to be the religious imperative. In the writings of Savarkar, Golwalkar and Upadhyaya, *dharma* was never associated with an unambiguous valorization of democracy. It is, for example, entirely conceivable that an anti-Western Hindu nationalist imaginary could claim democracy as arising from 'ancient Hindu culture'. However, democracy, rather than inhering in *dharma*, is always and already its exterior in Hindu nationalist conceptions, and rarely, if ever, elaborated in positive terms. Democracy is characteristically conceived in Hindu nationalism as other than *dharma*. Similarly, there is no discussion about the potential juridical or political institutions that can possibly have the legitimacy, authority or competence to stipulate and pronounce on what is *dharmic* or *adharmic*. While after the mid-1960s the Vishwa Hindu Parishad stepped into this role of authorizing disciplinary guidance on *dharma*, of significance is the inexplicitness in Integral Humanism regarding the structures of governance for '*dharmic* constitutionality' in a future Hindu rashtra.

Like Golwalkar, Upadhyaya proposed a 'unitary constitution' for India based on the village council (*panchayat*) system. In his view, the federal Union of States should be replaced by a 'unitary government' in order to achieve the ideal of 'integrated Bharat'. This idea of 'integrated Bharat' flowed from Upadhyaya ideology in which the 'national soul' or *chiti* had to be 'awakened' to its destiny and its *virat* ('life force') enabled so as to fulfil it. The key administrative unit in his 'integrated Bharat' was the village *panchayat*. Above this, should be a second tier based on *janapada sabhas* – assemblies of people based on regional language or dialect. Both the *panchayat* and the *janapada* were conceived by Upadhyaya as traditional, 'natural' 'Bharatiya' administrative structures. The *janapada sabha* would have greater authority than existing municipalities but less than the legislative assemblies. States would be abolished, as would all legislative authorities that lay between the Lok Sabha and *janapada sabhas*. Instead the heads of *janapada sabhas* would form provincial bodies with 'enough administrative or governing powers so that the encroachment of the forces of regionalism on national unity could be halted' (Bhishikar 1991: 183–4). The provincial *janapada sabha* heads would be under the authority of the Lok Sabha which would hold sovereign power. Upadhyaya did not stipulate how the *panchayats* or the *janapada sabhas* would be formally constituted.

This social and political system was thought by Upadhyaya to be a decentralization of power, rather than its concentration in the Centre, and aimed to maintain the integrated unity of India by defeating 'separatist', regionalist and secessionist tendencies. But clearly, the locus of legislative authority in such a scheme would shift towards the centre while local legislative power would be reduced. While similar ideas were already present in various Gandhian and socialist movements, their importance in Upadhyaya's philosophy was their intimate association with the RSS goal of Hindu rashtra, the latter a fulfilment of *dharma*. Of importance was Upadhyaya's transcendental conception of *dharma* as a metaphysical law, a way of life, that unique contribution of India that provides direction not just to Indians but to all humanity. This was related to Upadhyaya's conception of *moksha* through which 'Man' finds itself as simultaneously realized in itself, its family, its society, its nation, in humanity and in the entire cosmic existence. One might conceivably understand the appeal of these ideas for those who wish to believe that 'Man' is both the centre of, and possesses the capacity to apprehend, all existence: however, in Upadhyaya's political philosophy, such ideas are cohesively integrated with Hindu rashtra (Golwalkar, Upadhyaya and Thengadi 1991: 46–54, Bhishikar 1991).

The imagined 'Hindu rashtra' represented in the Jana Sangh vision was paradoxical, since a 'Hindu rashtra' counterposed to (primarily) Pakistan could be seen to maintain the symbolic integrity of India's *post*-Independence territorial borders, threatened externally by Pakistan (and communist China), while unable to convincingly make the (unrealistic and hence increasingly lesser) claim that Pakistan should be reunited with India. If Nehruvianism represented amicable cooperation with neighbouring states, Hindu nationalism consolidated around a new, post-Independence symbolic territory of a powerful India premised on a permanently aggressive stance towards external and permanent enemies. It is hence unclear how this could functionally relate to the different Hindu nationalist vision of 'Akhand Bharat' ('undivided India'). A similar orientation was apparent with regard to China. While communism was perceived as a pre-eminent threat, China (because of Buddhism) was also imagined in Hindu nationalist discourse as the ancient 'cultural partner' of India. In the case of both Pakistan and China, 'foreign ideologies' (respectively Islam and Marxism) had illegitimately usurped an original territory that belonged to the descendents of Vedic tradition.

This ideological structure of a present enemy that was primordially part of the self, but that has betrayed and thus denied the fulfilment of self, is of interest and modifies somewhat an elementary psychoanalytic reading of an uncomplicated, unfractured 'other' of Hindu nationalism. In one movement, the 'other' is conceived to be the same as the self, the symbolic desire being to appropriate it entirely within the self, while this 'other' is also simultaneously radically 'other' and to be annihilated in its identity. This unstable movement is less an ambivalent or undecidable orientation than one that allows both symbolic and 'pragmatic' gestures to coexist, the former as the claim for 'Akhand Bharat' that can never be disposed of, and the latter conceiving parts of 'Akhand Bharat' as foundational threats to selfhood.

There is a theory of ideology at work here that barely moves beyond vulgar conceptions of 'false consciousness' and which also has consequences for how self-hood is imagined. From the perspective of the Hindu nationalist imaginary, if Indian Muslims (or Pakistanis) are simply under the sway of a false ideology against which Hinduism can be measured as a pre-eminently superior civilizational rather than ideological form, then it should be an elementary matter for those who are conceived as originally 'Hindu' and who left that allegiance, even if by force, to 'awaken' to Hinduism's evident superiority. Yet the problem that threatens the integrity of Hindu nationalist claims is that this does not happen; given a 'second chance', as it were, the followers of other faiths disavow and do not 'return' to Hinduism even though their religions are conceived as purely ideological and even though Hinduism supposedly has a far greater and superior genealogy. Paradoxically, this is an admission of the substantial power of non-Hindu religious *ideologies*. Similarly, the ceaseless repetition of claims about Hinduism's superiority betray an acknowledgement that 'Hinduism' is in some way wanting (if it was not, the 'problem of otherness' would not exist) and thus direct a disciplinary attention toward Hinduism itself. However (and this is the second problem facing Hindu nationalism) that Hinduism is already conceived to be completed and giving, in its religious and philosophical learning, the best possible direction available to humankind. This is precisely the point where Hindu nationalism foundationally relinquishes Hinduism and projects itself as an *ideological* substitution for the latter. It is for such reasons that Hindu nationalism has been unimportant for any theological, epistemological, metaphysical or philosophical advancement, but significant for the substitution of Hinduism by materialist concerns of territory, culture, xenology and state power.

The Evolution of the Jana Sangh

Christophe Jaffrelot has illustrated the evolution of the Jana Sangh from its inception as comprised of 'sangathanist' political strategies in the early to mid-1950s based on RSS ideology and organization, a 'hybridization' of its sangathanist strategy from the early 1960s, a strategy of integration into the political mainstream and 'moderation' of its Hindu nationalism during the 1960s, and finally the 'mixed strategy' during the troubled period of the 1970s (Jaffrelot 1996: 153, 159, 193). In the early to mid-1950s, Jana Sangh goals were based on the strategic and long-term consolidation of 'Hindu society' through

> the creation of a militant network dedicated, like the RSS, patiently to imposing its vision of the world over a long period by working at the grassroots. Up to the early 1960s the Jana Sangh's leaders considered that they had to resist any drift into propaganda or alliances that would be counter to party ideology. (Jaffrelot 1996: 153)

However, Jana Sangh was entering a public sphere of representative politics in which they had little experience. Most Jana Sangh activists only had knowledge of local Arya Samaj and RSS agitations. Hence, there were contending pressures on the Jana Sangh during the 1950s: one pushing towards constitutional politics and the other towards local activism (Graham 1993: 34), the pressures reflecting a sociological divergence between constitutional politics and social movements. Both directions would involve working with politicians and organizations that had not arisen from within the RSS nor shared its ideology or discipline. Perhaps an additional pressure was of affiliation with the RSS itself.

The Jana Sangh's involvement in the Kashmir agitation (*satyagraha*) during 1952–3 illustrated these various tendencies. The Jana Sangh worked with the Jammu-based Praja Parishad, the Ram Rajya Parishad and the Hindu Mahasabha in opposition to Sheikh Abdullah's attempts to 'constitutionally' consolidate the special status of Jammu and Kashmir. The aim of the *satyagraha* was to demand full integration of Jammu and Kashmir into the Indian Union, rescind its special status and disallow its constitutional autonomy. The Praja Parishad however defended the power of feudal landlords (mainly Dogras) against land reforms that would give greater economic power to small tillers; the Hindu Mahasabha allied itself with and depended on the support of princely states, feudal power and Hindu orthodoxy; the Ram Rajya Parishad defended Hindu 'upper' caste orthodoxy and was opposed to reforms in untouchability. In each instance, the orientation of these three bodies went against the RSS and Jana Sangh goals of organic economic cooperation, 'anti-feudal modernization' and opposition to untouchability. Attempts at mergers between the Mahasabha, the Praja Parishad and the Jana Sangh hence failed, as the Jana Sangh had (at this stage of its development) few qualms about alienating the princes, the *zamindars* or Hindu orthodoxy (Baxter 1971: 128–33). The futility of the Kashmir agitation (and the arrest and deposing of Sheikh Abdullah by Nehru in 1953), the incarceration of Jana Sangh leaders by the Jammu and Kashmir government, and the death of Mookherjee, a recognised national political figure, while in detention (U. P. Mookherjee, not dated) led to a crisis of leadership and strategy in the Jana Sangh under its president Mauli Chandra Sharma and general secretary Deendayal Upadhyaya. This led to further, failed attempts during the early 1950s to merge with the newly formed Praja Socialist Party and with the Hindu Mahasabha. Into the 1960s, this lead to a reorientation in its political strategy that indicated both a pragmatic and an ideological shift away from the RSS's 'sangathanist' strategy.

During the early 1960s, in the face of massive Congress presence in the Lok Sabha and state legislatures, in comparison with its own very poor political representation, the Jana Sangh turned towards social and economic issues. The Jana Sangh appealed to urban and rural middle classes and their economic interests, rather than simply rehearsing issues which would guarantee a small Hindu nationalist constituency (such as Kashmir or cow protection). It also demonstrated a willingness to negotiate alliances with non-RSS sympathizers, especially the non-Communist parties. Its organizational strength was centred primarily in Madhya Pradesh and the 'Hindi belt' in northern India (Jaffrelot 1996: 159). Hindu 'traditionalism' and 'orthodoxy' had allied itself with the ruling Congress power and in this sense, Congress, while remaining a 'secular' party in national government could secure or procure the interests of Hindu 'traditionalists' at state and local level. The 'Congress system' for example could allow political space for those like K. M. Munshi, who could otherwise be viewed as Hindu nationalists. This also left the Jana Sangh little room for ideological or political manoeuvre (Jaffrelot 1996: 160–1).

Hence, an instructive and perhaps surprising set of alliances, that continue to thrive in the BJP today, were formed with socialist leaders such as Ram Manohar Lohia and Jayaprakash Narayan. It has been argued that it was precisely the influence of socialist leaders such as Lohia and (in the early 1970s) Jayaprakash that dragged the rightist Jana Sangh out of its marginal position and allowed its entrance into the political mainstream (Malik and Singh 1994: 32). The attraction of the Jana Sangh for the smaller socialist parties was often related to the organized and disciplined cadre that the Jana Sangh brought to any coalition. Leaving aside the question of opposition to Congress hegemony, there were important ideological ambiguities in Jana Sangh and RSS visions of nationalist, indigenous, corporatist economic and social policy which could be sutured with economic socialism based on 'anti-imperialist', 'self-reliance' or *swadeshi* precepts.

Furthermore, following the death of Nehru in 1964, the 1965 war with Pakistan, the consequent devaluation of the rupee, and the poor performance of Indira

Gandhi's Congress during the 1967 elections (Congress' majority in the Lok Sabha was reduced from about 200 to less than 50 seats; it also lost about 3,400 state legislative seats), there emerged from the late 1960s the so-called 'multi-party system' at national as well as state levels. The Jana Sangh hence became an important component in the arithmetic logic of state coalition governments. After the 1966–1967 elections, the Jana Sangh entered coalition governments in Madhya Pradesh, Uttar Pradesh, Haryana, Bihar and Punjab state. The Jana Sangh gained experience of coalition electoral strategies with minor parties, and formed long-term associations with Hindu 'royalty' (such as Vijaya Raje Scindia) and sections of India's industrial capitalist class. It cultivated a militant Hindu nationalist constituency through campaigns against Urdu, for the banning of cow-slaughter, and for a militarily strong India. But while it appealed to a selective northern Indian Hindu electoral constituency, it could also be portrayed as a responsible party that attempted to reflect broad Indian interests (Puri 1980).

The 1970s and the 'Emergency'

It was the period of Indira Gandhi's rule, and most importantly the impact of the Emergency (June 1975 – February 1977) that determined the fortunes of Hindu nationalism on both the party political and extra-parliamentary, mass cadre front. Indira Gandhi's Congress party had mobilized on an anti-poverty platform during the 1971–2 national and state elections that resulted in a stunning victory for Congress, reversing its poor showing since 1967. Of additional importance in late 1971 and early 1972 was India's military success against Pakistan which led to the formation of Bangladesh. However, the consequent period of Congress hegemony, opportunism and corruption was seen to signal a dramatic change in India's political culture. Indira Gandhi's political stature after the invasion of east Pakistan was on the wane and her anti-poverty oratory was ineffectual; conversely, the rate of inflation and the prices of fuel and basic foodstuffs continued to rise. Mass protest movements against poverty and political corruption by mainly student groups grew in this period, and were centred around Gujarat and Bihar states. In 1975, a High Court found Indira Gandhi guilty of electoral irregularities. In this year, the 'Gandhian socialist' leader Jayaprakash Narayan launched a people's movement (the Janata Morcha) that called for the dismissal of the Congress government in Bihar state. Jayaprakash also called for 'total revolution', the latter intended to appeal to both socialist constituencies and to elements who desired a 'revolution' in political ethics and propriety. Previously, in 1973 the student-led Navnirman (reconstruction) movement in Gujarat had similarly demanded the resignation of the governing assembly in the state.

Following the death of Golwalkar in 1973, Balasaheb Deoras became *sars-anghchalak* of the RSS and oriented the organization towards an activist political direction (Andersen and Damle 1987: 209–10, Jaffrelot 1996: 257). Jana Sangh and RSS cadres had participated in both the Gujarat and Bihar movements. In 1975, the Jana Sangh, following Jayaprakash, called for a united people's front of all the non-Congress parties and organizations, which would organize joint actions in parliamentary and extra-parliamentary arenas based on a common programme of opposition to Indira Gandhi's Congress government. In the months prior to the declaration of Emergency, the resolutions adopted by the RSS's Akhil Bharatiya Pratinidhi Sabha (its national central assembly) are instructive. In March 1974, the RSS issued a statement that condemned the attacks upon it from Congress and the Communist Party of India following the violence that erupted in the aftermath of the student and public protests in Gujarat and Bihar (Rashtriya Swayamsevak Sangh 1983: 76). This archetypal resolution condemned, and distanced the RSS from, the 'lawlessness and chaos' in those states. It also reflected the paranoid style of RSS politics by claiming that 'foreign loyalties and foreign designs', by which it meant Communists, were aiming to capture state power by instilling nationwide disorder. This resolution called upon its cadres to extend their 'hearty cooperation to every such effort from any direction' that was working for 'patriotism' and against 'the present atmosphere of all-round corruption and selfishness' (Rashtriya Swayamsevak Sangh 1983: 77). A year later, the RSS's Akhil Bharatiya Pratinidhi Sabha (national assembly) issued a statement again condemning Communist 'infiltration' and calling on *swayamsevaks* 'to exert themselves, with determination, to speed up the expansion of Sangh work throughout the country, heedless of any malicious propaganda indulged in by anti-nationalist and self-seeking elements' (Rashtriya Swayamsevak Sangh 1983: 77). In June, Indira Gandhi, claiming she feared a far right-wing or military coup in India, instructed the president to declare a 'national emergency' and suspend constitutional constraints. This gave Gandhi virtually unlimited powers to undertake actions deemed to be in the 'interests' of the nation. All the leaders of India's opposition parties were arrested and imprisoned or put under house arrest (for up to two years) and northern India's press and media was heavily censored or proscribed.

Aside from the extreme imperatives of political expediency, the RSS's and Jana Sangh's political alliances with Gandhian and socialist organizations before, during and after the Emergency period require further explanation. Of importance was a strand in Gandhite anti-poverty activist ideology of 'upliftment' that, perhaps in a contradictory way, dovetailed into the Jana Sangh's 'modernizing' strategy. Gandhi's earlier *sarvodaya* ('upliftment' of rural and village communities out of poverty) strategy was to be followed by Vinoba Bhave's (1895–82) *bhoodan yagna* (land gift movement) from the early 1950s, which later expanded into the *gramdan* and *jivandan* movements. Both the latter emphasized a cooperative sharing of land and labour resources for the collective 'upliftment' of (typically) rural village communities.

Jayaprakash ('JP') Narayan (1902–79), a worker in the *bhoodan yagna* movement, had previously been active in the non-cooperation movement and was a key founder of the Marxist-influenced Congress Socialist Party. However, after Independence, and in particular after the assassination of M. K. Gandhi, his ideology shifted from Marxism towards one that emphasized a tiered, decentralized and cooperatively organised Indian social formation of autonomous village councils ('republics') based on a democratic version of the *panchayat* system. This can be seen as a synthesis of a 'modernizing' Gandhianism and an anarcho-socialist utopianism. Of salience was the importance given by Jayaprakash to values and ethical principles, particularly those understood as informed by Gandhianism. One can see the unmediated appeal of Jayaprakash's ideology for Jana Sangh and RSS cadres. Golwalkar had also idealized the *panchayat* system. More importantly, Jayaprakash's vision could result in an ideological shift within the Jana Sangh without committing the latter to abandon its Hindutva foundation. 'Gandhian utopianism' of the kind promoted by Jayaprakash contained progressive and highly conservative resources and crucially *both* were important for the Jana Sangh. Similarly, the socialist aspects of Jayaprakash's ideology was resonant among the RSS and Jana Sangh cadres formal commitment to 'equality' and the redistribution of wealth. In important respects, Deendayal Upadhyaya's ideology of 'Integral Humanism' is awkwardly close to organic-utopian aspects of Gandhi's philosophy; conversely 'Integral Humanism' has had a long-standing appeal for some Gandhians. It is a moot point whether Upadhyaya's ideology can be seen as a direct syncretism of Gandhite-'JP' ideology with the RSS ideal of Hindu rashtra. (Of additional significance is that the Janata Party of which the Jana Sangh was a key component, was in principle committed to Jayaprakash's political ideology. Similarly, in 1975 Jayaprakash dismissed charges that the RSS was 'fascist' (Andersen and Damle 1987: 211)). It was from such influences that the founding ideology of the Bharatiya Janata Party was determined at its inception to be 'Gandhian socialism'.

The Emergency period was the second time that the RSS had been banned in India. Under Emergency powers, Indira Gandhi also amended the Constitution of India in 1976, making it, allegedly 'for the first time', constitutionally secular. (If the unnerving point is that the term 'secular' was inserted into the Preamble to the Constitution under the forty-second amendment during India's most authoritarian period since gaining Independence, article 25 (2) (a) already provided powers to the state to regulate and restrict 'any economic, financial, political or other secular activity associated with religious practice'.) The RSS and the Jana Sangh leadership were imprisoned, as were the leadership and activists of left and communist parties, and the (Maududist) Jamaati-i-Islami.

The Emergency period, while often considered in popular memory primarily as an attack on the left, was definitive in its impact on the strategy and ideology of the RSS in the late 1970s and into the 1980s. More than anything else, it confirmed for the RSS its own imagination of its centrality, necessity and power in India, as well as its role in rescuing the 'Hindu nation' from totalitarian 'secular' dictatorship (Sahasrabuddhe and Vajpayee 1991). During their incarceration, RSS cadres formed links with organizations that were traditionally political enemies. Aside from socialist, Marxist and communist activists, this also included Jamaati-i-Islami activists. Of 12,986 individuals imprisoned during the Emergency, political affiliation was recorded for 6,346 individuals. Of these, just over 65 per cent were members of the RSS or Jana Sangh, about a quarter were members of the Communist Party of India (ML) or the Socialist Party, and a small percentage were members of other parties (see especially Jaffrelot 1996 and Puri 1980 on this; figures based on Jaffrelot 1996: 276). The large number of individuals for whom political affiliation was not recorded may confound this interpretation, as indeed might the large number of people arrested and imprisoned during Emergency for allegedly 'non-political' reasons. However, the relatively high percentage of RSS and Jana Sangh activists among those imprisoned during Emergency is salient in understanding both the changed strategy of the RSS during the 1980s and 1990s and the considerable importance the RSS now attaches to its role during the Emergency period.

In April 1977, the RSS's Akhil Bharatiya Karyakari Mandal issued a statement of tribute to the fighters against the Emergency. Of significance was the absence of criticism of communism and of calls to uphold law and order, both of which were so prominent in its 1974–5 resolutions. Instead there was lavish praise for diverse sectors of Indian society, and especially the *sangh* cadres for their struggles against Indira Gandhi's dictatorship. This was a new political language for the RSS, knitting together its deal of national harmony and social integration with a characteristically non-RSS discourse of liberty, democracy, injustice, tyranny and vigilant struggle (Rashtriya Swayamsevak Sangh 1983: 80–1).

Perhaps most surprisingly, in 1977 and 1978, the RSS called upon its workers to 'initiate measures to remove the sense of alienation' of Muslims and Christians from the Hindus. Furthermore, the RSS reported that

> a large number of persons following different ways of worship such as Islam, Christianity, [Zoroastrianism] have participated in the congregations organized for the purpose by the RSS workers at different places, and exchanged views. As result of these get-together the communication gap among the different followers of different religions has narrowed down and to an extent mutual goodwill and amity developed. (Rashtriya Swayamsevak Sangh 1983: 83–4)

Following the RSS supreme leader, Deoras' meeting with Christian and Muslim leaders, the RSS's national assembly exhorted 'all citizens in general and R.S.S.

Swayamsevaks in particular to further expedite this process of mutual contact by *participation in each other's social functions*' (Rashtriya Swayamsevak Sangh 1983: 84, emphasis added). Such sentiments can be viewed as consequences of the optimism in Indian public culture in the aftermath of the ending of Emergency, but they nevertheless reflected, though for a very short period (see Rashtriya Swayamsevak Sangh 1983: 91), a different orientation to religious minorities, the latter still articulated together with the need for national integration, but with a liberality that perhaps could not be imagined in the Golwalkar period (see also the attacks in Goel 1997 to nominal attempts at dialogue by senior RSS leaders with some Muslim representatives in the mid-1990s).

The RSS's early 1990s narrative (Sahasrabuddhe and Vajpayee 1991) of its role in the Emergency is instructive and its language of heroism emblematic of its bumptious style. The large size of this tome is indicative of the RSS's attempt to place itself and the anti-Emergency *satyagraha*s organized by its *swayamsevaks* as the main and only consistent underground opposition to Indira Gandhi's Emergency. The anti-Emergency *satyagraha*s were called for by Jayaprakash Narayan in late 1975 and organized under a federation of parties and organizations, the Lok Sangarsh Samiti (LSS). However, the RSS narrative downplays the role of other organizations; even Jayaprakash is barely mentioned. Instead, the pre-eminent role of *sangh* workers and volunteers is portrayed as central to and decisive for the struggle against Emergency.

> A history of the struggle of the times of Emergency written without referring to the revolutionary work of these underground [mainly Sangh] workers would be like the Mahabharat written without acknowledging the fundamental contribution of Lord Shri Krishna – although it is true that today the common people are more attracted towards political power and Shri Krishna did not ascend the throne of Hastinapur after the Mahabharat war. All his efforts were directed towards the establishment of Dharma Rajya, not for achieving power for himself. (Sahasrabuddhe and Vajpayee 1991: 31)

This is characteristic RSS political language. The RSS is said to neither seek nor require any recognition for its selfless, anonymous work for the nation, yet at the same time its central heroic role is ceaselessly promoted (indeed compared to that of Krishna) and that of other organizations rebuffed, the latter seen as disorganized and divided (Rashtriya Swayamsevak Sangh 1983: 308). Hence, the RSS claims that of those who participated in the anti-Emergency *satyagraha*s, over 78 per cent (35,310) were associated with the *sangh parivar*; similarly, of those arrested under the MISA (Maintenance of Internal Security Act) imposed during the Emergency, almost 71 per cent (16,373) were associated with the *sangh parivar* (based on data in Sahasrabuddhe and Vajpayee 1991: 212–17, and excluding figures supplied for Akali Dal activists). However, this text is part of deeper and more recent revisionist and vanguardist project aimed at morally rehabilitating the RSS by exclusively identifying it with the history and 'remembrance' of both the anti-colonial and anti-Emergency struggles, significantly extending its own particular ideology to represent or substitute for 'the people'.

The Rise of the Bharatiya Janata Party

Following the end of the Emergency in 1977, Indira Gandhi's Congress party lost the general election and the Janata coalition headed by Morarji Desai won 295 of the 405 seats it contested; it also gained over 40 per cent of the popular vote. The Janata coalition formed a slight majority in the Lok Sabha (though the total non-Congress opposition held over two-thirds of Lok Sabha seats). The founders of the Jana Sangh, organized around long-term RSS members Lal Krishnan Advani and Atal Behari Vajpayee, were also key member of the Janata coalition. This was the first time since just after Independence that Hindu nationalists, and the first time ever that RSS members had held political power at the centre, as key members of a ruling coalition. This period of experience in government was to convince both Vajpayee and Advani that a Hindu nationalist party could become a viable party political force and the main opposition party in India. The coalition, however, was short lived and Indira Gandhi's Congress (I) party was returned to power in January 1980. Previously, the 'Jana Sangh' faction of the Janata Party had come under consistent criticism for its association with the RSS and with Hindu communalist interests. Key RSS and ex-Jana Sangh members of the Janata Party left the latter to form the Bharatiya Janata Party in 1980 (on the BJP see Malik and Singh 1994, Jaffrelot 1996, Mishra 1997, Hansen and Jaffrelot ed. 1998, Ghosh 1999 – the latter sources have been drawn on below; the burgeoning apologias for the BJP include Raghavan 1996, Thakur and Sharma 1999).

The early BJP under Vajpayee, claiming a heritage that the Jana Sangh had forged during its association with Jayaprakash Narayan and during its anti-Emergency activities, constitutionally declared its political ideology to be 'Gandhian Socialism'. Vajpayee also strategically viewed the BJP as an alternative to Congress (I), which could replace the Janata Party as the main opposition. 'Gandhian Socialism' was in all important respects a slogan under which the BJP could articulate in 'indigenous' registers the material needs and spiritual or moral values that Vajpayee considered important for India's post-Emergency development, while also presenting itself as a modernizing and scientifically-oriented political party. Similarly, alongside 'nationalism and national integration', 'democracy' and 'value-based politics', the BJP adopted what it called 'positive secularism'. This was an ambiguous concept ultimately based on the Hindutva view that Hinduism was not a religion and could not be other than 'secular'. However, in 1993 Vajpayee was himself to say that *dharma nirapeksh*, the indifference of the state to religion, was neither secularism nor a reflection of the dominant (Hindutva) 'ethos' of India (Raghavan 1996: 81–2). Hence 'positive secularism' could seemingly incorporate both the existing conception of *sarva dharma sambhava* (the view that the orientation of the state should be to conceive of all India's religions as 'equal') and the view that treating minority religions differently through what were conceived as 'special privileges' or 'concessions' would advantage them in comparison with Hindus (Malik and Singh 1994: 62). Similarly, both the separate terms under the designation 'Gandhian socialism' were from the inception of the BJP to grate against Hindu nationalist sensibilities for whom Gandhi had been an enemy, Gandhianism represented an anti-modernizing economic philosophy, and socialism represented a 'foreign', Marxist-inspired imposition (Andersen and Damle 1987: 228–9).

Paradoxically, it was during the period of the early- to mid-1980s of what is considered Vajpayee's relatively moderate, liberal steering of the BJP towards centrist political ground that Indira Gandhi's Congress (I) party, in power from 1980, was directly appealing to 'Hindu nationalist' voters through a series of explicitly religious symbolic gestures, manifested in Indira Gandhi's highly publicized attendance at Hindu religious temples and shrines (including the inauguration of the Hindu nationalist Bharatmata Mandir in Hardwar), seeking the blessings of the Hindu religious hierarchy, appealing to Hindu voters in Jammu, and launching military operations against Khalistani separatists in Punjab, which led to the storming and military occupation of the Golden Temple in Amritsar in June 1984 ('Operation Bluestar'). The latter action was followed by the assassination of Gandhi in October of that year, an extremely violent Hindu backlash against Sikh minorities, and the installation of Rajiv Gandhi as Prime Minister. However, the sweeping Congress (I) victory (and the defeat of the BJP) at the 1983 Jammu and Kashmir assembly polls based on a direct appeal to Hindu interests in Jammu had demonstrated that an electoral strategy based on majority communalism could be highly successful. This was a factor that the BJP had not yet directly exploited.

The BJP formed strategic alliances with other smaller parties, including the Lok Dal and Congress (Socialist) during state elections in 1982, and called for an anti-Congress front in 1983. However, it had little support beyond sections of urban Hindu, predominantly Hindi-speaking northern Indian voters (its main pockets of local electoral support were in Madhya Pradesh, Jammu, Delhi, Rajasthan, Uttar Pradesh, Maharashtra and Himachal Pradesh). During the 1984 general election, it won only two seats in the Lok Sabha. Vajpayee's ostensibly 'moderate' strategy was seen to have failed and Lal Krishnan Advani became BJP president in 1986.

Manufacturing the Hindu Vote Bank

From 1980 through to the end of the decade, there were several events in India that signalled the rise of an aggressively Hindu, anti-Muslim sentiment that had the potential to be consolidated into a distinct Hindu electoral constituency or Hindu vote bank for the BJP. Of importance was a new and increasingly vociferous discourse, often cultivated by the VHP, of 'Hinduism under threat' or 'under siege' in India as a result of the activities, real or perceived, of Muslim and Christian minorities and of secessionist or regionalist movements such as in Assam, Darjeeling, Mizoram and Nagaland. Events of importance included the mass conversions of 'untouchables' to Islam in Meenakshipuram, Tamil Nadu in 1981; Rajiv Gandhi's overturning of the Supreme Court ruling of 1985 on the Shahbano case (the court ruling had effectively dismissed the legitimacy of Muslim personal law in India); the emergence from 1984 of organized mass campaigns by the VHP for the building of a Ram temple on the site of the medieval Babri mosque in Ayodhya, Uttar Pradesh; secular protests against, and Hindu nationalist defence of the self-immolation of the widow Roop Kanwar in Rajasthan in 1987; and the Finance Ministry's banning of Salman Rushdie's *The Satanic Verses* in India in late 1988 following lobbying by Muslim MPs and organizations. 'Communal violence', directed against Muslim and Sikh communities, increased dramatically in India during the 1980s. In addition, the increased tension in Jammu and Kashmir from the mid-1980s, continued Sikh grievances in Punjab (and the active mobilization of anti-Sikh hysteria by Congress (I)), and the civil war in Sri Lanka between (Hindu) Tamils and a chauvinistic Sinhala-Buddhist government politically compounded what has been called India's 'crisis of governability' (Kohli 1990).

The BJP under Advani moved towards an openly Hindutva position after the mid-1980s. Deendayal Upadhyaya's Integral Humanism philosophy was adopted as its ideology from 1985 and supplemented with the idea of 'cultural nationalism' (*sanskritik rashtriyavad*). In the wake of the Meenakshipuram conversions, the VHP launched a nation-wide *ekatmata yagna* (Hindu unity and integration ritual). Aside from demanding the building of a Ram temple at the Babri masjid in Ayodhya, the VHP had also launched campaigns for 'the liberation of Krishna's birthplace' in Mathura and for 'the liberation of the Kashi Vishwanath temple complex' in Varanasi. In its 1989 general election campaign, the BJP formed electoral alliances with mainly V. P. Singh's new Janata Dal party, as part of the National Front alliance created by Narasimha Rao in 1988. While the thrust of the BJP campaign was directed against Rajiv Gandhi's Congress (I) party, criticizing both the dynastic nature and probity of the latter, the BJP also campaigned on a militant Hindutva agenda based on the building of the Ram temple at Ayodhya, the scrapping of article 370 of the Indian constitution, which granted Kashmir an exceptional status in comparison with other states in the Indian Union (historically, because of the recognition of its majority Muslim population), the replacement of India's Minorities Commission with a Human Rights commission, and legislation for a 'uniform civil code' that would apparently govern all personal and familial relations among Hindus, Muslims and other religious communities (Malik and Singh 1994: 83–5, Ghosh 1999: 94). The BJP dramatically increased its representation in the Lok Sabha from the two seats won in 1984 to eighty-six.

V. P. Singh's National Front coalition government, in power from 1989, adopted an ambivalent attitude to the Ram temple issue. Conversely, it attempted to consolidate its electoral victory by deciding in 1990 to implement the recommendations of the 1980 Mandal Commission report, which provided for reservations in public sector employment and in higher education for 'other backward castes'. The Mandal Commission recommendations would have considerably increased the 'lower-caste' base of public sector employment, the latter traditionally conceived as the preserve, indeed stronghold of 'upper' caste groups. This resulted in an 'upper' caste backlash and the public self-immolation of brahmin and 'upper' caste students in the summer of 1990. In August 1990, L. K. Advani launched his *rath yatra*, a mass procession through some ten northern Indian states, starting from the Somnath temple in Gujarat and intending to finish in October at the Babri *masjid* in Ayodhya, Uttar Pradesh at which work would be started to build the Ram temple. The *yatra* was led by Advani riding in a DCM Toyota jeep decorated as 'Rama's chariot'. Predictably, considerable communal violence followed in its wake, and aptly demonstrated BJP methods of 'national' and 'social integration' (*samarajik samarashtha*). Advani, the leader of a national political party and member of the Lok Sabha, considered it appropriate to undertake extra-parliamentary action of disputed legality, and with inevitably violent consequences, for the cause of Hindutva.

The reasons often given for Advani's decision to launch the *rath yatra* relate to the Hindu vote bank that the BJP (and the VHP) had been cultivating since the mid-1980s and that was threatened as caste loyalties came to the fore in the aftermath of the implementation of the Mandal report. It is thus significant that, as part of BJP-VHP-RSS symbolic strategy, the *rath yatra* often had a token dalit or Muslim presence. Advani said that it was irrelevant whether or not the Babri mosque had been built over an existing Ram temple; of importance was the *belief* among Hindus that it had replaced the temple, as well as the *symbolism* of Ayodhya and Ram in the Hindu religious-popular imagination. It is clear that the Hindutva forces were attempting to displace the issue of caste discrimination in favour of another political configuration in which 'backward' castes and those outside the caste system could be 'sutured' into an 'integrated' Hinduism (itself a part of a much older sangathanist strategy, though now deploying a different method based on the use of popular symbols and the mass media). In this sense the *yatra* could be interpreted as an anti-Mandal strategy.

However, the BJP was also willing to take considerable political risks during this campaign by magnifying and enforcing other political and religious cleavages, including within Hinduism, and creating large-scale social and political disorder through a singular strategy that appealed to northern Indian mainly upper- and middle-caste devotional (*bhakti*) traditions centred on the Rama mythology. The BJP's uses of disorder are in sharp contradiction with its Hindutva ideal of 'social integration' and 'social harmony', this perhaps also indicating how Hindu nationalism is incapable of fulfilling a 'requisite' of national sovereignty – 'perpetual peace'. Advani was arrested in Bihar under the orders of its chief minister Laloo Prasad Yadav who, like Mulayam Singh Yadav, chief minister of Uttar Pradesh, was determined to prevent the *yatra* from reaching Ayodhya. Nevertheless, VHP *kar sevaks* ('religious volunteers') continued to Ayodhya and attempted to raise saffron flags over the dome of the mosque. The arrest of Advani and the withdrawal of BJP parliamentary support led to the fall of the V. P. Singh National Front coalition government in late 1990.

During the mid-term general elections the following year, Rajiv Gandhi was assassinated by a suicide bomber associated with factions of the Tamil 'liberation' movement in Sri Lanka. Consequently, P. V. Narasimha Rao became Congress (I) president. During the 1991 election, the BJP had campaigned on the slogan 'Towards Ram Rajya' (the mythological 'rule of Ram'). Its election manifesto declared it to be 'the party of Nationalism, Holism and Integral Humanism' and exactly reproduced Savarkar's definition of Hindutva:

> From the Himalayas to Kanya Kumari, this country has always been one. We have had many States, but we were always one people. We always looked upon our country as Matribhoomi, Punyabhoomi [Motherland and Holyland]. (Bharatiya Janata Party 1991)

The Hindutva political language of the 1991 BJP manifesto was deceptive in crucial respects. For example, its one apparently affable declaration that 'Hindus and Muslims are blood-brothers' did little more than rehearse the old Savarkarite formula that Muslims were originally 'biological' Hindus, while appearing to say something else. Hindu-Muslim conflict, it stated, resulted from 'historical reasons'. Similarly, the 'restoration' of the Ram temple at Ayodhya, the latter 'a symbol of the vindication of our cultural heritage and national self-respect', was articulated as a 'symbolic righting of historical wrongs, so that the old unhappy chapter of acrimony could be ended, and a Grand National Reconciliation effected'. This was a precise, if coded, use of Hindutva political language that raised the real or imagined spectre of the Mughal period in which Hindus were conceived as victims; the onus thus fell squarely on India's contemporary Muslims to accept that one of their mosques 'super imposed' on the Ram temple must be removed. Other Hindu nationalist themes also emerged clearly among the BJP's 1991 electoral promises: the deleting of article 370 from the Indian constitution; 'a common civil law'; the scrapping of the Minorities Commission; Deendayal Upadhyaya's proposed constitutional changes for *panchayat raj* (the latter conceived as Vedic); the banning of cow and bullock slaughter; the ideal of womanhood as *matri-shakti* (reflecting the power of women through their 'motherhood role'); the preservation of the ancient cultural heritage of India; the establishment of cultural heritage centres in all Indian districts; the screening of Hindu religious epics on television in vernacular languages; the encouragement of Sanskrit study; and, importantly, to 'give our Defence Forces Nuclear Teeth'. On the Mandal issue, the BJP claimed to support reservations 'broadly on the basis' of the Mandal recommendations but stated ambiguously that:

> the reservation policy should be introduced taking into consideration socio-economic ethos. Reservation policy should be used as an instrument of social justice and promoting social harmony as well. The question of reservation has to be viewed with open mind free from prejudices of any kind. (Bharatiya Janata Party 1991)

Narasimha Rao's Congress (I) won the election. However, the BJP increased its seats in the Lok Sabha to 120 and gained twenty percent of the popular vote. As Vajpayee had intended, the BJP had become the main opposition party. Moreover, the BJP now controlled Madhya Pradesh, Himachal Pradesh, Rajasthan and the prize state of Uttar Pradesh.

In early December 1992, Hindutva *kar sevaks* marched again on Ayodhya and this time the Babri masjid was illegally destroyed in an atmosphere of Hindutva triumphalism that paradoxically caused revulsion across India. (The term *kar seva* is related to work undertaken for religious purposes, including building religious centres, in the Sikh tradition – it does not have a traditional meaning in Hinduism.) The Narasimha Rao government dismissed the BJP-controlled states (the Uttar Pradesh BJP government resigned soon after the demolition of the mosque) and assumed central control over all four ex-BJP states. In the 1993 state assembly elections, the BJP did not recapture its lost states with an absolute majority. It lost Himachal Pradesh and Madhya Pradesh to Congress (I). It was forced into forming a perhaps surprising coalition government in Uttar Pradesh with an alliance of the Bahujan Samaj Party and the Samajwadi Party, the latter two parties having ostensibly gained prominence on the basis of appealing to dalit and Muslim tactical voting *against* the BJP. The BJP formed the government of Rajasthan but with less than half the seats. However, it won the new 'state' of Delhi outright (Ghosh 1999: 100–1, Malik and Singh 1994: 208).

The 1990s – Extremism or 'Moderation'?

During the period 1991–6, the BJP has been seen to moderate its strategy, diluting its militant Hindutva philosophy, making appeals to Muslim and dalit voters, and, importantly, being seen internationally as a moderate and responsible party. This was reflected in a movement away from Advani and back to Vajpayee's leadership. However, the manifestations of the BJP in power at state level by no means represented a 'moderation' of Hindutva. The BJP took control of Gujarat and Maharashtra states in the mid-1990s assembly elections, the latter in an alliance with the violently Hindutva Shiv Sena (on the Shiv Sena, see Gupta 1982, Lele 1995, Heuze 1995). That the BJP at federal level could *in principle* ally itself with a xenophobic and violent party whose leader has repeatedly demonstrated unqualified veneration for Hitler is instructive. If sections of the national and parliamentary BJP were aiming to secure a 'moderate' political ground for technological progress and economic investment in a global period, its Hindutva cultural nationalism could however be interpreted in diverse and autonomous ways by local BJP activists, the latter often having strong regional links with the RSS, the VHP or with non-RSS Hindu nationalist groups.

The BJP entered the 1996 general elections on a platform 'for a strong and prosperous India'. The BJP reiterated its ideal of 'one nation, one people, one culture' but appeared to modify somewhat its Hindutva declaration of 1991. India was to be 'a country where *every citizen* regards this land of ours, this Bharat-bhoomi, that stretches from the Indus to the seas, as his *sacred motherland*' (Bharatiya Janata Party 1996, emphasis added). However, this interpellation was ambiguous, because it can also be read as stipulating that every Muslim and Christian citizen regard India, in Savarkar's sense, as their 'sacred motherland'. It is as difficult to take seriously the BJP claim to represent 'positive' or 'genuine secularism' if *every citizen*, secular, agnostic, atheist, or religious had to conceive their country as 'sacred'. The manifesto also declared the ancient cultural heritage of India as 'Hindutva':

> Hindutva is a unifying principle which alone can preserve the unity and integrity of our nation. It is a collective endeavour to protect and re-energize the soul of India, to take us into the next millennium as a strong and prosperous nation. Hindutva is also the antidote to the shameful efforts of any section to benefit at the expense of others . . . On coming to power, the BJP Government will facilitate the construction of a magnificent Shri Rama Mandir at Janmasthan in Ayodhya which will be a tribute to Bharat Mata. This dream moves millions of people in our land; the concept of Rama lies at the core of their consciousness. (Bharatiya Janata Party 1996)

The dual strategy of the national BJP – ambiguously projecting moderation, inclusivity and responsibility (in the figure of Vajpayee) while appealing to Hindu nationalism and cultivating a national Hindu vote bank (as symbolized by Advani) – has more-or-less remained up to the present.

This was highly apparent from 1991, but of significance from 1996 was the attention paid by the BJP to the radically different economic and political global environment, and the rise of new information and scientific technologies to which India had to respond. The BJP was apparently strongly committed to the deregulation of the Indian economy (vociferously criticizing the stalling of previous Congress (I) liberalization reforms initiated by Rajiv Gandhi against India's 'permit raj'), while exposing India to the chill winds of economic globalization in a staggered manner – what the BJP termed 'calibrated globalization' – that would ensure a degree of protectionism for key industrial, public and private service sectors. The BJP argued that neither India's resurgence as a global economic competitor nor the protection of India from western cultural influences as a result of globalisation were possible without strengthening India's ancient cultural heritage. A proud and confident Hindutva cultural nationalism (*sanskritik rashtriyavad*) emerges here both as a precise response to political, economic and social globalization and as the means for India's economic, political, technological and military rejuvenation on the world stage. However, the precise nature and degree of economic globalization, and the inevitable social and cultural globalization that both precedes the former and can pave the way for its expansion, is subject to significant tension with the BJP, between it and its socialist coalition partners, and between the BJP and the RSS. The BJP won 161 seats to the Lok Sabha and, for a fortnight, took over role of the government of India under the leadership of Vajpayee. It however lost a vote of non-confidence and H. D. Deve Gowda's National Front government took power.

In the 1998 elections the BJP won 297 Lok Sabha seats. The opposition led by Sonia Gandhi's Congress and the United Front campaigned on a platform of secularism and protection of minorities and raised the spectre of fascism in India if the BJP took over the reins of government. Congress and its allies secured 134 seats and the remaining parties accounted for 106 seats. Hence, the BJP came to power at the head of an unwieldy, and perhaps unlikely coalition, the unstable alliances of which continue to dominate contemporary Indian politics, particularly in the case of the demands upon the government by Jayalalitha's AIADMK. Mainly as a result of the withdrawal of support by the latter, Vajpayee lost another vote of confidence in October 1999 and new elections were called. The BJP, as head of the National Democratic Alliance, campaigning on the basis of its earlier *National Agenda for Governance*, won again by a slim majority but increased its seats in the Lok Sabha to 182. Its share of the popular vote was just over 25 per cent. However, the BJP government has faced not just formidable constraints from its coalition partners but also the realities of government.

Hindutva Bound

The political constraints on the BJP are revealed in the stark differences between its explicitly Hindutva-based 1998 election manifesto and the '*National Agenda for Governance*' agreed with its coalition partners, which does not make any mention of Hindutva. The 1998 BJP manifesto is, if anything, a far denser elaboration of the kinds of primordialist Hindu nationalism discussed in earlier chapters. The manifesto presented a sweeping vision of *Bharatvarsha*'s and *Bharat Khand*'s unique and primordial civilizational superiority since Vedic times, the cradle of all world civilization, the progenitor of the message of universal humanity thousands of years before the League of Nations and the United Nations were conceived. It was the 'ancient Indian mind', it claimed, that shaped the Constitution of India that guaranteed equal treatment to all faiths. The manifesto listed the Hindu, Jain, Buddhist and Sikh texts that comprised the national tradition alongside the 'Indian traditions of the Muslims, Christians and Parsis'. The BJP, rather fancifully, claimed itself as the true inheritor of the struggle for Independence. The manifesto reiterated the previous policy of the BJP regarding the Ram temple, the uniform civil code, article 370, the ideology of Integral Humanism, an attack on 'pseudo-secularism', a policy of 'positive secularism' as 'justice for all, appeasement of none', and the importance of cultivating and furthering Hindutva, the latter declared to be 'secular'. The 'Ramjanmabhoomi' movement is described in flamboyant terms as 'the greatest mass movement in post-Independence history', which 'reoriented the disoriented polity in India and strengthened the foundation of cultural nationalism'. Aurobindo's view that *sanatan dharma* was equivalent to Indian nationalism is evoked, as is Vivekananda, Bankimchandra's *Bande Mataram* and Gandhi's 'Ram Rajya'. The BJP also proposed economic liberalization, calibrated globalization and a new informatics policy to make India an information technology superpower. While proposing a 'new culture of national consensus' in which the BJP would 'not practice political untouchability' against any party, the BJP also attacked the Congress policy of 'negativism and confrontation' and declared that the choice facing the electorate was between 'nationalism and a Foreign Hand'. These various themes represent a characteristic ideological tension between an imagined Hindutva ideal of harmonious 'social integration' and the necessity of antagonism against critics of Hindutva.

The 1998 manifesto included a commitment, which is also present in the *National Agenda for Governance* agreed by the BJP-led National Democratic Alliance, whereby the BJP would 'appoint a Commission to comprehensively review the Constitution of India in the light of the past 50 years and make suitable recommendations' (Bharatiya Janata Party 1998). The BJP has not explicitly declared which articles of the Constitution are in need of 'review', or indeed why this is necessary. However, the BJP has an ideological aversion to at least two of the terms within the Preamble of the Constitution that defines India as a 'sovereign socialist secular democratic republic' comprised of a union of states. The BJP is also committed to the rescinding of article 370 (relating to Kashmir), and it has made various promises regarding religious, regional and linguistic minorities, scrapping the Minorities Commission, a 'uniform civil code', cow protection, the 'protection' and promotion of Hinduism, Hindu religious education, the Babri *masjid* and other mosques, economic deregulation, non-alignment, *sanskritik rashtriyavad* and Hindutva.

As in its previous (1996) election manifesto, the BJP rejected 'the notion of nuclear apartheid', said it would actively oppose attempts to impose a 'hegemonistic nuclear regime by means of CTBT, FMCR and MTCR' and made a commitment to 're-evaluate the country's nuclear policy and exercise the option to induct nuclear weapons'. However, aside from the nuclear option and a modified critique of the languages of 'majority and minority', the *National Agenda for Governance* agreed with its coalition partners contained none of the main Hindu nationalist policies declared in its 1998 election manifesto. The most important price the parliamentary BJP had to pay in order to assume government was to apparently abandon its commitment to its founding ideological backbone of Hindutva and of the policies that flowed from it. In power, the BJP government has not only faced the political constraints of coalition, but also the realities of coalition arithmetic and of administration and governance that have functionally exposed the limitations of its political experience. This was most apparent following its decision to detonate nuclear devices at Pokharan near the border with Pakistan in 1998. This resulted in immediate retaliatory tests by Pakistan, which assured not 'Resurgent India' but raised the threat of mutual destruction fuelled by a now more equalized nuclear capability, a disastrous south Asian nuclear arms race, and ignominy heaped upon the BJP leadership both domestically and internationally.

Conclusion

The BJP's emergence as a party of economic liberalization that is seriously attuned to a changed global environment is in ideological contradiction with its lineage and its inheritance of an RSS philosophy based broadly on *swadeshi*, some form of redistributivism and a concern to promote the interests of traditional sections of north India's middle classes who, together with the poor, would be threatened by economic globalisation. In these changed circumstances, it is unclear what the RSS can mean by *swadeshi* or how the BJP's 'Integral Humanism', itself predicated on an hermetically enclosed social system, can function in a global environment.

In the late 1990s, these differences became apparent following renewed attacks by the *sangh parivar* on the BJP for apparently abandoning its Hindutva agenda in the coalition government, as well as disagreements about the nature, pace and direction of 'calibrated globalization'. The BJP also launched a major review of liberalization that would lead to a second set of economic reforms in the early years of the new millennium. The views of one of the BJP's four national general secretaries and an important RSS ideologue, K. N. Govindacharya (who can be viewed as on 'political secondment' from the RSS), are important in this respect. The position presented by him was one in which transnational foreign investment was to be encouraged – multinational corporations would be free to make profits if they would invest capital, generate currency for foreign exchange and create new jobs in India. However, they would also be evaluated and judged on their social and cultural influence and propaganda, which could not be at the expense of India's own cultural heritage, her economic exploitation or an unbridled consumerism and materialism. The ideological tensions between 'RSS economic nationalism' and 'BJP economic globalization', however 'calibrated' the latter is intended to be, are severe and reflect not simply an RSS concern about rising poverty, unemployment and the potential failure of small Indian businesses unable to compete in a global market, but the cultural and social impact of globalization on the 'Hindu ethos' it believes requires protection. While Govindacharya has argued that *swadeshi* does not mean isolationism or protectionism, it is unlikely that the BJP can steer a third way between *parivar* 'economic nationalism' on the one hand and unfettered market reforms and economic globalization on the other.

The second major ideological and political tension concerns Hindutva itself and of the forms of Hindu nationalist governance that an unconstrained BJP government at the centre would impose on the Indian polity. In its 1998 election commitments, the BJP's intentions, combining social and political authoritarianism with economic liberalism and economic nationalism, are clear. A clear BJP majority government poses a serious threat to India's secular, democratic and federal organization of state and civil society, and to India's religious minorities. While the Hindu vote bank of the BJP is impermanent and motile, and its support base is restricted to mainly northern India's Hindi belt, Maharashtra and Gujarat, the BJP has consistently increased its share of the popular vote in every general election it has contested (7.4 per cent in 1984, 11.5 per cent in 1989, 20.1 per cent in 1991, 20.3 per cent in 1996 to 25.6 per cent in 1998). While this does not approach anything like the 41 per cent of the popular vote gained by the Jana Sangh / Janata coalition in 1977 following the unique conditions of Emergency, it does reflect a significant trend. Moreover, the activities and impact of the Hindu nationalist movements extends well beyond the electoral fortunes of the parliamentary BJP. The mid- to late-1990s have witnessed the extraordinary rapidity and zeal with which BJP controlled states, and the Hindutva movements unleashed within them, have inducted their vision of 'Hindu rashtra' into the institutions of state governments and civil society.

–7–

The Authoritarian Landscape of the
Vishwa Hindu Parishad

There would be nothing to object to if one uttered 'Mara' [instead of 'Rama'] reversing the order of syllables, while chanting the Name. We read of the pure of heart having attained [salvation] even by chanting it in an erroneous manner and we can believe this to be true. However, what are we to say of sinners who, although their pronunciation is perfect, chant the *mantra* of *Ramanama* ['Ram's name'] in order to nourish their sins? That is why I am afraid of any propaganda for *Ramanama*. (M. K. Gandhi, *Hindu Dharma*)

Introduction

The RSS's core ideology and organizational method are novel products of the twentieth century. The distinctive emphasis on xenological nationalism, modernity and 'science', and its rational, algorithmic apprehension of the human personality and of the social formation have led some to typify it as reflecting essentially a 'secular nationalist' methodology that can claim no foundational basis in the affective, devotional, metaphysical or vernacular beliefs and practices of traditional, ordinary or folk Hinduism (Nandy et al. 1995). One aspect of this argument has some force: the RSS has, perhaps until recently, found what may be called superstitious, obscurantist and non-rational beliefs and practices within Hinduism as bordering on the abhorrent. The organization of Hindu practice through *sampraday* affiliation and *jati* membership is also disagreeable for an organization that privileges Hindu organic solidarity rather than what it perceives as illegitimate differentiations that weaken Hinduism. Since its inception, the RSS has sustained a foundational critique of what it has perceived as the historical failure of Hindus; the RSS was indeed founded on the belief that the reasons for 'the failure' of Hindus to 'repel foreign invaders' were to be found in Hindus, if not elements of Hinduism or Buddhism. Similarly, those aspects of Hindu symbolism and mythology that were privileged by the RSS were selectively ones that emphasized 'secular' concerns of territory, military power and organized strength, rather than those of belief, ritual, devotion, philosophy and personal or metaphysical apprehension of the divine. The putatively religious symbolism employed by the RSS has traditionally centred on the medieval Mahratta confederacy, the 'guru' symbolism of the saffron flag, and its distinctly idiosyncratic renderings of some traditional religious festivals (such as Makara Sankranti and Raksha Bandhan) as part of the six main RSS *utsavs* that it celebrates (although its founder Hedgewar did cultivate a devotionalism around Bajrang, the Marathi version of the God Hanuman). These were regional and 'temporal' symbols that could not have purchase outside their limited *shakha* enclaves. Nevertheless, the RSS claimed be the society in microcosm that it wanted the Indian social formation to become, and hence considered itself best placed to articulate the totality of Hindu society, including, apparently, all of its religious beliefs. It was thus inevitable that the RSS would have to confront, and negotiate with, the structures of actually existing caste and *sampraday* Hinduism and attempt to restructure the latter according to its overarching vision of a strong and unified Hindu Samaj and Hindu Rashtra.

The Formation of the Vishwa Hindu Parishad (VHP)

On 29–30 August 1964, at the instigation of Madhav Golwalkar, the RSS's second *sarsanghchalak*, some 150 delegates representing different Hindu sampradaik traditions were invited to, and over sixty attended, a meeting at the Sandipani Sadhanalaya (ashram) of Swami Chinmayananda (who died in 1993) in Bombay at which it was decided to inaugurate a new organization to represent all Hindus (information on the early VHP meetings has been obtained from the VHP's *Hindu Vishwa* July 1982, van der Veer 1994, McKean 1996, and from the VHP's Web site, which published some of the founding letters and reports of its first three meetings, and overlaps in content with the *Hindu Vishwa* edition). Previously, RSS *pracharak* Shivram Shankar Apte had met with regional Hindu leaders and the titular heads of *sampradays* (particular religious 'traditions') and *panths* ('sects') in various parts of India in order to garner opinion on a new Hindu body. In 1963, Chinmayananda, founder of the Chinmaya Mission, had explored the prospect of convening a world Hindu council in order to develop a common platform of Hindu *dharma* across the diversity of Hindu sects and which would be agreeable to the diversity of opinions among Hindu *dharmacharyas*. Chinmayananda presided over the inaugural meeting of the VHP whose attendance included Golwalkar, V. G. Deshpande and S. S. Apte, Sant Tukadoji, Swami Shankarananda Saraswati from Yoganandeshwara math, K. M. Munshi (the Gujarati writer and Hindu nationalist) and representatives of Sikh bodies, including the Shiromani Akali Dal. The initial aims and objectives of the VHP were: to take steps to consolidate and strengthen Hindu Society; to protect, develop and spread Hindu values – ethical and spiritual – in the context of modern times; and to establish and strengthen contacts with and help all Hindus living abroad.

The VHP's definition of 'Hindu' as one that 'embraces all people who believe in, respect or follow the eternal values of life, ethical and spiritual, that have evolved in Bharat' is a syncretism of Savarkar's Hindutva (and reproduces the 'civilizational' discourse of the latter) and the idea of *sanatan dharma*. As Peter van der Veer has pointed out, the VHP's definition shares considerable epistemological space with mainstream academic discussions that also view Hinduism as a civilization rather than a religion (van der Veer 1994: 134). The VHP also reflected an unambiguous RSS sangathanist strategy. Of additional significance was the 'global' aim of the VHP. Representatives from Kenya and Trinidad had attended the inaugural meeting, and from its inception, the VHP, unlike the RSS during the 1960s, had adopted an international perspective that was to bear fruit in the coming decades among Hindus in the south Asian diaspora. It is a moot point whether this objective reflected the wishes of *sampraday* heads such as Chinmayananda, who were to soon develop their overseas missionary movements, or whether it appeared to give nominal substance to the idea of a '*world* council'. At this inaugural meeting, Swami Shankarananda expressed the urgent need to 'rouse the Hindu nation' against the 'menacing conversions to Christianity and Islam, which are spreading like a conflagration in our country'. It was also decided at this meeting to create an advisory council of the *shankaracharyas*, the heads of all *sampradays* and sects, and various *sants*, gurus, 'personalities, thinkers and philosophers respected all over the country'. The VHP resolved to forbid any officer of any political party from holding office in its executive body; this was a demonstration of its apparently non-political orientation.

The second meeting of the VHP was held in November 1964 in New Delhi and chaired by Chinmayananda, with Jaya Chamaraja Wadiyar, the Maharaja of Mysore accepting presidentship of the VHP. Apte had become VHP general secretary at its inauguration, starting a tradition in which senior RSS executives, rather than religious leaders, were to hold this office. While the *shankaracharyas* of Sringeri, Puri, Dwarka and Kamkoti had sent messages, they did not attend this meeting. However, the then *shankaracharya* of Bhanpura *pith*, Satyamitranand Giri apparently did attend. The third meeting of the VHP executive council was held on May 27–28 1965 in the Summer Palace of the Maharaja of Mysore, at which the draft constitution of the VHP was discussed.

It was decided at the inaugural VHP meeting to organize a world Hindu *sammelan* during the Kumbh Mela on 22–24 January 1966 in Allahabad. This event was attended by a claimed 25,000 delegates, of which some 250 were from abroad. By this stage, the VHP had secured the attendance of two *shankaracharyas*, from Sharda peet in Dwarka and Govardhan peet in Puri, as well as the ex-*shankaracharya*, 'Mahamandaleshwar' Satyamitranand Giri. Satyamitranand was of considerable significance both in furthering the aims of the VHP, especially outside India, and in developing an early and distinctly territorial form of devotionalism – a 'geopiety' that sacralized symbolic devotion to the land, and was the precursor to the VHP's 'semiological' political strategy from 1979. At the *sammelan*, he called on Hindu society to kindle *brahmatej* and *kshatriyatej*. The resolutions passed at the *sammelan* included: making Sanskrit teaching compulsory in secondary education; banning cow slaughter; reconversion of those who had left Hinduism through 'violence, coercion and temptations exerted on them by people of other faiths', particular attention being focused on 'the sinister activities of Christian missionaries amongst the Tribals'; and strengthening ties and promoting *dharma* among Hindus in India and abroad.

The *sammelan* resolved to appoint a Vidvat Parishad ('Council of the Learned') 'to compile a minimum code of conduct and cultural guide' for Hindus to strengthen Hindu *samskars* in society. This was framed as the preparation of

> a charter of 'Hindutva', to *prescribe* a common code of 'Laukika' [mundane or ordinary] and 'Daivika' [extra-mundane or religious] conduct in conformity with our ancient heritage and in consonance with the needs of the modern world. (Resolution on convening of Vidvat Parishad, January 1966, http://www.vhp.org, emphasis added)

The VHP rather audaciously considered itself as the legitimate body for directing *both* the secular and religious conduct of all Hindus. While codes of personal and religious conduct typically attach to affiliation with a particular *sampraday*, 'Hinduism' does not recognize a single body of injunctions that govern the conduct of all the traditions and sects that 'comprise' it, nor a single organization or 'ecclesiastical' body that stipulates such injunctions. The 'Council of the Learned' was comprised of the *shankaracharya* of Dwarka, the Maharaja of Mysore, C. P. Ramaswamy Aiyer, Swami Chinmayananda, Ramprasad Mookherjee, Golwalkar and Sant Tukadoji.

The VHP's constitution was agreed in late April 1966. This established the VHP's executive committee and its two main bodies, the board of trustees and the governing council. Of the twenty-two initial trustees, only three can be said to have been religious leaders – Swami Chinmayananda, Sant Tukadoji and Satguru Jagjit Singh (representing Namdhari Sikhs). No Hindu religious leaders were apparent among the fifteen members of its 1966 governing council. The presence of Golwalkar on the 'Council of the Learned' and board of trustees, commenced a tradition in which the RSS *sarsanghchalak* was also a member of the VHP's controlling body, just as the VHP general secretary was a senior RSS officer. This does not imply that the RSS controlled the VHP, but the converse is evident – that the most senior RSS leadership knew about and participated in formulating VHP national policy and strategy. The VHP established a central office in New Delhi (its Bombay office functioning as a provincial branch), a monthly journal (*Hindu Vishwa*), and a 'short and general' training seminar for its own *pracharaks*. The VHP resolved to create a nationwide and state-level structure. Of significance was the decision in 1966 to open VHP centres in Assam, Madhya Pradesh, Gujarat, Maharashtra and elsewhere to:

acquaint our brethren residing in hills and forests, scheduled castes and other backward groups, with the Hindu ways of life and to introduce among them simple ways of worship and devotion to Hindu deities and thereby stabilize them within our common Hindu fold. (VHP Executive Committee Resolution 27.04.1966, from J. R. Gupta, 'The evolution of a full-fledged organization', http://www.vhp.org/englishsite/a-origin_&_growth/evolution.htm)

The rather unwieldy structure of the VHP took shape during the 1970s and 1980s and included not just the Board of Trustees (from 1988 this could have a maximum of 101 members from India and abroad), the Governing Council and a board of Patrons (the latter appointed by the Governing Council), but a number of sub-structures including: a Standing Committee (established 1970) of up to fifteen members of the Governing Council, empowered to formulate policies and implement promptly the work of the Board of Trustees and Governing Council; a 'board of holding trustees'; a sub-committee of the Governing Council to frame and implement by-laws of the VHP; and a national and international branch structure.

The VHP is organized according to state-level units that have their own branches at *vibhag* (a zonal division of groups of states in India), provincial (about 30 mainly state-level bodies), district (a geographical unit containing a population of approximately one million), *prakhand* (covering a population of about one hundred thousand) and sub-*prakhand* levels (*khand* and *upkhand*, covering areas containing populations of about ten thousand or less than two thousand respectively.) In 1999, the VHP reported almost 19,300 'administrative units' at *prakhand* and sub-*prakhand* levels. In addition, the VHP also has *vibhags* (departments) working in some eighteen different project areas. These include its youth, women's and 'tribal' work. Internationally, the Vishwa Hindu Parishad reported affiliated bodies in eighteen countries. In 1984, it was recommended that the relation of the VHP branches outside India to the VHP in India be such that 'the VHP central office, New Delhi and its Board of Trustees is the Supreme Body having jurisdiction over the entire organization of the world' (VHP Executive Committee Resolution, 27.04.1966). In other words, the policy and organization of VHP branches in the diaspora was to be directed from India.

The Shankaracharyas

The presence of two *shankaracharyas* at the 1966 *sammelan* was significant. The importance of the 'four' *shankaracharyas* for the VHP is related to the power they wield within (especially brahminic, Sanatanist and northern Indian) Hinduism. However, the *shankaracharyas* cannot be conceived as an ecclesiastical structure *of* Hinduism. The legitimacy of the *shankaracharyas*, or the authority of any one of them, can be questioned. Indeed, the authority of the *shankaracharyas* is often not acknowledged either within their own ostensible spheres of influence or from within a broader Indian Hinduism. The brahminic strictures, limits to 'theological' influence, and the competition between *shankaracharyas* can create obstacles for the VHP's integrationist project.

In some dominant Hindu traditions, the early medieval Indian philosopher and theologian Sankara (c. 700–750), the *adi* (original or first) *shankaracharya* was said to have attempted to unify various *sannyasin* orders under the *dashnami* (ten 'names' or orders) *sannyasi* tradition. He is said to have established four monasteries (*maths*), each headed by a *shankaracharya*, in order to geographically consolidate his *advaita* tradition across India. Currently, these are based at Sharda *math*, Dwarka (in Gujarat, the western *math*), Govardhan *math*, Puri (in Orissa, the eastern *math*), Sringeri *math* (in Sringeri, Karnataka, traditionally the southern *math*) and Jyotirmath (Badrinath, near Hardwar, Uttar Pradesh, the northern *math*). Historically, there have not only been numerous other *dashnami sannyasin* monasteries in India but also a multitude of swamis claiming inheritance of the *shankaracharya* mantle in one or other *math*, or who otherwise name themselves *shankaracharyas*. The Kanchi Kamakoti Peetam (in Kanchipuram, Tamil Nadu) headed by Swami Chandrasekharendra Saraswati until 1954, and then by Swami Jayendra Saraswati, both adopting the *shankaracharya* title, is significant in this respect and has jostled for prestige as the southern *math* against the more traditionally recognised Sringeri *math* (see especially Sundaresan not dated). The right of succession to the northern (Badrinath) *math* is claimed by at least three swamis, including Swami Vasudevananda Saraswati and the existing *shankaracharya* of Dwarka, Swami Swarupananda Saraswati. Swami Nischalananda, titular head of Puri *math*, has also been recently challenged. These disputes demonstrate an alternative sphere of hegemonic contestation within 'upper' caste Hinduism that can work against the organizational and political aims of the VHP. Some *shankaracharyas* make the same demands as the Hindutva movement but also contest the hegemonic encroachments of the VHP in its claim to represent 'pan-Hinduism'. Vasudevananda is considered close to the VHP (Jaffrelot 1996: 356) or 'firmly in the Sangh camp' (Lochtefeld 1996: 110). Conversely, Swarupananda opposed the VHP's *shilanyas* at the Babri masjid, proposed his alternative ceremony, and insisted that a Ram temple be built at the site of the mosque – though not under the VHP's direction or leadership (Sundaresan not dated). Nischalananda (of Puri) has been close to the VHP and has, for example, led conversions of Christians to Hinduism (*India Today*, 31 July 2000), while his recent challenger Swami Adhokshajananda, is apparently opposed to the VHP and close to Congress (Sundaresan not dated). Jayendra Saraswati of Kanchi *math* has both opposed 'conversions' to Christianity and called for 'a national debate on religious conversions' along the lines proposed by the BJP. The organization of the *shankaracharya* tradition in the contemporary period hence reflects not stasis but a dynamic structure that has its own uneven momentum.

The VHP and Hindutva Social Movement

The VHP's activities until the early 1980s were relatively limited. However, during the early 1980s, the VHP substantially increased its activities, holding a number of Hindu Samajotsavs (Hindu Unity events) and *sammelans* in Karnataka, Delhi, Jammu, Kanyakumari, Ranchi, Tirupati and Maharashtra (Bhattacharya 1991: 130). In 1979, it held a second World Hindu Conference at which it proposed a six-point 'code of conduct' for all Hindus. Hindus were expected to worship the Sun at dawn and dusk (reflecting the *suryanamaskar* ceremony of RSS *shakhas*); wear the 'Om' symbol around their neck and use the symbol on personal artefacts; revere and keep in their homes the *Bhagavad Gita* as *the* 'sacred' book of the Hindus; maintain a shrine to the family deity and worship it daily – the onus on family religious observance placed on the male head of the household; grow a *tulsi* (holy basil) plant; and regularly attend temple, *gurudwaras* and other centres of faith (McKean 1996: 110–11). Similarly, in 1998 the VHP held a *dharma sansad* (religious congress) in Taylorsburg, Pennsylvania, attended by the VHP president Ashok Singhal, to develop a similar 'code of conduct' for Hindus living in the west (*India Abroad*, 28 December 1998); this was followed by a second *dharma sansad* in September 1999 held in Austin, Texas. The Indian VHP's *achar samhita* (code of conduct) for all Hindus was significant in stipulating sun worship, the 'Om' symbol and the *Bhagavad Gita* as central to universal Hindu practice. The VHP's elevation of the Gita has been noted as reflecting an emulation of the sacred book of the 'semitic' traditions (Jaffrelot 1996: 348).

The *achar samhita* is also important for what it leaves out: the four Vedas are considered universal sacred books of divine origin in (especially northern Indian Hindu) traditions in a way that the *Bhagavad Gita* is not, the latter, as part of the *Mahabharata*, belonging to the more 'secular' epic tradition. Presumably, either the Vedas were considered too sacred to allow all Hindus to have them in their homes (since they are traditionally the preserve of the 'pure' male brahmin priesthood), or the Vedas would not serve the functions of political mobilization which a *bhakti* text that could be read as inculcating a Hindu 'will to action' potentially could.

However, during its 'Ramjanmabhoomi' campaign 'to liberate the birthplace of Rama' by destroying the medieval Babri masjid at Ayodhya in Uttar Pradesh, the VHP elevated the *Ramayana* as the privileged text of Hinduism. This strategy has been similarly viewed as both 'semitizing' and creating a 'syndicated' Hinduism (Thapar 1985), in this case by proposing one God (Rama), 'one' book (the Valmiki and Tulsidas versions of the numerous south Asian and south-east Asian Rama stories) and one holy city (Ayodhya) (Thapar 1989, 1991: 159–60; on the histories and variety of Rama legends within and outside India, see Brockington 1984, Richman 1991). This characterization of Hindutva as 'semitizing' Hinduism is problematic. While this is not the intention of adherents of this thesis, under a singular 'semitic' appellation, the hugely varying manifestations of Islam and Christianity can be dehistoricized and socially disembedded; conversely, the idea that Hinduism could share such characteristics may be considered disagreeable. It is also by no means clear that Hindutva strategy is preoccupied with 'semitizing' Hinduism.

The importance attached to both the *Bhagavad Gita* and the *Ramayana* can be seen as a syncretism of a 'kshatriyization' strategy with *bhakti* traditions. In this, the privilege accorded to brahminism is left more-or-less intact, but a flexible kshatriya political space is created through which the allegiance of the mass of caste Hindus, and those outside the caste system, can be cultivated. Overall, this can be seen to reflect a political and symbolic method based on a reconfigured brahmin-kshatriya caste alliance.

The strategy of the VHP from the early 1980s was as seemingly multifarious as it was changeable. The first plank of VHP strategy was the creation of a political space that appealed to, and allowed the entry of, a wide range of independent *mahants* (local temple administrators), *sannyasins* and relatively minor local or regional *dharmacharyas* who were seeking greater social and political influence but who were, with a few exceptions (such as *mahant* Avaidyanath), kept external to the VHP's structures of power (Lochtefeld 1996: 107). It was not the mass of lower status *sannyasin* supporters of the VHP who were given political or public platforms, unless they uncritically reheased RSS-VHP themes (Basu 1993: 95–6). However, the VHP has also been keen to organize public unity forums of important *sampraday* and *panth* leaders, ascetics and well-known *kathakars* that *portray* a united 'Hindu front' of *dharmacharyas*. Conversely, organized mass congregations of *sadhus*, such as the Akhil Bharatiya Akhara Parishad, have opposed the VHP's political Hindutva agenda. This has included vehement opposition from the extremely influential Juna Akhara, as well as the Niranjan and Udaseen *akharas* for using Hindu symbols and events, including religious festivals and the Kumbh Mela, for political purposes. In the VHP's visual material (such as the various videos it produced), it is noticeable both how many ascetics are present at VHP events, typically depicted as a mass of saffron-clad followers, sometimes officiating at 'religious' rituals that the VHP has orchestrated, and how few are heard speaking. The spoken voice has been restricted to figures such as Avaidyanath, the *sannyasinis* Sadhvi Rithambara and Uma Bharati, and RSS-VHP senior officers, such as Ashok Singhal, the VHP's general secretary, and *acharya* Giriraj Kishore, the VHP's senior vice-president.

The restriction of the diversity of religious voices is in sharp contrast to the semiological proliferation of religious-nationalist and devotional icons, tokens and symbols. The VHP undertook the development, initially tentatively, of a political semiology based on symbols that could appeal to the affectiveness and emotion of *bhakti* (devotionalism) among Hindus without requiring Hindu devotees to abandon their attachment to their traditional deities, forms of worship or *sampradays* and, apparently, without causing a cognitivie dissonance or in other ways disrupting those beliefs (Lochtefeld 1996, Basu 1993).

Of considerable significance is that a strategy involving devotion was used, rather than the more austere paths of esoteric knowledge or physical practice that exist in (especially upper) caste Hinduism. This required the formulation of novel overarching nationalist religious symbols, which cannot be said to have traditional endorsements within Hinduism, but which could nevertheless not be explicitly opposed either. One key symbol was that of Bharatmata, a devotional rendering of the Mother Goddess as equivalent to the geographical territory of 'Akhand Bharat'. Strictly speaking, Bharatmata is not a devotional figure for any Hindu tradition, nor does worship of Bharatmata complete any extant sampradaik tradition – 'she is nobody's Goddess' (Lochtefeld 1996: 105). Nor indeed does worship of Bharatmata signify the symbolic unity of either Hinduism or of the religions traditions and *sampradays* that comprise it. However, neither could a devoted Hindu *contest* her worship without appearing to counter the meaning of affective devotionalism in Hindu traditions. Similarly, the worship of Bharatmata does not rupture allegiance to other forms of worship. In the Hindutva symbolic imaginary 'Bharatmata' *stands in for* 'Hindu Rashtra', and worship of the latter, so important in the RSS *shakha* regime, could be eminently problematic for the ordinary Hindu devotional sensibility, not least because in the Hindu pantheon there is not a single Hindu God that symbolizes 'Hindu Rashtra' itself. In this context, it is significant that the Hindu Rashtra *mandirs* advocated in the earlier Hindutva *sangathan* period by Swami Shraddhanand and Savarkar were displaced by Satyamitranand Giri's Bharat Mata *mandir* in Hardwar as a key Hindutva symbol in the 1980s. The *mandir* was consecrated in May 1983 during a ceremony attended by the Dwarka *shankaracharya* and some 100,000 devotees. During a period when Congress (I) was exploiting the religious Hindu vote, Indira Gandhi also attended and performed *aarti*. The temple was also a focus for the VHP's 1983 *ekatmata yagna* ('sacrifice for unity') (McKean 1996: 148–9).

Caste, Symbols and Myths: Brand(ish)ing Hinduism

The importance of the novel syncretism of selected *bhakti* symbols, 'upper' caste *yagnas* and *yatras*, *varnashramadharma*, and a strictly 'secular', 'geo-pious' symbolism of landscape, geography, territory and boundary requires noting (and confounds the view of a 'semitization' of Hinduism). In the aftermath of the 1981 Meenakshipuram conversions, the VHP organized two *jnana rathams* ('chariots of religious wisdom') in Tamil Nadu. Two vans, carrying idols of the (mainly south Indian) deity, Murugan, travelled across Tamil Nadu, crossing each others paths, and at each stop, 'lower' caste and 'untouchable' people were encouraged to offer devotion to, and bathe the idols. The RSS described this in the following way:

> The Jnana Ratham project of VHP gave one more powerful thrust to the movement for Hindu social harmony. The Ratham was specially taken to the backward rural areas. Harijans and other neglected sections were amongst those most exposed to the [Dravidian parties'] anti-religious propaganda assaults. But now, Lord Murugan, installed by Shri Kanchi Shankaracharya and Shri Pejawar Mathadheesh in the Jnana Ratham, was Himself coming to their humble hamlets and huts to give darshan – an opportunity denied to them for centuries. Their devotional fervour had to be seen to be believed. At one place, there was a regular stream of devotees who started pooja and abhisheka in the afternoon which came to a close only after midnight. (Seshadri 1988: Chapter 5)

This is a political manipulation of an extremely important regional deity of caste Hinduism 'travelling' across the physical landscape of Tamil Nadu in order to simultaneously counter conversions to Islam among lower and 'untouchable' castes, oppose Dravidian, anti-north Indian and anti-brahmin ideology, attempt to interpellate 'untouchables' with an hierarchical caste-devotional Hinduism, and elide in their entirety the social and economic grievances of 'untouchables' that arise from caste Hinduism. Moreover, the strategy of involving individual acts of *puja* (prayer) and *abhishek* (a ritual in which an idol is bathed) can appear to be giving something to 'untouchable' communities – namely the opportunity to bathe an idol representing a God who is not traditionally their own. It also placed the onus on those communities (rather than 'upper' caste Hindus) to undertake *this task*, rather than one that might address the oppression of scheduled castes and dalits by caste Hinduism. Strategically, this was undertaken in the cause of their alleged 'upliftment' into Hinduism. While this may be seen as the wreaking of an insult upon a gross injustice, its significance was the multi-accentual use of singular religious symbols in order to achieve a political goal. This is a hegemonic strategy of 'upper' caste Hinduism: the VHP has never undertaken a *yatra* that has brought the world-views, animist beliefs, deities, and secular or religious practices of tribal and 'untouchable' people to 'upper' caste neighbourhoods and insisted that brahmins adopt these in place of their own religions.

In November 1983, the VHP organized a month long nation-wide *ekatmata yagna*. A *yagna* is traditionally a caste Hindu 'sacrifice' ritual, typically performed by the brahmin priesthood, and its use in this context was novel. *Ekatmata* means 'unification', to make Hindus into one, but also can have nationalist connotations of a singular mother(land) (*ek mata*) and a single 'national' soul (*ek atma*). The *yagna* was rather different to the sangathanist strategies of earlier decades. Earlier sangathanists focused their activities regionally and in urban theatres – the city space was organized or divided through religious affiliation. The VHP method is based on syncretizing the symbol of national space with an existing religious ecology of *bhakti* and *puja* that can be redirected towards new deities of land, geography and monument:

> The Yajna's focus was three caravans carrying Ganges water: one from Kathmandu to Rameshvaram, one from Ganga Sagar to Somnath, and one from Hardwar to Kanyakumari. The caravans traveled across the continent on pilgrimage routes, converging at midpoint in Nagpur, the headquarters of the RSS. Along the way the Ganges water carried by the caravans was mixed with water from local rivers, to demonstrate symbolically the country's unity . . . it was conducted amid extensive publicity, and sales of Ganges water along the way generated considerable revenue. (Lochtefeld 1996: 105)

This traversal of India (and Nepal) manufactured, and appeared to appropriate, a new religious-territorial landscape. The six towns and cities contain important pilgrimage sites for Hindus and Buddhists, and the *yagna* also chose routes passing through numerous other religious sites, converging on Nagpur, the Maharashtrian home town of the RSS. In addition, there were some 90 shorter processions and the *yagna* involved the participation of almost 60 million individuals (Andersen and Damle 1987: 135).

The 'deities' of Ganga (the Ganges river) and Bharatmata, neither of which are, strictly speaking, traditionally used for *bhakti*, were combined with an overarching focus on *yagna* (sacrifice) and *yatra* (pilgrimage, symbolized by the processions) (Jaffrelot 1996: 361). Characteristically, water-river and land-territory were the objects of deification. These strongly connote the founding primordial myth of Aryan Hindutva, and hence the VHP's strategy can be viewed as an 'aryanization' of *bhakti*. While there certainly exist traditions of taking Ganges water to local shrines, the sale of Ganges water during the *yagna* was an inversion of the traditional ritual pilgrimage to and bathing in the Ganges. Basu et al. (1993:63) have commented that such activities signalled a commodification of Hinduism based on its commercialization – vending mythology. Similarly, James Lochtefeld has argued that during such events the VHP showed 'a media mastery and an eye for symbols that would put most ad agencies to shame' (Lochtefeld 1996: 105). This was start of the VHP's populist branding strategy of Hinduism. While this can be viewed as the cultural invigoration and innovation that accompanies all cultural nationalisms, its intolerance was foregrounded.

In the VHP's 1983 *ekatmata yagna* there were other innovatory aspects of its methodological strategy of loading affect onto symbol which became definitive in its subsequent campaigns. Most significant was the importance of journeys from one part of India to another and the concomitant process of carefully selecting symbolic sites. The journey from Kathmandu to Rameshvaram illustrated the novelty of this. While both contained important pilgrimage sites, the latter town in Tamil Nadu is mythologically related to the Rama of the epic period (and said to bear Rama's 'footprints' before he crossed the seas to Lanka) but is also important to Shiva devotees, whereas Kathmandu, while conceivably important for Hindu devotionalism, is primarily known for its Buddhist shrines, in particular the *disputed* site of Bodhnath. Nepal is privileged in Hindutva discourse as a 'Hindu state' and its two autocratic kings (Mahendra until 1972, and then Birendra) have been avid supporters of the VHP and vice versa. Nevertheless, historically the two sites represent different religious traditions and for which it would be difficult to use the single term *bhakti*. The linking of both sites through the journey was a displacement of their distinct traditions by the symbols of territorial Hindutva.

It is worth noting the significance of the two privileged terms *yagna* and *yatra* in the VHP's strategies of political mobilization during the 1980s and 1990s; the terms signify, respectively, an *arya*-Vedic (rather than strictly devotional) brahminic practice and an asceticism traditionally and scripturally associated with upper castes. With the one possible exception of *rashtra-bhakti* (devotion to the Hindu nation), *bhakti* does not feature regularly in the titles of VHP campaigns. Nevertheless, of considerable importance is the way the VHP has combined the traditionally brahminic *yagnas* (and *havans*), as well as the *yatra* traditions of ascetic pilgrims, with the more popular traditions of *bhakti*, *puja* based on *murtis*, *abhishekh*, darshan and *aarti*. Indeed the use of *aarti* in the form of mass, public *maha-aartis* by the Shiv Sena, the Bajrang Dal and the VHP to directly confront Muslims at Friday prayers in Bombay, and Christians in recent years, was a strategically provocative, violence-oriented transformation of the peaceful practice of offering devotion to and receiving blessing from the deities. While novel, the practices are very different from the formulaic and austere nationalist rituals of the RSS. *Yatras* became politically important in the nineteenth century as a procession of idols through *urban* spaces, as in the Ganesh festival popularized by Tilak. The VHP's combination of idolatry with the *yatra* tradition of pilgrimage, and hence a journey, created a *national* procession of political symbols. The aim of the VHP is not to make caste Hindus more religious or devotional but to make them more political.

The VHP and Bhakti

The articulation of *bhakti* under overarching symbols of *yagna* and *yatra*, while strongly suggestive of a hierarchical brahminic discourse, should not imply that *bhakti* in itself has been unimportant to the VHP. On the contrary, the appeal to and at the same time modification of *bhakti* affect is central to VHP technologies of hegemony, especially in conditions of limited literacy. However, with the exception of *smarta* influences, *bhakti* is so strongly linked to particular deities or worship traditions that mobilizing on a national scale one *bhakti* symbol was a potentially problematic undertaking. The key problem the VHP had to negotiate was the utilization of devotional symbols and deities that could appeal to the majority of Hindus without alienating any specific devotional tradition.

This was most apparent in the VHP's role in the 'Ramjanmabhoomi' campaign to destroy the Babri masjid at Ayodhya and in its place build a temple to the mythological god Ram. In traditional Hindu beliefs, Ram existed in the mythic time of the *treta yuga*, though the latter was 'historicized' by the VHP to somewhere between 90,000 and 100,000 years ago. The VHP's strategy from the mid-1980s combined new, developing and experimental rituals with novel iconic represent- ations. The 1988 'Ram *shila pujas*', whereby bricks inscribed with the god Ram's name were 'sacralized' (consecrated) and then worshipped in puja activities in a nationwide (indeed international) campaign systematically organized by the VHP, illustrated the inventiveness of such rituals. The bricks, wrapped in saffron cloth and displayed in temples and public sites, became the intended object of devotional reverence. (The VHP advanced the majesty and grandeur of Hindu civilization by creating a nation of brick devotees.) Alongside the *shila pujas* was the organization of *mahayagnas* (mass 'sacrifice' rituals) which served as the basis for the dissemination of VHP propaganda, as well as Ram *padukas*, *prasad*, *gulal*, *pataka* and Ram *jyotis*. Finally, mass public processions of consecrated bricks converging on Ayodhya were organized (Panikkar 1997: 95, 155–6.) If worshipping *bricks* or organizing their public procession had no precedent in Hinduism, what were the existing processes of 'enchantment' among the Hindu supporters of the Ram campaign in Indian civil society that allowed and condoned such a rapid and drastic politicization of their religious traditions?

VHP strategy has also involved what Basu et al. (1993) have called the controlled and strategic proliferation of a vast number of iconic representations of Ram, typically juxtaposed with images of the proposed temple. This was under- taken using the print media, videos, posters and flyers, hoardings and stickers. Ram was already a familiar and popular icon since the widespread, although relatively recent, use of Ram iconography in secular and public environments, domestic shrines and on calendars, posters, comic books, and Diwali and other greeting cards. (The development of what are now the dominant Hindu iconic representations in graphic print ephemera and temple effigies requires more discussion than can be provided here; however, the post-1960s print representations have surprisingly little semblance to the older traditions of Hindu iconography, including those during the colonial period, and have to be seen as a novel form.) These representations of Ram were by and large of a noble, patriarchal (though sometimes feminized) civility, typically a portmanteau of Ram figured centrally, Sita and Lakshman standing on either side, and Hanuman in a gesture of reverence, his weapon on the ground. Ram holds his bow upright but is non-threatening. The presence of figures other than Ram decentre him and invoke a range of layered connotations and narratives that are not simply about Ram's power, nor even a simple celebration of his victory against the mythological king of Lanka, Ravan. If one can speak of a dominant connotation, it is one of peaceful rule and plenitude. (It is necessary to register here an earlier quotidian meaning of 'Ram' as simply 'God', and especially the post-Gandhian connotation of 'Ram' as *both* Ishwar and Allah, and which the VHP has purposefully focused on and fractured through its demands that Muslims be forced to say 'Jai Shri Ram!' as a demonstration of their 'love' for and allegiance to 'Hindu Rashtra'. Also, the traditional relationships between devotee and religious representation, ritual, myth or litany are exceedingly complex, but largely exclude the idea that the gods or goddesses are sources of emulation or to be 'imitated'.)

A characteristic VHP visual representation, however, has Ram alone, purposefully and angrily striding through turbulent waters and under a dark sky, not facing the viewer, his unambiguous intention to use his weapons – the God has clearly been angered (Kapur 1993, Basu et al 1993, Davis 1996). A representation of a magnificent temple to Ram is usually juxtaposed with this image. The overdressed, overpatterned and highly garlanded body of former representations is gone. Ram's skin tone is also consistently lightened.

For many northern Indian devotees of Ram, no representation of Ram could be feasibly contested, since each could in principle be a 'valid' representation if invoking some aspect of the narrative of the northern Indian tradition of Tulsidas' *Ramacharitmanas*. However, while Ram's *throne* has been frequently represented in popular iconography, there is no tradition of the representation of Ram's *temple*. It is unclear what the semiology of a Ram temple can invoke from the actual narratives of Tulsidas' *Ramacharitmanas* or Valmiki's *Ramayana*. Hence, the VHP's transfiguration of Ram iconography summons a leap from the mythic time of the *Ramayana* to the historical time of the medieval period of the first Mughal emperor, Babar and to the contemporary demand of the VHP to destroy the masjid at Ayodhya. Aside from this particular representation, the VHP also skilfully deployed a number of other Ram images including ones of Ram in a cage and Ram as a young child (*Bhaye Prakat Kripala*, a VHP-RSS video produced by Jain Studios). Such representations were characteristically juxtaposed with more traditional images of Ram, creating a motile chain of significations that could easily lead from the 'feminized' Ram of the domestic shrine to the VHP's militant kshatriya Ram. The 'caged Ram' evoked the locking of the gates of the Babri masjid in late 1949 following the 'miraculous appearance' of Ram idols in the mosque and the violence that ensued as some Hindus demanded rights over the mosque. Similarly, the representation of Ram's childhood is novel, this depiction clearly intended to appeal to Krishna devotees for whom the latter's variously coy and mischievous childhood antics have been a source of popular iconic representation.

However, the representation of Krishna has also been militarized. Govinda, the flute playing cowherd surrounded by admiring *gopis*, the amorous represent-ations of Radha-Krishna, the child Krishna stealing ghee from an urn, and Krishna as the infinite and timeless Vishnu of the *Bhagavad Gita*, have been displaced by a depiction of Krishna alongside Arjuna, both mounted on their chariot situated on the battlefield of Kurukshetra, sounding the conch that calls forth their armies to battle against their enemies. That Arjuna's enemies are also his kin and whom he is under a moral compulsion to kill is suggestive. The mythic time of the Mahabharata battle is transposed to the Hindutva war against Muslims, Christians, 'pseudo-secularists' and Hindu 'traitors'. Of significance in the Hindutva use of the *Bhagavad Gita* is not the complex ethical and moral epistemology that it contains, nor, indeed, the dispersed ending of the *Mahabharata*, but instead the primitive message that any kind of violence, if undertaken for the protection of dharma, is a bounden obligation, regardless of the abhorrence of violence for any individual sensibility. Hence, violence becomes an unavoidable religious duty under *dharmic* principles for anyone who claims to be a Hindu. Leaving aside the bleak rendering of Hinduism, this is a highly unethical position, containing no moral or ethical principles, only an elementary code of collective narcissism. The sensibility here is singularly about violence and killing and there is a glaring absence of an ethics of collectivism, responsibility, love or care that can include the 'other', indeed even include others who may be dissenting Hindus. In the propagation of such self-absorbed, nihilistic ideological positions, the Hindutva movement is unleashing many demons for the future.

The use of the two epics by the VHP, both of which conveniently contain a monumental and decisive war, as well as symbolic representations from the Puranas, highlights its differentiated, hierarchical and strategic deployment of *bhakti* motifs and associated political rituals. The text of the epics and the Puranas and the multifarious iconic representations that have traditionally accompanied them become part of a primitive strategy of palimpsest in VHP hands: the content of the actual texts of Hinduism are overwritten with slogans of strength, honour, obligation, violence and war. A hierarchy of text is still retained, travelling from the Vedas and Upanishads to the Puranas and Epics, but also including the Buddhist Tripitaks, the Jaina Agamas and the Sikh Granth Sahib (in Hindutva discourse all the latter are offshoots of Aryan-Vedic religion). However, the contents of these texts are neither excavated nor elaborated. Strictly speaking, the texts are not recuperable in Hindutva discourse because they do not contain anything like a singular, incontestable, uncompounded message, nor indeed anything like an injunction to create a Hindu rashtra. Hence, the Vedas (the first of which could conceivably be used to figure a militaristic discourse, but would have little popular appeal) and the Upanishads (the main ones of which are absorbed in metaphysical explications) are reduced to bare slogans that are claimed to demonstrate Hinduism's primordiality, its universal message of humanism, its indisputable tolerance, and its narrative of a unique landscape and chosen people. The Epics and some of the Puranas on the other hand mainly function to elaborate a new militaristic Hindu identity that traverses *sadhus* and ordinary Hindus alike. The *Manudharmashastra* is invoked in the cause of a greater Hindu integration that elides caste and tribal injustices and differences. The contents of Buddhist and Jaina texts are characteristically ignored.

The militaristic thrust of the VHP's vernacular *bhakti* discourse also reflects another hierarchical layer, that of kshatriya caste belonging exemplified as martial valour or *kshatriyatva* (Pinch 1996: 146–7). This demonstrates how the role of *varnashramadharma* in Hindutva discourse is not simply symbolic but can have important practical manifestations. Claims to kshatriya caste belonging have often functioned as markers of upward caste mobility for sections of vaishya, shudra, 'other backward' castes and for some groups outside the caste system. In this sense, the kshatriyization of *bhakti* traditions by the VHP can both dovetail into existing caste mobility claims (kshatriya caste reforms), and can provide a new route for potential acceptance into a higher caste status for groups who wish to make these claims. It is significant in this respect that Valmikis, an upwardly mobile section of the *bhangi* (sweeper) caste were mobilized in violence against Muslim communities, the *violence itself* seemingly exemplifying a different caste claim while leaving the taxonomy and hierarchy of caste intact (Basu 1993: 91–2). The name 'Valmiki' of course also connotes an association with the *Ramayana*. Advani's *rath yatra* in 1990 had a single dalit and a single Muslim riding Ram's 'chariot'. Similarly, the VHP's *shilanyas pujan* (the laying of the foundation stone) at Ayodhya was undertaken by a dalit. In both cases, these token but nevertheless potent presences were intended to convey the symbolic assumption of an 'upper' or 'higher' caste role for those formally outside caste Hinduism. Unlike the previous *sangathan* movements, it is through the dense intertwining of *bhakti* symbols with *varnashramadharma* and *kshatriyatva* that the VHP can systematically deploy caste affiliation and apparent caste mobility under the greater conception of Hindutva within which the structure of caste is left more or less in place (even the dalit leader Ambedkar has been appropriated by the RSS and VHP for the cause of Hindutva – for example, Aggarwal 1993). However, if kshatriya caste reforms of an earlier period allow an apparent *symbolic* mobility, this is completed before such mobility intrudes upon brahmin caste membership. It remains to be seen to what extent existing, socially embedded caste and religious structures will allow such processes once they move beyond the purely symbolic and gestural.

Monuments, Mortar and Muslims

The 'Ramjanmabhoomi' campaign of the VHP and BJP was supplemented by two other temple campaigns. The first was the 'liberation of Krishnajanmasthan' at Mathura, Uttar Pradesh. Mathura is traditionally considered the mythological birthplace of Krishna and the VHP has demanded the destruction and 'relocation' of mosques adjacent to a Krishna temple. Similarly, the VHP has demanded the restoration of the Kashi Vishwanath temple complex at Varanasi, the latter an important Shiva shrine in north India, and the removal of adjacent mosque buildings. In each case, the centre of Hindu devotional worship, the Hindu *mandir*, becomes valorized solely because of its alleged association with mosques. This method, fixated on the religious desacralization and nationalist sacralization of monument, is evocative of other forms of authoritarian nationalism. The three main VHP temple campaigns, appealing to Krishna and Shiva devotees, alongside those of Ram, while appearing to envelop the Vaishnava and Shaiva traditions of northern India, have focused on monumental architecture that is made to evoke the early and later medieval period, and hence 'the Muslim invasion of India'. The third, Shakta tradition in Hinduism was symbolically encapsulated by the VHP through its use of both Bharatmata and Durga symbols. This transfiguration of vernacular *bhakti* traditions around Ram and Krishna, Shiva and Durga is such that the privileged objects of devotional veneration are displaced from the mythologies, beliefs, morals and ethics of the Puranic religious traditions to bricks, mortar and marble. This demotion of complex and variegated devotional traditions can be seen as their de-sacralization. For religious devotees in the 1990s, their gods and goddesses were indissociable from Muslims, monuments and territory in the Indian public sphere. Of significance, as in the late nineteenth century, was the de-privatization of religious devotion and the de-sacralization of religious contemplation. The domestic shrine, universal in caste Hinduism, and its associated space of personal contemplation of and comfort derived from the deities is irrelevant to VHP discourse, indeed a potential hindrance to the politicized, public space of anti-Muslim Hinduism that the VHP seeks to create (though of considerable ethnographic interest is whether and how the meanings of personal-affective forms of domestic worship have been transformed through these Hindutva processes). The VHP's paradoxical contribution to vernacular Hindu *bhakti* 'theology' may be to evermore associate it with Islam. Indeed, a new VHP campaign has focused on a *tomb*, the sandstone mausoleum of the sixteenth-century emperor Sher Shah of Sur in Sasaram, Bihar. Adjacent to the mausoleum complex is a Hindu temple built in 1977 which the VHP wishes to expand into the site of the complex.

Violence against Minorities: the Hindutva Discourse of Punishment

The illegal construction of the Ram temple in Ayodhya started soon after the destruction of the Babri masjid in 1992 and has gathered pace since (*The Hindu*, 19 June 1998, *Indian Express*, 31 December 1998). The destruction of the mosque brought in its wake an unprecedented attack on Muslim communities in late 1992 and early 1993, both in northern and also, uncharacteristically, southern Indian towns and cities. In Bombay, this destructive campaign was planned and systematic, as Muslim communities, individuals, business and homes were methodically marked out and targeted, mostly by Hindu crowds under the direction of the Shiv Sena (Padgaonkar 1993, Srikrishna Commission Report). Aside from their anti-Muslim character, the Bombay events had a range of other compounded and contributory causes relating to land redevelopment and organized crime (Masselos 1996). Nevertheless, it has been estimated that some 60 per cent to 67 per cent of the 784 people who died in Bombay after the Ayodhya events were Muslims.

A judicial commission of enquiry headed by Justice B. N. Srikrishna was instituted by the Maharashtra state government under the instructions of Prime Minister P. V. Narasimha Rao. Its initial brief was to investigate the causes of the Bombay events, though the Shiv Sena – BJP joint government that took control of Maharashtra state expanded the commission's area of inquiry to consider the serial bomb blasts in Bombay that occurred in March 1993 and believed to have been undertaken by those with criminal underworld connections, and whose importance for the Shiv Sena and the BJP was that they were Muslim. The Srikrishna report, however, identified responsibility for the cause of the riots with the Hindutva camp, in particular the activities of the Shiv Sena, its aggressive leader Bal Thackeray, its publication (*Saamna*) and some BJP activists:

> [The] Commission's view is that though several incidents of violence took place during the period from 15th December 1992 to 5th January 1993, large scale rioting and violence was commenced from 6th January 1993 by the Hindus brought to fever pitch by communally inciting propaganda unleashed by Hindu communal organizations and writings in newspapers like 'Saamna' and 'Navakal'. It was taken over by Shiv Sena and its leaders who continued to whip up communal frenzy by their statements and acts and writings and directives issued by the Shiv Sena Pramukh Bal Thackeray. The attitude of Shiv Sena [was] reflected in the 'TIME' interview given by Bal Thackeray [he stated that Muslims should 'be driven out of India' and there was 'nothing wrong' with treating them as Jews were in Nazi Germany]. (Srikrishna Commission Report, Volume 1, Chapter 3, section 1.2)

The commission found that not only were the Shiv Sena instrumental in the Bombay pogroms but that Shiv Sainiks and Hindu rioters had acted with the collusion and participation of officers in the Bombay and state police. This included police murders of Muslims (Srikrishna Commission Report, Volume 1, Chapter 5, section 1.30). The report confirmed an alarming pattern of police indifference to, collusion with and active participation during Hindutva attacks on Muslim (and latterly Christian) communities, including during the VHP-BJP Ayodhya campaigns. The report has not to date been acted upon. The Shiv Sena – BJP joint government of Maharashtra dismissed it, its representatives claiming that it was 'anti-Hindu, pro-Muslim and one-sided', and Bal Thackeray remains free to expound his admiration for Hitler and Nazism.

The differential Hindutva political languages regarding legality, Muslim and Christian minorities, Hindu majorities, democracy and secularism should be noted. In the Hindutva ideological universe, the illegal destruction of the Babri Masjid and the building of the Ram temple is conceived as 'secular' and 'legal', whereas the presence of a mosque since 1528 is 'communal' and 'appeasing' of minorities. Similarly, it is considered genuinely 'secular' to organize a Hindu 'Council of the Learned' and follow the dictates of the VHP and of the *shankaracharyas* and *dharmacharyas* that support it, but 'pseudo-secular', 'communal', or 'appeasing' to elicit the opinions of imams and bishops. Explicitly appealing to the Hindutva or 'Hindu vote' is 'secular', whereas appealing to Muslim voters is 'communal appeasement'. It is 'secular' and 'democratic' to institute 'Hindu values' in the constitution of a state in which about eighty-five percent of the population is Hindu; however Christian values are anti-national and the desires and aspirations of minorities are 'non-democratic' (*Sunday*, 13 February 1993).

Virtually all socio-economic indicators show that in comparison with the total Indian or the Hindu population, Muslims in India have less or far less than proportionate representation in government employment, in higher-level government employment, in industrial business, in the receipt of credit loans, in the financial sector, in terms of levels of literacy, or in further and higher education; conversely, Muslims have a higher or far higher that proportionate representation in terms of poverty, illiteracy and unemployment (an 'appeased minority' indeed!). The Hindutva claim about an electoral 'Muslim vote bank' in existence since Independence and both exploited by Congress and forming the basis for Congress 'appeasement' of Muslims has also been comprehensively rejected (Ghosh 1999). An extremely potent Hindutva myth, which has deliberately focused on Muslim fertility, claims that because of a higher fertility rate and the practice of polygamy, the Muslim population of India will increase until the Muslims are a majority in the future. This is characteristically encapsulated by a grim Hindutva phrase, distorting an earlier birth-control campaign slogan: *ham do hamara do, ham panch hamara pachhis* ('we [Hindus] are two and we have two, we [Muslims] are five and we have twenty-five'). However, Muslims have the lowest polygamy rate of *any* religiously denominated population group in India. This Hindutva emphasis on demographic fertility, the prominence given to Muslim women's fertility, and the imagined consequences of Hindu 'extinction' reproduces a 'Malthusian' tradition that has characterized Hindu nationalism since the turn of the century. Its sexual resonances are suggestive, specifically the unspoken anxiety about Hindu male sexual potency and the fear of the literal emasculation of the Hindu male.

The VHP and Christians

Despite the unprecedented violence associated with the Ayodhya campaign (the worst violence since Partition), the VHP has stridently continued its Hindutva campaigns and has adopted explicitly political agendas on, for example, scrapping article 370 and Kashmir's special constitutional status, preventing undocumented migration from Bangladesh, abolishing the Minorities Commission and instituting what it wishes to call a 'uniform civil code'. In the late 1990s, the VHP turned its attention towards Christian minorities, especially Christians living in 'tribal' areas or working among 'tribal' groups. Christians constitute a minute proportion of the population of India, less than three percent. From the early 1980s, the VHP, in a further transformation of the *shuddhi* activities of previous Hindu nationalist organizations, undertook mass conversion campaigns among syncretic Hindu-Muslim groups and among Christian tribals. The VHP called such activities *paravartan*, or 'homecoming' rituals, emphasizing that those who had adopted other faiths were to 'come back' to their 'original', 'natural' faith, Hinduism, and hence their *homeland*. Significantly, the *paravartan* oath did not emphasise the conscientious, voluntary adoption of systematically articulated Hinduism, but instead the abandonment of 'wrong traditions' (Lochtefeld 1996: 108). A number of swamis formally independent of the VHP also launched conversion activities among tribal groups, reflecting an extant sangathanist tradition in which dalits and tribals were considered to be 'owned' by Hinduism – they just did not know this and hence had been led astray by 'the beef-eating denominations' through what the VHP termed 'inducements', 'fraud' and 'coercions'.

Underlying the VHP and the RSS orientation to Christianity was a narrative of a global Christian conspiracy, orchestrated by an alliance between the Pope and Catholic Church in Rome and American Christian fundamentalists. If this betrayed a striking ignorance of contemporary Christianity, one important reason for this focus was the rise of 'the foreigner', Italian-born Sonia Gandhi, widow of Rajiv, as leader of the Congress Party, who contested the elections of 1998 on an 'anti-fascism', pro-secularism platform. Various other alleged activities compounded an already paranoid VHP-RSS vision, including the US Christian evangelical and fundamentalist AD2000, Joshua Project 2000 and the Celebrate Messiah 2000 campaigns, each of which aimed to 'provide the gospel for every person by the year 2000'. However, these projects had little if any influence in India and the key targets of VHP, BJP and Hindu Jagran Manch ('Forum for Hindu Awakening') activities were traditional institutions of Indian Christianity. Of additional significance was the winning of the Nobel Prize in Economics by Amartya Sen in 1998, the prize seen by the VHP working president Ashok Singhal as another example of a worldwide Christian conspiracy to promote an 'alien' religion in India through the anti-poverty, educational and developmental programmes that Sen advocated (*Indian Express*, 28 December 1998).

The events in Dangs district, Gujarat before December 1998 – January 1999 illustrated the evolving nature of the Hindutva social movement at local levels. Since the Ayodhya events of 1992, several new Hindutva organizations have come to prominence, in particular the Bajrang Dal and the Hindu Jagran Manch. The Bajrang Dal ('Hanuman's Army') is one of two youth offshoots of the VHP, the other being the women's youth wing, the Durga Vahini. During the mid- to late-1990s, the Bajrang Dal represented what is best termed a disorganized, poly-cephalous, amorphous and violent social movement. While it had a state and district-based organization and a loosely federal structure with an overall national convenor, its membership procedure was based on a nominal declaration of affiliation, the ritual of which varied from state to state. In Gujarat, Bajrang Dal affiliates undertake an initiation ritual in which the neophyte is presented with a *trishul* (trident) and declares allegiance to its stated 'ideology' of *seva, sanskar, suraksha* ('service', 'Hindu culture' and 'self-defence' – the same three terms consistently appear in BJP, VHP and RSS manifestos and policy statements). Even the RSS was moved to say that 'All the riff raff, the rejects of society. And the discards of the Sangh Parivar. These are the people who find refuge in the Bajrang Dal' (*India Today*, 8 February 1999).

The Bajrang Dal, the Hindu Jagran Manch and other similar organizations represent the third stage of the evolution of RSS-created organizations (the *sangh parivar*) and represent a strong potential for the consolidation of Hindu supremacist ideology that bears little relationship with, or experience of being socialized into, the formal ideology of Hindutva that animates the Sangh. It is likely that the disorganized Hindutva social movement will in time throw up its own charismatic national leaders and consolidate around organizational centres and ideological poles that will be distinct from those of the RSS and VHP. The Shiv Sena already provides one such model and has declared ambitions to spread beyond the confines of greater Maharashtra.

The recent Hindutva hostility to Gujarat's Christians largely commenced in 1997 with Swami Ashimananda's 'reconversion' campaigns among Christian tribal populations. The Waghai-based *sadhu* Ashimananda, a worker of the Vanavasi Kalyan Parishad, a VHP body working among tribal populations, also initiated a local Bajrang Dal branch. Likewise, Ashimananda was associated with the Hindu Jagran Manch, a new organization that surfaced in south Gujarat. The increasing violence against Christian tribal populations, their homes and places of worship had been reported to the state Minorities Commission from 1997. However, the violence against Christians intensified following a Hindu Jagran Manch agitation against the 'conversions' of tribals to Christianity in late June 1998 (*Indian Express*, 28 July 1998). On Christmas Day (1998), the Hindu Jagran Manch, together with local VHP, Bajrang Dal and BJP activists, organized a similar protest in Ahwa against 'mass conversions' of Hindus to Christianity. The opposition to the December protest by local Christians was followed by a massive conflagration involving thousands of Hindus and Christians. This led to a renewed, systematic attack on Christians. The BJP did not condemn outright the role of the VHP and the Hindu Jagran Manch in the violence in Gujarat in December (*Hindustan Times*, 31 December 1998). Leaders of the Gandhian Sarvodaya movement in Gujarat, reflecting an earlier association with some Hindu nationalist tendencies, led a delegation to Vajpayee which called for a ban on conversions to Christianity in Dangs district. Vajpayee in turn called for a 'national debate' on religious conversions (*Rediff on the Net*, 5 January 1999, *Indian Express*, 10 January 1999).

Meanwhile, on 5 January 1999 at Peth, Nasik, Vidhyashankar Bharati, the *shankaracharya* of the Karveer peet, together with Swami Ashimananda, 'reconverted' almost forty tribal Christians to Hinduism (*Indian Express*, 01 June 1999). At a Vishal Hindu Sammelan organized by the Dharmarakshan Samiti (Society for the Protection of Hindu Religion), the *shankaracharya* demanded that Christian missionaries leave tribal areas: 'Request them once, twice, thrice and if they do not refrain from their activities, then take the next step.' The six resolutions passed at the *sammelan* were:

- The government should not allow and protect unauthorised churches
- Educational institutions in which due respect is not paid to the national flag and national anthem should be banned
- Bharatmata poojan [prayer to the 'Holy Motherland' as conceived in a 'Hindu' idiom] should be made compulsory in all educational institutions on August 15 [Independence Day] and [January] 26 [Republic Day]
- Converted tribals should be requested to return to the Hindu fold and missionaries should be asked to leave tribal areas by March 31, failing which they would be responsible for any consequences from April 1
- Converted tribals should be stripped of reservations and facilities applicable to Hindu tribals
- A ban should be imposed on foreign funding of missionary activities. (*Indian Express*, 01 June 1999)

Some VHP leaders did, for a very brief period, dissociate themselves from the Hindu Jagran Manch, and the then RSS *sarsanghchalak* Rajendra Singh appeared to condemn the attacks on Christians and their places of worship. It was also claimed that Bajrang Dal activists had no involvement in the anti-Christian atrocities in Gujarat (*Indian Express*, 3 January 1999, *Indian Express*, 5 January 1999). However, another discourse rapidly emerged. Ashok Singhal, VHP president, characteristically dismissed the anti-Christian violence, claiming that 'foreign hands', namely Christian leaders from abroad, were behind the violence, their aim being to project India and Hinduism in a bad light (*Rediff on the Net*, 29 December 1998). However, other reports demonstrated the involvement of *sangh parivar* activists in Hindu Jagran Manch agitations. VHP and BJP leaders

helped in organising and also participated in [Hindu Jagran Manch] rallies, held in Ahwa and other parts of Dangs on the Christmas day . . . Notwithstanding the denials emanating from Delhi, Gujarat Youth BJP vice-president Devarshibhai Joshi said the Manch is an outfit of the VHP, working in tribal areas. It is an umbrella organization of all those attracted to Hindutva, Joshi said, adding, significantly, 'Almost every one of its members holds dual citizenship' . . . [Activists] of the VHP, BJP and other Sangh Parivar outfits were present in the HJM rallies at Tokarwa, Dolarwa, Vyara and Ahwa. Amongst those at Tokarwa was BJP MLA from Bardoli Rajanikant Rajwadi. 'I was looking after the arrangements', he said, trying to absolve himself of any links. Rajwadi, who is national secretary of the Adivasi Morcha of the BJP, said, 'HJM is a separate organization but, ideologically, we are one and have the same objective'. Also present at Dolarwa was the VHP district vice-president, Subhas Takkar (Rajkotwala). He told this reporter that he had been in the RSS for 25 years. 'The RSS asked me to work for the VHP so I am in the VHP. Tomorrow, I may be asked to work for some other organization. The RSS is the parent body; the VHP, Bajrang Dal and HJM are its branches'. (*Indian Express*, 4 January 1999)

The anti-Christian violence rapidly spread from Dangs district to Surat in Gujarat, and then to Orissa, Bihar and elsewhere. In Madhya Pradesh the rape of four nuns by a mob in Navapada village, Jhabhua district, in September 1998 had been preceded by a spate of attacks and arsons on Christian churches, schools and missions (*The Week*, 11 October 1998, *The Hindu*, 14 October 1998). In Manoharpur village, Orissa, Australian-born Christian missionary Graham Stewart Staines and his two sons, aged seven and ten, were burned to death on the night of 22–23 January 1999 by a Hindutva crowd chanting 'Jai Bajrang Bali'. The banner of the Bajrang Dal had also been unfurled during previous attacks on Muslims allegedly led by Dara Singh (*India Today*, 8 February 1999). During the commission of enquiry into the Staines' murders led by Justice D. P. Wadhwa, it was alleged that Dara Singh had attended RSS *shakhas* (*The Hindu*, 8 May 1999). He was also said to be a Bajrang Dal activist and a member of a cow-protection society who had allegedly been sent by the Bajrang Dal to Orissa to 'cleanse' the area of 'evil minorities' (*Rediff on the Net*, 27 January 1999). He also allegedly had strong associations with the BJP (*Indian Express*, 9 May 1999).

The Staines murder and the widespread anti-Christian incidents did, for a brief period put the BJP and VHP on the defensive. However this was quickly displaced by a reiteration of 'a world-wide Christian conspiracy' to account for the international media attention following the Staines murders, emphasizing again the manner in which RSS truth claims are created so as to appear strictly 'irrefutable'. K. N. Govindacharya, one of the BJP's general secretaries and a major RSS ideologue elaborated this same theme: the international spotlight on India as a result of anti-Christian atrocities only confirmed an international Christian conspiracy to destabilize the BJP government. Ominously, the Home Ministry issued a circular instructing the police to undertake a census of the Christian population of Gujarat. Christian schools in the state also received a further circular requesting information on their 'country affiliations and foreign funds'.

The VHP's 'Hindu Agenda'

In 1997, in the prelude to the 1998 general elections, the VHP under the presidentship of V. H. Dalmia and the working presidentship of Ashok Singhal issued what it called the *Hindu Agenda* and urged all political parties to adopt it, though its clear target was the BJP. The BJP's 1998 election manifesto reproduced almost exactly many of the Hindutva themes of the VHP document. The VHP's *Hindu Agenda* strongly reiterated its belief in the ancient and primordial land of the Hindu race, the Arya Rashtra (Aryan Nation) or Hindu Rashtra, which had been under 'slavery' for one thousand years and had, since becoming 'divided Bharat' upon Independence, been subject to 'foreign-oriented thought' that left 'this most ancient, glorious and cultural civilization . . . powerless, helpless and orphaned in its own country', at the mercy of 'anti-national elements' appeased by policies of 'pseudo-secularism' (Vishwa Hindu Parishad, *The Hindu Agenda*, 1998). This ceaseless iteration of a narrative of 'Hindu hurt' and Hindu frailty is undertaken, in the same breath, with an aggressive promotion of Hindutva.

The VHP called on 'all political parties' to protect 'in every manner' the *honour* and 'interests' of Hindus. The word 'honour' has notable resonances. The VHP's demand that the state institutionalize the protection of the majority 'community' of Hindus is strictly anti-democratic, a primitive equivalence of 'democracy' with religiously delineated majority rule. It characteristically justified this through the assertion that Hindutva and nationalism in 'Bharat' were synonymous. The VHP, while apparently arguing for 'real secularism', included the following demands in its *Hindu Agenda*, most of which were inextricably linked with new proposed federal or state legislation. Some of its demands are worth quoting at length, because they starkly clarify the VHP's future aims:

[Point 2.] . . . *Only* 'Bharat' which has the ancient, glorious and historical connotations will have constitutional recognition. [7.] The *anti-national* activity of religious conversion of Hindus by force, fraud or false propaganda by exploiting the innocence [and] the poverty of backward communities will be *strictly banned*. [8.] All foreign remittances to non-governmental agencies, social, religious or service organizations or individuals will be *stopped*, so that the money and material so received is not misutilised for religious conversion and other *divisive conspiracies*. [13.] Secessionist demands and propaganda in Kashmir or anywhere else in the country, or indulging in violent activity will be *ruthlessly repressed*. Secessionist demand will be a *strict penal* anti-national offence. [16.] Universally recognised, well-developed and scientific language Sanskrit will be made a *compulsory* subject of study throughout the country. [18.] Teaching of Bharatiya culture and Dharma will be made *compulsory*. [19.] The status of second official language accorded by certain states to Urdu in foreign script will be *withdrawn*. [20.] The *distorted presentation* of modern, social and cultural history of Bharat will be re-written by honest, patriotic and learned historians and archaeologists. The teaching syllabus shall be accordingly reformed. [21.] Singing of 'Vande Maataram' everyday will be *compulsory* in all educational institutions. [22.] Pooja, Archana and religious construction activities of math, mandirs and ashrams will be deemed a charitable activity and will be entitled for exemption from the income tax. [23.] A specified portion of Government revenue shall be earmarked for the various Dharmic, charitable objects of the taxpayers. [26.] Pilgrimages shall be made tax-free. Ministries shall be established at the centre and in the states to restore the glory of pilgrim centres and to develop them as also to facilitate and encourage pilgrimage. [27.] Drinking and non-vegetarianism will be discouraged by the Government. All meat export from the country will be *banned*. All big mechanical abattoirs will be closed. [31.] Any denigration of, or disrespect to, any faith including Hindu culture, belief or tradition, or any venerated character, by audio-visual, written or spoken means will be a *penal offence* and *strictly enforced*. [35.] The old and glorious historical names of towns, roads and places will be restored. [36.] Prominent Hindu festivals will be declared national holidays. [37.] The rights and privileges accorded to scheduled castes and scheduled tribes will be *withdrawn* on their conversion. [38.] In view of the unimpeachable historical, literary and archaeological evidence, the Places of Worship (Special Provision) Act, 1991 shall be suitably modified/repealed. (Vishwa Hindu Parishad, *The Hindu Agenda*, 1998, emphases added)

The authoritarianism of these demands, their legislative thrust and their thorough embedding in a language criminalizing minorities and opponents of the VHP is disquieting. These points, alongside the usual VHP-BJP demands regarding Kashmir, the Minorities Commission, so-called 'Bangladeshi infiltration', cow protection, the Ram temple and a 'uniform civil code', cannot be conceived as even tenuously 'secular'. The VHP's *Hindu Agenda* reflects the will to institutionalize an authoritarian, aggressive and intolerant form of Hindu nationalist governance, from the constitution of the Indian union downwards. Together with the BJP's 1998 election manifesto, which also demanded a 'comprehensive review' of India's constitution, it provides a grim vision of what a politically, administratively and legally unconstrained Hindu nationalism working within and outside parliamentary frameworks might mean for India's constitutionality and forms of post-independence secular government. Even if a lenient reading might conceive of the BJP as India's domestic version of the 'New Right', in an assessment of both the VHP's *Hindu Agenda* and the BJP's 1998 election manifesto, it is difficult to think of a description other than 'fascism' that can aptly characterize the authoritarian intensities and will to institutionalize Hindutva power that these two documents represent.

The Return of Aryanism

In recent years, Aryanism has also re-emerged in dramatic, if unsurprising, ways. The Aryanist claims of the Hindutva movement have been shrill, and are the basis for a huge and diverse range of transnationally organized projects. While they characteristically and uncritically rehearse many of the nineteenth century Aryanist themes described in Chapter 1, the focus today concerns the status of the Indus Valley civilization. During the 1920s the ruins of a vast, ancient, relatively advanced urban civilization were discovered in northern colonial India. Numerous other sites have since been discovered across northern India and (mainly) within Pakistan, with the two main centres of the civilization identified as the large cities of Mohenjodaro and Harappa. The Indus Valley civilization was broadly contemporaneous with the main ancient riverine civilizations in central Asia and Africa, but much larger in geographical reach. The written script of the Indus Valley civilization has not been deciphered. The scholarly consensus is that the Indus Valley script represents a non-Indo-European, non-Indo-Aryan language that existed before the Vedic Sanskrit period.

It was claimed earlier this century by British archaeologists, such as Mortimer Wheeler, that the state of some of the ruins of the Indus Valley civilization provided direct evidence of a conquering and destructive 'Aryan invasion' against the original inhabitants of India. This view has also been rejected in post-war scholarship, the general consensus being that the Indus Valley civilization declined over a considerable period of time, possibly due to a combination of environmental and ecological factors. The scholarly consensus against a destructive 'Aryan invasion' is important. Instead there took place complex and multiple processes of migration by relatively technologically unsophisticated, agro-pastoral *arya*-speaking tribes over an extremely long period of well over a thousand years, and in the main well after the decline of the Indus Valley civilization. Linguistic and non-linguistic evidence for the migration *into* India of *arya*-speaking tribes is overwhelming. Those tribes are also thought to have probably arrived from a region bordering Iran and India, and probably separated from rival Avestan tribes. Consequently, *arya* speakers were exogenous to India. Later syncretism with the cultures that existed eventually gave rise to Sanskrit-based Vedic culture which developed, in a far later period, into what we know as Hinduism. However, the existence of a pre-Vedic, pre-Aryan civilization in India, and the migration of speakers of Aryan languages into India also implies that the 'originary' foundations of 'Hinduism' are exogenous to India.

Hence, over the last decade there has emerged an enormous body of autodidact and dilletantist literature published in India and the US (indeed, also Pakistan – reflecting another current of archaic nationalist legitimation for a recently born nation) preoccupied with demonstrating that Aryans were indigenous to India, had then migrated to central Asia, Europe and elsewhere (indeed everywhere that ancient civilizations have been found), and that India is the original Aryan homeland. The most contentious of its claims is that the Indus Valley civilization was Aryan, its language Sanskritic, and its gods and goddesses Vedic. The Indus Valley civilization has also been erroneously redesignated in Hindutva literature as the 'Indus Saraswati civilization', because 'Saraswati' is a Rig Vedic deity, a later Hindu name for a goddess, and an unidentified river. (Archaic Avestan literature also refers to its version of 'Saraswati'.) Hindutva adherents have claimed that 'Saraswati' refers to an ancient river bed in the north and north-west of the subcontinent recently discovered by Landsat imaging, demonstrating again the older Hindutva Aryanist obsessions with river, water and landscape, though the actual referent of the Avestan and Rig Vedic literature is unknown. Central to Hindutva claims is the resurrection of an earlier European idea, the basis of Romantic and early Enlightenment attacks on clerical authority and the biblical chronology of humankind, that India received the first revelation and was the cradle of world civilizations. However, Hindutva supporters of these views contend that the denial of Aryan autochthony in India is an example of 'racist', 'colonialist' and 'Christian' chauvinism (although their anger at recently discovered Western racism is not matched by anything like a similar rage at caste – some disagreeable aspects of the latter are ascribed to 'Muslim influences', whereas *varna* is unhesitatingly defended as a natural order). Hindutva writers are arguing against late nineteenth- and early twentieth-century paradigms that few contemporary scholars accept. However, their interventions, against what they have dubbed the Western 'Aryan Invasion Theory' (AIT), in contrast to their 'out of India' (OIT) claims, have dramatically affected contemporary Indological and South Asianist disciplines within and outside India. Hindutva claims about the Indus Valley civilization have not been substantiated and contrary evidence is overwhelming (see variously Mallory 1989, Jha 1998, Sharma 1999, Thapar 'Hindutva and history', *Frontline*, 13 October 2000, Witzel and Farmer 'Horseplay at Harappa', *Frontline*, 13 October 2000). Adjacently, there are burgeoning projects determined to demonstrate that the Rig Veda contains, or the 'Vedic seers' had discovered,

Dalton's chemistry, Newton's laws of motion and gravitation, aeroplanes and helicopters, general and special relativity, radioactivity, quantum mechanics, and 'an astronomical code' or plan embedded in the numerical structure and arrangement of Rig Vedic hymns, evidence of advanced and sophisticated Vedic astronomical and scientific knowledge and computational abilities, betraying again the peculiar importance of claims about modern natural science and universalism in Hindutva discourse. These projects have had determinate effects especially in primary and secondary education (see below), but increasingly in higher education – the Indian University Grants Commission, for example, is planning to fund masters courses in Vedic astrology. 'Neo-Aryanism' has also shaped Hindutva's 'integrationist' political discourse. For example, in November 1998, union home minister L. K. Advani declared not only that Buddhism offered no new religion, but that Gautama Buddha was simply rehearsing the existing ideals of Indo-Aryan civilization. Most of these ideas were exhaustively rehearsed in eighteenth- and nineteenth-century Orientalism; the 'paradox' of Hindu nationalism is that it remains the last loyal practitioner of Orientalist and colonial reason in India.

Conclusion: State-induced 'Shakha Education'

In 1994, in a case related to the use of religious appeals during election campaigns, the Indian Supreme Court ruled that an electoral appeal based on using the terms 'Hindutva' and 'Hinduism' was not in itself 'corrupt practice' under the 1951 Representation of the People Act. In its judgement, the Supreme Court declared that 'Hinduism' and 'Hindutva' referred to the way of life in India and were not corrigible as religions, in the way that the latter are normally understood (on the Hindutva deposition to the court, see Jois 1996). This desecularization is based on the legal legitimation of precisely the mythological primordialism that has been the concern of earlier chapters.

Such processes of accelerated desecularization have been highly apparent in the policies and directions of BJP states since the mid-1990s, particularly since the coming to power of BJP-led governments in 1998 and 1999. Murli Manohar Joshi, a long-term RSS member and BJP minister for human resources development with responsibility for education, instigated proposals for changes in school textbooks to reflect the Hindutva world view, as well as proposals 'to amend the right to education of minorities' (*Hindustan Times*, 21 October 1998). The changes were intended to make the primary and secondary school curricula 'Indianized, nationalized and spiritualized'. In the BJP-controlled states, this meant a literal incorporation of the textbooks used in RSS secondary and primary schools into government schools in Gujarat, Rajasthan, Delhi and elsewhere. The textbooks extols 'Greater India' as the Aryan homeland and the birthplace of humanity, and from whom the Persians, Greeks, Egyptians and Native Americans and indeed

Jesus (said to have roamed the Himalayas) gained their knowledge and wisdom. The pre-*arya* Indus Valley civilization is described as Vedic. Aryan culture is the core of Indian culture. India had however been invaded for 3000 years by 'greedy marauders' against whom the gods and then the Hindus fought. Muslim rule is described as foreign rule, spread by the sword. The followers of Islam are said to remain unincorporated into India because of their intolerant faith. Prominence is given to Tilak, Aurobindo Ghose, Lajpat Rai, Bipinchandra Pal and the alleged role of Hedgewar and the RSS as key leaders in the Independence movement. In political science textbooks, a chapter on Deendayal Upadhyaya's ideology of an 'ideal Dharmarajya' has been inserted (Taneja not dated). One examination question in Uttar Pradesh asked 'If it takes four sevaks to demolish a mosque, how many does it take to demolish twenty?' In Rajasthan, a guide on essay writing skills includes the following conversation between a teacher and a pupil:

> 'Student: Master, what has India achieved by doing the nuclear tests? Was it a right step? Teacher: Undoubtedly it was correct, India has achieved a huge success . . . Economic sanctions do not matter. The country should first become powerful. Only the powerful are listened to. Now we can talk about world peace aggressively.' (*Guardian*, 25 January 2000)

In Gujarat, a current history and civics textbook states that 'Aryans were the most illustrious race in history. They were a tall, fair complexioned, good-looking and cultured people.' In a social studies text, Hitler is described as 'instilling the spirit of adventure in the common people'. The Holocaust is not mentioned (*Guardian*, 25 January 2000). The Hindutva focus on children, youth and ideological inculcation, and the attention given to educational institutions, seen as the prime vehicles for the cultural reproduction of the 'Hindu nation', is supplemented by the miserable fictions of the Hindutva curricula. The RSS has arrived at the stage where it can inject the repugnant contents of its *shakha* curriculum into the institutions of the state.

–8–

Conclusion

The movement to centre stage in contemporary Indian politics of what was in the 1920s a tiny northwest Indian cult obsessed with Hindu supremacism, order, conformity and obedience raises theoretical and political issues of considerable complexity. A partial explanation is offered by the intensification since the 1980s of ethnic, religious and nationalist resurgence in various parts of the world as a 'paradox' of processes of economic, social and technological 'globalization' and their concomitant uncertainties – especially outside the West where the impact of globalization has been both asymmetric and inextricably linked to the economic immiseration and socio-political marginalization of large populations. However, the dramatic rise of Hindu nationalism has also unravelled older, if now seemingly provisional, certainties about the meanings of secularism and secular nationalism for national populations living under, and immediately amenable to the charm of religions. The persistence of Hindu nationalism also poses sharp questions about the understanding of religious and cultural politics that informed the national, anti-colonial movement of Gandhi and Nehru.

It has been the argument of this book that while the Hindutva movement is of relatively recent lineage, both 'Hindu' and Hindu nationalist political and ideological formations have been far more influential since the nineteenth century than their post-Nehruvian designation as marginal tendencies might suggest. Ideologies of archaic primordialism have formed the core political lexicon of Hindu nationalist, and many Indian nationalist, tendencies. If archaic Indian civilizations have provided resources for both Indian and Hindu nationalism, it has also allowed for a thematic convergence between these different projects. At critical moments since the nineteenth century, abstracted conceptions of Hinduism have functioned to justify for both the superiority, however conceived, of 'the Hindu ethos' as a basis for their nationalisms. This has even been the case when Indian nationalism was articulated (for example, by M. K. Gandhi) in principled anti-communal, 'caste upliftment' and religious pluralist terms, an abstracted Hinduism being claimed to provide for the greatest co-existence of diversity.

Back to the Future

The Hindutva investment in primordialist, archaic and mythological fictions is a characteristic method of cultural nationalism, and is seen as essential for the cultural and 'moral' regeneration and invigoration of an imagined 'historic community'. It is a form of archaic modernization that demonstrates how post colonial cultural nationalism, even though its content is 'primitivist', has an irreducibly evolutionary vision against which the West can be measured as antediluvian, out-moded and irrelevant (Hutchinson 1987). However, if Hindu cultural nationalism is a mainspring for the 'moral' innovation of a delineated 'Hindu community', the 'moralities' being generated in the xenological cultures advanced by the BJP-VHP-RSS are preoccupied with narcissistic self-aggrandizement and revulsion at the independent existence of autonomously formed identities that are not completed within their narrow Hindutva ideology. How indeed *are we* to account for the late twentieth century postcolonial demand that a nation must be considered literally *sacred* by all its citizens?

As P. C. Chatterji has cogently demonstrated, even if one concedes Hinduism's alleged capacity for diversity and tolerance, genuine secularism is radically incompatible with Hindu religious and scriptural precepts, not least because scriptural Hinduism (*dharma*) can demand the totalizing arrangement and moral ordering of *every* aspect of life, secular or otherwise. Hence, a commitment to secularism necessarily implies that the state has powers to intervene in the social and political regulation, control and restraint of Hindu (and all other) religious customs, practices, and indeed Hindu *dharma* as a whole, while guaranteeing the individual rights of religious belief and congregation (Chatterji 1995). Moreover, for a multi-religious, multi-ethnic, multi-caste, pluralist and democratic federal nation such as India, the obligation to ensure state regulation and restraint of religious conduct falls on the majority – Hindus. To be sure, optimism in a renewed Indian secularism is problematized from a number of directions, including the religious nature of the genealogy of secularism in the West, the meanings of secularism and secular cultural politics in religiously governed civil societies and private spheres, and the thorough historic association of Indian 'secularism' with the anti-communal management of already reified religious communities. However, commitment to a painstakingly meticulous, heterogeneous, novel and visionary secular renewal is of a radically different epistemological order from one committed to the institutionalization and religious sacralization of Hindutva nationhood and its stern irrationalities.

The major problem that has faced Hindu nationalism since its inception is that its ideology has never been equivalent to the expression of national identity of India or Indians. It is for such reasons that the recent efforts of the Hindutva movement have been directed to both appropriating for itself the memory of Indian anti-colonial and anti-authoritarian struggles, and attempting to make its parochial concerns grandly stand in for the totality of Indian nationalism. Hence, the BJP describes the Ramjanmabhoomi movement as the greatest movement for *national liberation* since Independence. Similarly, those Hindutva tendencies whose Aryanism has been unleashed in recent years describe their primordialist projects as the 'decolonization' of the Hindu mind. These Hindutva languages of 'national liberation', 'anti-colonialism' and 'anti-imperialism' are curious, not simply because of the formally post-colonial conditions in which they are emergent, nor because of the absence of Hindutva organizations from Indian anti-colonial movements: the massive anti-colonial freedom movement for independence, and the virtually miraculous consolidation of the Indian nation state in uniquely troubled circumstances in the aftermath of colonialism, nationwide religious conflict, and the horrors of Partition, remains a definitive marker of sophisticated nationalist accomplishment that Hindu nationalism has been unable to match.

Bibliography

Aggarwal, S. K. (1993), *Dr Ambedkar on Muslim Fundamentalism*, New Delhi: Suruchi Prakashan.

Agnes, F. (1995), 'Redefining the agenda of the women's movement within a secular framework' in Sarkar and Butalia eds.

All India (Akhil Bharat) Hindu Mahasabha (1942), *Resolutions adopted by the Working Committee at its Meetings held at New Delhi on the 29th and 30th and the 31st August 1942, under the Presidentship of Veer Savarkar*, Calcutta: Bhowanipore Press.

—— (1943), *All-India Hindu Students' Conference, Second Session, Presidential Address by N.C. Chatterjee, Amritsar 28th December 1943*, Calcutta: Bhowanipore Press.

—— (1944), *26th Session of All India Hindu Mahasabha, Presidential Address by Syamaprasad Mookerjee, 24th December 1944*, New Delhi: All India Hindu Mahasabha.

—— (1946), *Hindu Mahasabha on Cabinet Mission Proposal*, Calcutta: All-India Hindu Mahasabha.

—— (1947), *The Presidential Address of Mr. L. B. Bhopatkar at the Rajputana Provincial Hindu Conference held at Pushkar on 27th November 1947*, Calcutta: All India Hindu Mahasabha.

—— (1948a), *The Moslem Minority Problem – a letter addressed to the* Hindusthan Times, *New Delhi, and published in part in the paper on the 21st November, 1948*, New Delhi: All-India Hindu Mahasabha.

—— (1948b), *Full Text of the Proceedings of Working Committee meeting held at New Delhi on 14th & 15th February 1948*, New Delhi: All India Hindu Mahasabha

—— (1949b), *Mahasabha's New Stand*, New Delhi: All India Hindu Mahasabha.

—— (1949c), *Full Text of the Resolutions adopted by the Working Committee on 10th and 11th September 1949*, New Delhi: All India Hindu Mahasabha.

—— (1949a), *Address of Welcome by the Chairman of the Reception Committee, Calcutta Session December 1949*, Calcutta: Akhil Bharat Hindu Mahasabha

—— (1950a), *Mahasabha and its Ideals, December 1950*, Calcutta: Bharat Publications.

—— (1950b), *Text of Resolutions, 29th Session, Poona 1950*, Poona: Akhil Bharat Hindu Mahasabha.

—— (1951), *Election Manifesto of the Akhil Bharat Hindu Mahasabha as adopted by the Working Committee in its meeting held in August 1951 in New Delhi*, New Delhi: Akhil Bharat Hindu Mahasabha.

—— (1952), *Presidential Address by Shri N. C. Chatterjee, M.P., 30th Session, Bhopal, (28th December 1952)*, New Delhi: All-India Hindu Mahasabha.

—— (1953), *Full Text of the Resolution adopted by the Akhil Bharat Committee on 23rd August, 1953*, New Delhi: Akhil Bharat Hindu Mahasabha.

—— (1954), *31st Session, Hyderabad (held on 7th, 8th and 9th May 1954) Full Text of Resolutions and Report of the Mahasabha*, New Delhi: Hindu Mahasabha Bhawan.

—— (1959), *44th Annual Session, Varanasi 20th Feb 1959, Presidential Address by Prof Ram Singh*, New Delhi: Akhil Bharat Hindu Mahasabha.

All India Varnashrama Swarajya Sangh (not dated), *Memorial on the Hindu Marriage and Divorce Bill (Submitted to the Joint Committee of the Parliament on behalf of the orthodox Hindu population of India)*, Banaras: All India Varnashrama Swarajya Sangh.

Alter, J. (1992), *The Wrestler's Body: identity and ideology in north India*, Berkeley: University of California Press.

Anand V. S. (1967), *Savarkar: a study in the evolution of Indian nationalism*, London: Cecil & Amelia Woolf

Andersen W. K. and Damle S. (1987), *The Brotherhood in Saffron: the Rashtriya Swayamsevak Sangh and Hindu revivalism*, Boulder CO: Westview Press

Anonymous (not dated), *1. Straight Issue of Bare Survival before the Hindus and the Clear Duty. 1. Who is actually responsible for Pakistan-demand, and the present tragic situation in the country?* Delhi: The National Publications.

Appadorai, A. ed. (1973), *Documents on Political Thought in Modern India*, 2 volumes, London: Oxford University Press.

Argov, D. (1967), *Moderates and Extremists in the Indian National Movement 1883–1920, with Special Reference to Surendranath Banerjea and Lajpat Rai*, London: Asia Publishing House.

Azad, A. K. (1988), *India Wins Freedom*, London: Sangam Books.

Badrinath, C. (1993), *Dharma, India and the World Order*, Edinburgh: Saint Andrew Press.

Bacchetta, P. (1996), 'Hindu Nationalist Women as Ideologues' in Jayawardena and de Alwis eds.

Banerjee, S. (1995), 'The woman Shiv Sainik and her sister Swayamsevika' in Sarkar and Butalia eds.

Basu, A. (1995), 'Feminism inverted: the gendered imagery and real women of Hindu nationalism' in Sarkar and Butalia eds.

Basu, C. (1913), *Hindutva* [in Bengali].

Basu, K. and Subrahmanyam, S. eds. (1996), *Unravelling the Nation: sectarian conflict and India's secular identity*, New Delhi: Penguin Books

Basu, T. (1993), *Khaki Shorts and Saffron Flags: a critique of the Hindu right*, New Delhi: Orient Longman.

Baxter, C. (1971), *The Jana Sangh – a biography of an Indian political party*, Bombay: Oxford University Press

Bayly, C. A. (1983), *Rulers, Townsmen and Bazaars: north Indian society in the age of British expansion, 1770–1870*, Cambridge: Cambridge University Press.

—— (1998), *Origins of Nationality in South Asia: patriotism and ethical government in the making of modern India*, Delhi: Oxford University Press.

Bayly, S. (1995), 'Caste and "race" in the colonial ethnography of India' in Robb, P. ed. *The Concept of Race in South Asia*, Delhi: Oxford University Press.

—— (1999), 'Race in Britain and India' in van der Veer, P. and Lehmann, H. eds, *Nation and Religion – perspectives on Europe and Asia*, New Jersey: Princeton University Press.

Bengal Provincial Hindu Sabha (1938), *Under False Colours – statement on 'Bengal Hindu Sabha'*, Calcutta: Bengal Provincial Hindu Sabha.

Bengal Provincial Hindu Mahasabha (n.d.), *Mahasava Parliamentary Board, Bulletin No. 1. the Coming Elections. Congress Vs. Mahasava – Questions and Answers*, Calcutta: Bengal Provincial Hindu Mahasava.

Bhabha, H. K. (1994), *The Location of Culture*, London: Routledge.

Bharatiya Janata Party (1991), *Towards Ram Rajya. Mid-Term Poll to Lok Sabha, May 1991: Our commitments*, New Delhi: Bharatiya Janata Party.

—— (1995), *Supreme Court on 'Hindutva' and 'Hinduism' and L. K. Advani's Statement*, New Delhi: Bharatiya Janata Party.

—— (1996), *For a Strong and Prosperous India: Election manifesto*, New Delhi: Bharatiya Janata Party.

—— (1998), *Vote for a Stable Government and an Able Prime Minister: Election manifesto*, New Delhi: Bharatiya Janata Party.

Bhatt, C. (1997), *Liberation and Purity: Race, new religious movements and the ethics of postmodernity*, London: UCL Press.

—— (1999), 'Primordial Being', *Radical Philosophy* 100, April.

Bhattacharya, N. (1991) 'Myth, history and the politics of Ramjanmabhumi' in Gopal ed.

Bhishikar, C. P. (1991), *Pandit Deendayal Upadhyaya: Ideology and Perception, Part V, Concept of the Rashtra*, New Delhi: Suruchi Prakashan.

Bluntschli, J. K. ([1895] 1971), *The Theory of the State* [second edition], Freeport NY: Books for Libraries Press.

Bose, S. C. (1997a), *An Indian Pilgrim – An unfinished autobiography*, [S. K. and S. Bose eds.], New Delhi: Oxford University Press.

—— (1997b), *The Indian Struggle 1920–1942* [S. K. and S. Bose eds], New Delhi: Oxford University Press.

—— (1988), *The Essential Writings of Netaji Subhas Chandra Bose*, [S. K. and S. Bose eds.], Delhi: Oxford University Press.

Brass, P. R. (1990), *The Politics of India since Independence* (*The New Cambridge History of India IV:1*), Cambridge: Cambridge University Press.

Brockington, J. L. (1984), *Righteous Rama: the evolution of an epic*, Delhi: Oxford University Press.

Brown, E. C. (1975), *Har Dayal: Hindu revolutionary and nationalist*, Arizona: University of Arizona Press.

Cashman, R. (1970), 'The Political Recruitment of God Ganapati', *The Indian Economic and Social History Review*, VII, 3: 347–73

—— (1975), *The Myth of the 'Lokamanya': Tilak and mass politics in Maharashtra*, Berkeley: University of California Press.

Casolari, M. (2000), 'Hindutva's Foreign Tie-up in the 1930s: archival evidence', *Economic and Political Weekly*, 22 January.

Chande, M. B. (1992), *Shree Ram Janma Bhoomi*, Nagpur: M. B. Chande.

Chandra, B. (1987), *Communalism in Modern India*, New Delhi: Vikas.

Chari, S. ed. (not dated), *A Fruitful Life*, Delhi: Bharat Prakashan.

Chatterjee, B. C. (1986), *Sociological Essays: Utilitarianism and Positivism in Bengal*, [translated and edited by S.N. Mukherjee and M. Maddern], Calcutta: Rddhi.

—— (1992), *Anandamath*, New Delhi: Vision Books.

—— (1994), *Bankimchandra Chatterjee: Essays in Perspective*, New Delhi: Sahitya Akademi.

Chatterjee, N. C. (1953), *Demand for Enquiry into the Detention and Death of Dr Syama Prasad Mookerjee, Speech by Sri N. C. Chatterjee, M. P. in the House of the People on Friday, the 18th September 1953*, New Delhi: All-India Hindu Mahasabha.

Chatterjee, P. (1986), *Nationalist Thought and the Colonial World: A derivative discourse?* London: Zed Books.

Chatterji, P. C. (1995), *Secular Values for Secular India*, New Delhi: Manohar.

Chaturvedi, S. (1972), *Madan Mohan Malaviya [Builders of Modern India Series]*, New Delhi: Publications Division, Ministry of Information and Broadcasting Government of India.

Childe, V. G. (1926), *The Aryans*, London: Kegan Paul.

Chirol, V. ([1926] 1972), *India*, Freeport NY: Books for Libraries Press.

Chitkara, M. G. (1997), *Hindutva*, New Delhi: APH Publishing.

Curran, J. A. (1951), *Militant Hinduism in Indian politics: A study of the RSS*, New York: International Secretariat Institute of Pacific Relations.

Dalmia, V. (1997), *The Nationalization of Hindu traditions: Bharatendu Harischandra and nineteenth-century Banaras*, Delhi, Oxford University Press.

Datta, P. K. (1993), 'Dying Hindus – production of Hindu communal common sense in early 20th century Bengal', *Economic and Political Weekly*, no. 44.

—— (1999), *Carving Blocs – Communal Ideology in Early Twentieth-Century Bengal*, New Delhi: Oxford University Press.

Davis, R. H. (1996), 'The Iconography of Rama's Chariot' in Ludden ed.

Dayananda, Swami ([1908] 1970), *Light of Truth*, New Delhi: Jan Gyan Prakashan.

Deodhar, V. N. (1991), *Pandit Deendayal Upadhyaya: Ideology and perception, Part VII, A Profile*, New Delhi: Suruchi Prakashan

Deshpande, B. V. and Ramaswamy, S. R. (1981), *Dr Hedgewar, the Epoch-maker: A biography*, Bangalore, Sahitya Sindhu.

Dharmavira (1970), *Lala Har Dayal and Revolutionary Movements of his Times*, New Delhi: Indian Book Company.

Douglas, M. (1991), *Purity and Danger: An analysis of the concepts of pollution and taboo*, London: Routledge.

Dumont, L. (1980), *Homo Hierarchicus: The caste system and its implications*, Chicago: University of Chicago Press.

Edwardes, M. (1971), *East-West Passage, The Travel of Ideas, Arts and Inventions between Asia and the Western World*, New York: Taplinger.

Enthoven, R. E. (1920), *The Tribes and Castes of Bombay*, Vol. 1, Bombay: Government Central Press.

Flora, G. (1993), *The Evolution of Positivism in Bengal: Jogendra Chandra Ghosh, Bankimchandra Chattopadhyay, Benoy Kumar Sarkar*, Istituto Universitario Orientale, Supplemento 75 (53) fasc. 2.

Forbes, G. H. (1975), *Positivism in Bengal, A case study in the transmission and assimilation of an ideology*, Calcutta: Minerva

Gandhi, M. K. (1997), *Hind Swaraj and Other Writings*, Cambridge: Cambridge University Press.

Gautier, F. (1996), *Rewriting Indian History*, New Delhi: Vikas.

Ghatak, K. K., (1991), *Hindu Revivalism in Bengal: Rammohan to Ramakrishna*, Calcutta: Minerva.

Ghose, A. (1925), *Dayananda, as viewed by Shri Aravinda Ghosh, with appreciation by A. J. Davies of America*, Lahore: Vedic Pustakalaya

—— (1971), *The Foundations of Indian Culture*, Pondicherry: Sri Aurobindo Ashram.

—— (1995), *The Secret of the Veda*, Twin Lakes WI: Lotus Light Publications.

—— (1997), *India's Rebirth*, Paris: Institut De Recherches Evolutives

Ghosh, P. S. (1999), *BJP and the Evolution of Hindu Nationalism: From periphery to center*, New Delhi: Manohar.

Goel, S. R. ed. (1997), *Time for Stock Taking – Whither Sangh Parivar?* New Delhi: Voice of India.

Golwalkar, M. S. ([1939] 1944), *We, or Our Nationhood Defined*, Nagpur: Bharat Publications.

—— (1956), *Shri Guruji – the Man and His Mission, on the occasion of his 51st Birthday*, Delhi: Bharat Prakashan.

—— (1958), *Justice On Trial, a collection of the historic letters between Sri Guruji and the Government (1948–49)*, Bangalore: Rashtreeya Swayamsevak Sangh.

—— (1966), *Bunch of Thoughts*, Bangalore: Vikrama Prakashan.

—— (1970), *Shri Guruji Meets Delhi Newsmen*, New Delhi: Suruchi Sahitya.

—— and Upadhyaya D. and Thengadi, D. B. (1991), *Integral Approach*, New Delhi: Suruchi Prakashan.

Goodrick Clarke, N. (1985), *The Occult Roots of Nazism*, New York: New York University Press.

—— (1998), *Hitler's Priestess: Savitri Devi, the Hindu-Aryan Myth and neo-Nazism*, New York: New York University Press.

Gopal, S. ed. (1991), *Anatomy of a Confrontation: the Babri Masjid-Ramjanmabhumi issue*, New Delhi: Penguin.

Gordon, L. (1990), *Brothers Against the Raj: A biography of Indian nationalists Sarat and Subhas Chandra Bose*, New York: Columbia University Press.

Gordon, R. (1975), 'The Hindu Mahasabha and the Indian National Congress, 1915 to 1926', *Modern Asian Studies*, 9 (2): 145–203

Goyal, D. R. (1979), *Rashtriya Swayamsewak Sangh*, New Delhi: Radha Krishna Prakashan.

Graham B. (1993), *Hindu Nationalism and Indian Politics: The origins and development of the Bharatiya Jana Sangh*, Cambridge: Cambridge University Press.

Grover, V. eds (1993), *V. D. Savarkar*, New Delhi: Deep & Deep Publications.

Gupta, B. D. (1972), *Sociology in India – an Enquiry into Sociological Thinking & Empirical Social Research in the nineteenth century – with Special Reference to Bengal*, Calcutta: Centre for Sociological Research.

Gupta, D. (1982), *Nativism in a Metropolis: The Shiv Sena in Bombay*, New Delhi: Manohar.

Halbfass, W. (1988), *India and Europe: An essay in understanding*, New York: State University of New York Press.

Haldar, M. K. (1989), *Foundations of Nationalism in India: A study of Bankim-chandra Chatterjee*, Delhi: Ajanta Publications.

Hansen, T. B. (1999), *The Saffron Wave: Democracy and Hindu nationalism in modern India*, Princeton, NJ: University of Princeton Press.

Hansen, T. B. and Jaffrelot, C. eds. (1998), *The BJP and the Compulsions of Politics in India*, New Delhi: Oxford University Press.

Hasan, M. (1991), *Nationalism and Communal Politics in India, 1885–1930*, New Delhi: Manohar

Heehs, P. (1998), *Nationalism, Terrorism, Communalism – Essays in Modern Indian History*, New Delhi: Oxford University Press

Heuze, G. (1995), 'Cultural Populism: the appeal of the Shiv Sena' in Patel and Thorner eds.

Hindu Mahasabha (1935), *Resolutions, Receipts and Payments Accounts, the Balance Sheets 1933 and 34 and the Report Oct. 1933 to April 1935, passed by the 16th Session of the Hindu Mahasabha held at Cawnpore on the 20th to 22nd April 1935, under the Presidentship of Shri Bhikhshu Ottama, Buddhist Monk of Burma*, New Delhi: Hindu Mahasabha.

Hindu Nationalist (1941), *Gandhi-Muslim Conspiracy*, Poona: R.D. Ghanekar, 1941.

Hingle, G. S. (1999), *Hindutva Reawakened*, New Delhi: Vikas.

Ispahani, M. A. H. (1970), 'Factors leading to the Partition of British India', in Philips, C. H., Wainwright, M. D. eds, *The Partition of India. Policies and Perspectives 1935–1947*, London: George Allen & Unwin.

Hobsbawm, E. and Ranger, T. eds (1983), *The Invention of Tradition*, Cambridge: Cambridge University Press.

Hutchinson, J. (1987), *The Dynamics of Cultural Nationalism*, London: Allen & Unwin.

Jaffrelot, C. (1996), *The Hindu nationalist movement and Indian politics – 1925 to the 1990s: strategies of identity-building, implantation and mobilisation (with special reference to Central India)*, London: Hurst.

Jammu Kashmir Sahayata Samiti (1991), *Genocide of Hindus in Kashmir*, New Delhi: Suruchi Prakashan.

Jayaprasad, K. (1995), *RSS and Hindu Nationalism: Inroads in a leftist stronghold*, New Delhi: Deep & Deep.

Jayawardena, K. and De Alwis, M. (1996), *Embodied Violence – Communalising Women's Sexuality in South Asia*, London: Zed.

Jha, D. N. (1998), *Ancient India in Historical Outline* [revised edition], New Delhi: Manohar.

Jhangiani, M. A. (1967), *Jana Sangh and Swatantra: A profile of the rightist parties in India*, Bombay: Manaktala.

Jog, B. N. (1991), *Pandit Deendayal Upadhyaya: Ideology and Perception, Part VI, Politics for Nation's Sake*, New Delhi: Suruchi Prakashan.

Johari, J. C. (1993-), *Voices of Indian Freedom Movement*, 10 volumes, New Delhi: Akashdeep Publishing House.

Jois, M. R. (1996), *Our Fraternity*, New Delhi: Suruchi Prakashan.

—— (1996), *Supreme Court Judgement on 'Hindutva' – An Important Landmark*, New Delhi: Suruchi Prakashan.

Jones, K. (1976), *Arya Dharm: Hindu consciousness in nineteenth-century Punjab*, Delhi: Manohar Press.

—— (1989), *Socio-religious Reform Movements in British India*, Cambridge: Cambridge University Press.

Jordens, J. T. F. (1981), *Swami Shraddhananda, His Life and Causes*, Delhi: Oxford University Press.

Kaviraj, S. (1995), *The Unhappy Consciousness: Bankimchandra Chattopadhyay and the formation of nationalist discourse in India*, Delhi: Oxford University Press.

Kapur, A. (1993), 'Deity to crusader: the changing iconography of Rama' in Pandey, G. ed.

Keer, D. (1988), *Veer Savarkar*, London: Sangam Books.

Kelkar, B. K. (1991), *Pandit Deendayal Upadhyaya: Ideology and Perception, Part III, Political Thought*, New Delhi: Suruchi Prakashan.

Kishwar, M. (1998), *Religion at the Service of Nationalism and Other Essays*, New Delhi: Oxford University Press.

Kohli, A. (1990), *Democracy and Discontent: India's growing crisis of governability*, Cambridge: Cambridge University Press.

Kohli, R. (1993), *Political ideas of M.S. Golwalkar: Hindutva, nationalism, secularism*, New Delhi: Deep & Deep.

Kulkarni, S. A. (1991), *Pandit Deendayal Upadhyaya: Ideology and Perception, Part IV, Integral Economic Policy*, New Delhi: Suruchi Prakashan.

Kulke, H. and Rothermund, D. (1988), *A History of India*, [3rd edition] London: Routledge.

Lahiry, A. (1968), *Meet The Challenge – Need for a New Political Party*, Calcutta: R. P. Bookwala.

Lajpat Rai, L. ([1915]), *The Arya Samaj – an account of its origin, doctrines, and activities, with biographical sketch of the founder*, Delhi: Renaissance Publishing House.

—— (1965), *Lajpat Rai, Autobiographical Writings*, Edited By V. C. Joshi, Delhi: University Publishers.

—— (1966a), *Lala Lajpat Rai – Writing and Speeches, Volume One*, Edited by V. J. Joshi, Delhi: University Publishers.

—— L. (1966b), *Lala Lajpat Rai – Writing and Speeches, Volume Two 1920–1928*, Edited By V. J. Joshi, Delhi: University Publishers

Lal Chand, R. B. ([1909] 1938), *Self-Abnegation In Politics*, Lahore: Central Hindu Yuvak Sabha.

Laqueur, W. (1996), *Fascism: Past, present, future*, Oxford: Oxford University Press.

Lele, J. (1995), *Hindutva: The emergence of the right*, New Delhi: Earthworm Books.

—— (1995), 'Saffronization of the Shiv Sena: the political economy of city, state and nation' in Patel and Thorner eds.

Leopold, J. (1970), 'The Aryan Theory of Race in India 1870-1920: Nationalist and Internationalist Visions', *The Indian Economic and Social History Review*, VII, 2: 271–97.

Bibliography

Lillingston, F. (1901), *The Brahmo Samaj and Arya Samaj in their Bearing upon Christianity: A study in Indian theism*, London: Macmillan.

Lochtefeld, J. G. (1996), 'New Wine, Old Skins: the sangh parivar and the transformation of Hinduism', *Religion* 2 (6), 101–18.

Lorenzen, D. N. ed. (1995), *Bhakti Religion in North India – Community Identity and Political Action*, Albany: State University of New York Press.

Ludden, D. ed. (1996), *Contesting The Nation – Religion, Community, and the Politics of Democracy in India*, Philadelphia: University of Pennsylvania Press.

Mack Smith, D. (1994), *Mazzini*, New Haven and London: Yale University Press.

Madan, T. N. (1987), 'Secularism in its Place', *Journal of Asian Studies*, 46: 747–58.

—— (1993), 'Whither Indian Secularism?' *Modern Asian Studies*, 27: 667–97.

—— (1997), *Modern Myths, Locked Minds, Secularism and Fundamentalism in India*, New Delhi: Oxford University Press.

Madhok, B. (1996), *R.S.S. and Politics: Story of Rashtriya Swayamsewak Sangh with special reference to its role in Indian politics*, New Delhi: Hindu Rajya Prakashak.

Majumdar, R, C. (1960), *Glimpses of Bengal in the Nineteenth Century*, Calcutta: K. L. Mukhopadhyay.

—— (1971), *History of the Freedom Movement In India, Volume I*, Calcutta: K. L. Mukhopadhyay.

Malik Y. K. and Singh, V. B. (1994), *Hindu Nationalists in India: The rise of the Bharatiya Janata Party*, Boulder: Westview.

Malkani, K. R. (1980), *The RSS Story*, New Delhi: Impex India.

Mallory, J. P. (1989), *In Search of the Indo-Europeans*, London: Thames & Hudson.

Marshall, P. J. (1970), *The British Discovery of Hinduism in the Eighteenth Century*, Cambridge: Cambridge University Press.

Marty, M. E. and Appleby, R. S. eds (1991), *Fundamentalisms Observed*, Chicago: University of Chicago.

—— *(1993), Fundamentalisms and the State*, Chicago: University of Chicago

Masselos, J. (1996), 'The Bombay Riots of January 1993: the politics of urban conflagration', in McGuire, J., Reeves, P. and Brasted, H. eds, *Politics of Violence, From Ayodhya to Behrampada*, New Delhi: Sage Publications.

Mathur, S. (1996), *Hindu Revivalism and the Indian National Movement – a Documentary Study of the Ideals and Policies of The Hindu Mahasabha, 1939–45*, Jodhpur: Kusumanjali Prakashan.

McCully, B. T. (1966), *English Education and the Origins of Indian Nationalism*, Massachusetts: Peter Smith.

McKean, L. (1996), *Divine Enterprise: Gurus and the Hindu Nationalist Movement*, Chicago: University of Chicago Press.

Mill, J. and Thomas, W. (1975), *The History of British India*, Chicago: University of Chicago Press.

Mishra, M. (1997), *Bharatiya Janata Party and India's Foreign Policy*, New Delhi: Uppal Publishing House.

Mookerjee, S. P. (1942), *A Phase of the Indian Struggle*, Nadia: Monojendra N. Bhowmik.

Mookerjee, U. P. (not dated), *Syamaprasad Mookerjee: His Death in Detention*, Calcutta: Uma Prasad Mookerjee.

Mosse, G. M. (1966), *The Crisis of German Ideology*, London: Weidenfeld & Nicolson.

Mukherjee, H. and Mukherjee, U. (1957), *'Bande Mataram' and Indian Nationalism (1906–1908)*, Calcutta: K. L. Mukhopadhyay

Mukta, P. and C. Bhatt eds. (2000), *Hindutva Movements in the West: resurgent Hinduism and the politics of diaspora, Ethnic and Racial Studies*, 23 (3): May [Special Issue].

Nagar, P. (1977), *Lala Lajpat Rai – The Man and His Ideas*: New Delhi: Manohar.

Nair, M. V. K. (1991), *How India Won Freedom*, New Delhi: Galaxy.

Nandy, A. (1983), *The Intimate Enemy: Loss and Recovery of Self Under Colonialism*, New Delhi: Oxford University Press.

—— (1985), 'An anti-secularist manifesto', *Seminar*, 314.

—— (1994), *The Illegitimacy of Nationalism: Rabindranath Tagore and the Politics of Self*, New Delhi: Oxford University Press.

—— and Trivedy, S., Mayaram, S. and Yagnik, A. (1995), *Creating a Nationality: The Ramjanmabhumi Movement and Fear of the Self*, New Delhi: Oxford University Press.

Nene, V. V. (1991), *Pandit Deendayal Upadhyaya: Ideology and Perception, Part II Integral Humanism*, New Delhi: Suruchi Prakashan.

Padgaonkar, D. ed. (1993), *When Bombay Burned – Reportage and comments on the Riots and Blasts from the Times of India*, New Delhi: UBS Publishers.

Pal, B. C. (1910), *The Spirit of Indian Nationalism*, London: Hind Nationalist Agency

Pandey, G. (1992), *The Construction of Communalism in Colonial North India*, New Delhi: Oxford University Press.

—— ed. (1993), *Hindus and Others: The question of identity in India today*, New Delhi: Viking.

Panikkar, K. N. (1997), *Communal Threat, Secular Challenge*, Madras: Earthworm Books.

Pareek, R. S. (1973), *Contribution of Arya Samaj in the Making of Modern India 1875–1947*, New Delhi: Sarvadeshik Arya Pratinidhi Sabha.

Parmanand, B. (1907), *Our Earliest Attempt at Independence*, New Delhi: The Hindu Outlook.

—— (1982), *The Story Of My Life*, New Delhi: S. Chand & Company.

Patel, S. and Thorner, A. eds (1995), *Bombay – Metaphor for Modern India*, Bombay: Oxford University Press.

Pattanaik, D. D. (1998), *Hindu Nationalism in India* (4 volumes), New Delhi: Deep & Deep.

Phillips, C. H., Singh, H. L. and Pandey, B. B. (1962), *The Evolution of India and Pakistan 1858 to 1947 – Select Documents*, London: Oxford University Press.

Pinch, W. R. (1996), *Peasants and Monks in British India,* Berkeley: University of California Press.

Poliakov, L. (1971), *The Aryan Myth: A history of racist and nationalist ideas in Europe*, London: Heinemann.

Prakasha, I. (1942), *Where We Differ – The Congress and the Hindu Mahasabha*, New Delhi: The Hindu Mission.

Puri, G. (1980), *Bharatiya Jana Sangh: Organization and Ideology – Delhi, a case study*, New Delhi: Sterling.

Rajagopal, A. (1996), 'Communalism and the consuming subject', *Economic and Political Weekly*, 2 February.

Raghavan, G. N. S. (1996), *A New Era in the Indian Polity – a study of Atal Bihari Vajpayee and the BJP*, New Delhi: Gyan Publishing House.

Rashtra Sevika Samiti (not dated), *Rashtra Sevika Samiti*, Jabalpur: Organization of Indian Women.

Rashtriya Swayamsevak Sangh (1983), *RSS Resolves – Full Text of Resolutions from 1950 to 1983*, Karnataka: Rashtriya Swayamsevak Sangh.

—— (1985), *RSS: Spearheading National Renaissance*, Karnataka: Rashtriya Swayamsevak Sangh.

Rastogi, G. (1991), *Our Kashmir*, New Delhi: Suruchi Prakashan

Ray, A. K. (1999), *Party of Firebrand Revolutionaries: The Dacca Anushilan Samiti 1906–1918*, Calcutta: Minerva.

Raychaudhuri, T. (1995), 'Shadows of the Swastika: historical reflections on the politics of Hindu communalism', *Contention*, 5: 141–62.

Richman, P. ed. (1991), *Many Ramayanas: The diversity of a narrative tradition in South Asia*, Berkeley: University of California Press.

Risley, H. H. (1903), *Census of India, 1901 (Volume 1) – India, ethnographic appendices: being the data upon which the caste chapter of the report is based*, Calcutta: Office of the Supt. of Government Printing.

—— (1908, 1915), *The People of India*, Calcutta: Thacker, Spink & Co.

Rothermund, D. (1986), *The German Intellectual Quest for India*, New Delhi: Manohar.

Sahasrabuddhe, P. G. and Vajpayee, M. C. (1991), *The People versus Emergency – a Saga of Struggle*, New Delhi: Suruchi Prakashan

Sarda, H. B. ([1906]1975), *Hindu Superiority: An attempt to determine the position of the Hindu race in the scale of nations*, New Delhi: Hindu Academy.

Sarkar, S. (1993), 'The fascism of the sangh parivar', *Economic and Political Weekly*, 30 January.

Sarkar, T. (1996), 'Educating the Children of the Hindu Rashtra: notes on RSS schools' in Bidwai, P., Mukhia, H. and Vanaik, A. eds, *Religion, Religiosity and Communalism*, New Delhi: Manohar

—— (1996), 'Imagining Hindurashtra: the Hindu and the Muslim in Bankim Chandra's writings' in Ludden ed.

—— and Butalia, U. eds. (1995), *Women and Right-Wing Movements – Indian Experiences*, New Delhi: Kali for Women.

Savarkar, V. D. ([1909]1947), *The Indian War of Independence 1857* [S.T. Godbole ed. trans.], New Delhi: Rajdhani Granthagar.

—— (1930), *Hindu Dhwaja*, Bombay: Veer Savarkar Prakashan.

—— (1941), *Veer Savarkar's 'Whirl-Wind Propaganda' (Statements, Messages and extracts from the President's Diary of his Propagandistic Years, Interviews from December 1937 to October 1941)*, Bombay: A. S. Bhide.

—— (1949), *Hindu Rashtra Darshan – A Collection of the Presidential Speeches Delivered from the Hindu Mahasabha Platform*, Bombay: G. Khare.

—— (1950), *The Story of my Transportation for Life*, Bombay: Sadbhakti Publications.

—— (1967), *Historic Statements*, Bombay: G.P. Parchure.

—— (not dated), *Thus Spake The Prophet! Warnings that were overlooked: a collection of writings and speeches of Veer Savarkar*, New Delhi: Akhil Bharat Hindu Mahasabha.

—— ([1923] 1989), *Hindutva*, Bombay: Veer Savarkar Prakashan

—— and Srivastava, H. (1983). *Five Stormy Years – Savarkar in London, June 1906–June 1911: a centenary salute to Swatantrayaveer Vinayak Damodar Savarkar*, New Delhi: Allied Publishers.

Schwab, R. (1984), *The Oriental Renaissance: Europe's rediscovery of India and the East, 1680–1880*, New York: Columbia University Press.

Sen A. P. (1993), *Hindu Revivalism in Bengal, 1872–1905: Some essays in interpretation*, Delhi: Oxford University Press.

Seshadri, H. V. ed. (1988), *RSS: A Vision in Action*, Bangalore: Jagarana Prokashana.

—— (1990), *Hindus Abroad – The Dilemma: Dollar or Dharma?* New Delhi: Suruchi Prakashan.

—— (1991), *The Way*, New Delhi: Suruchi Prakashan.

—— and Sudarshan, K. S., Rao, K. S. N. and Madhok, B. (1990), *Why Hindu Rashtra?* New Delhi: Suruchi Prakashan.

Sharma, R. S. (1999), *The Advent of the Aryans in India*, New Delhi: Manohar.

Shaw, G. and Lloyd, M. (1985) *Publications Proscribed by the Government of India*, London: The British Library.

Shraddhananda S. (1926), *Hindu Sangathan, Saviour of the Dying Race*, Delhi: Arjun.

—— (1961), *Swami Shraddhanand*, Bombay: Bharatiya Vidya Bhavan.

Singh, R (1993), *Ayodhya Episode: A Turning Point*, New Delhi: Suruchi Prakashan.

—— (1994), *Ever-Vigilant We Have To Be*, New Delhi: Suruchi Prakashan.

Spivak Gayatri, C. (1993), *Outside in the Teaching Machine*, London: Routledge.

Sundaresan, V. (not dated), 'The Jyotirmath lineage in the 20th century', posted on Indology website, http://www.ucl.ac.uk/~ucgadkw/position/shank-jyot.html

Swarup, R., (1991), *Whither Sikhism*, New Delhi: Voice of India.

Taneja, N. (not dated), 'In the Name of History', posted on website, http://www.secularindia.com/Inthenameofhistory.htm.

Thapar, R. (1985), 'Syndicated Moksha?', *Seminar*, 313.

—— (1989), 'Imagined religious communities? Ancient history and the modern search for a Hindu identity', *Modern Asian Studies*, 23 (2): 209–31.

—— (1991), 'A Historical Perspective on the Story of Rama' in Gopal ed.

—— (1992), 'The Perennial Aryans', *Seminar*, 400

—— (1996), *Ancient Indian Social History: Some interpretations*, London: Sangam Books.

Thakur, C. P. and Sharma, D. P. (1999), *India under Atal Behari Vajpayee – the BJP Era*, New Delhi: UBS Publishers.

Thengadi D.B. (1991), *Pandit Deendayal Upadhyaya: Ideology and Perception, Part I, An Inquest*, New Delhi: Suruchi Prakashan.

—— (1995), *Third Way*, New Delhi: Janaki Prakashan.

Tilak, B. G. (1919), *Bal Gangadhar Tilak: His writings and speeches – appreciation by Babu Aurobindo Ghose*, Madras: Ganesh.

—— (1936), *Gita-Rahasya: The Hindu philosophy of life, ethics and religion*, Poona: Tilak Bros.

—— (1956), *The Arctic Home in the Vedas: being also a new key to the interpretation of many Vedic texts and legends*, Poona: Kesari.

—— (1984), *The Orion, or Researches in to the Antiquity of the Vedas*, Mumbai: Damodara Savalaramaani Mandali.

Trautmann, T. R. (1997), *Aryans and British India*, Berkeley: University of California Press.

Trehan, J. (1991), *Veer Savarkar: Thought and action of Vinayak Damodar Savarkar*, New Delhi: Deep & Deep.

Upadhyaya, D. (1992), *Political Diary*, New Delhi: Suruchi Prakashan.

Upadhyaya, G. P. (1939), *Swami Dayanand's Contribution to Hindu Solidarity, Religious Renaissance Series No. 2*, Allahabad: Arya Samaj

Van der Veer, P. (1994), *Religious Nationalism: Hindus and Muslims in India*, Berkeley: University of California Press

—— (1997), *Gods on Earth: Religious Experience and Identity in Ayodhya*, Delhi: Oxford University Press.

Vanaik, A. (1997), *The Furies of Indian Communalism: Religion, modernity, and secularisation*, London: Verso.

Vishwa Hindu Parishad (1991), *History versus Casuistry: Evidence of the Ramjanmabhoomi mandir presented to the government of India in December–January 1990–91*, New Delhi: Voice of India.

Wolpert, S. (1977), *Tilak and Gokhale: Revolution and reform in the making of modern India*, Berkeley: University of California Press.

Yajnik, I. (1950), *Shyamaji Krishnavarma: Life and times of an Indian revolutionary*, Bombay: Lakshmi Publications.

Index

Index

Index

Index